*Wagner and Aeschylus*

by the same author

*Janáček's Tragic Operas*
(1977)

# WAGNER
# AND AESCHYLUS

The *Ring* and the *Oresteia*

## MICHAEL EWANS

CAMBRIDGE UNIVERSITY PRESS

*Cambridge*

*London   New York   New Rochelle*

*Melbourne   Sydney*

Published by the Press Syndicate of the University of Cambridge
32 East 57th Street, New York, N.Y. 10022 USA

First published in the USA and Canada in 1983 by
Cambridge University Press
First published throughout the rest of the world in 1982
by Faber and Faber Limited

Printed in the United States of America

Library of Congress Cataloging in Publication Data

Ewans, Michael, 1946–

Wagner and Aeschylus.

Bibliography: p.
Includes index.
1. Wagner, Richard, 1813–1883. Ring des
Nibelungen. 2. Aeschylus. Oresteia.
I. Title.
ML410.W15E9 1982   782.1′092′4   82-12762

ISBN 0-521-25073-0

# Contents

# Preface

Nietzsche once declared that 'no ancient work ever had as powerful an influence, as that of the *Oresteia* on Richard Wagner'.
Wagner expressed his deep love of Greek tragedy in general, and
the dramas of Aeschylus in particular, on many occasions. But
Nietzsche later came to recant the enthusiastic admiration which
had led him to portray Wagner, in *The Birth of Tragedy*, as the
true heir of the Greek tragedians. And for most subsequent
classical scholars Wagner's name is almost synonymous with
Romantic extravagance. Few have felt that there is any real
affinity between Wagner's stage works and those of the earliest
and most ascetic of the surviving Greek tragic poets. (The exceptions, however, are distinguished: Wolfgang Schadewaldt and
Hugh Lloyd-Jones.) Nor has the subject been adequately explored by Wagner's admirers, despite the enormous quantity of
comment which his life and work have evoked.

It has, of course, long been accepted that Wagner's ideal of a
festal community theatre for the enactment of dramas based on
myth was formed under the example of classical Greek tragedy.
Furthermore, Wagner instructed Gottfried Semper to design the
auditorium of the projected Wagner theatre for Munich (the
plans for which were later used in the construction of the Fest-
spielhaus at Bayreuth) after the pattern of the amphitheatres in
ancient Greek and Roman theatres. Greek influence on Wagner
is also clearly visible in his major theoretical writings, especially
in *Art and Revolution* (1849) and *Opera and Drama* (1850–1).
But it can be traced, far more importantly, in his subsequent

stage works. In this book, I shall argue that the example of Aeschylus' great trilogy is present in the procedures of the *Ring* at several major levels, from the overall concept of a cycle of three closely interrelated dramas—designed for consecutive performance and solely for festival occasions—right through to profound aspects of subject-matter and form.

To interpret the *Ring* in relation to the *Oresteia* is not merely to shed fresh light on Wagner's dramaturgy. Wagner's cycle is itself a special 'reading' of Aeschylus. His areas of qualified assent and overt or tacit dissent from Aeschylus suggest a reappraisal not only of Wagner's own artistic aims, dramatic strategy, and vision of life, but of Aeschylus' as well. Indeed, the relationship between Wagner and Aeschylus raises such a wide range of issues that any treatment must inevitably be selective. I am very conscious that my own viewpoint is a subjective one, and that I have been able to discuss only those aspects which I myself feel to be the most important.

I have not hesitated to dwell at times on fairly basic details of the plot and the patterns of action of the two trilogies. Drama is a direct medium, and careful attention to what actually happens in the theatre, as each work unfolds, seems to me to be very important. And so, after the two introductory chapters, this book treats the issues raised by the *Ring* and the *Oresteia* in the order in which they are brought before us in performance.

Aeschylus like Wagner directed the production of his work himself, and he composed the music for the lyric sections of his dramas as well as supervising the design of the costumes and acting the leading parts. From what little we know about the music of the early fifth century, the lyrics of Aeschylean tragedy would seem to have been written in a clear and straightforward style, to be sung in unison to a plain accompaniment from one single woodwind player. There is therefore an immense difference between the *Oresteia* and the *Ring* whose entire action is surrounded by one of the most sumptuous orchestral scores ever to have been written for the theatre. But Wagner insisted in all his theoretical writings (from *Opera and Drama* to his 1878 essay 'On the Application of Music to Drama') that in his theatre works, by contrast with traditional operatic practice, the music would be devoted exclusively to illuminating the action; and in order to proclaim this ideal clearly he even described the *Ring* in its subtitle as a 'stage festival play', and termed *Tristan und Isolde* a '*Handlung*', literally translating the Greek word *drāma* (action). Although his musical techniques for realizing it developed considerably as the *Ring* scores were composed, Wagner never deviated from this fundamental aim. I have, therefore, felt it proper, given that my subject is the influence on Wagner of a playwright, to confine my commentary on the music of the *Ring* to the manner in which the composer's musical inventions shed light upon the situations enacted on his stage. I have paid particular attention to the development and transformation of certain recurrent themes and motifs, since this is one of the principal musical means which Wagner uses to articulate the dramatic structure of the cycle.

I have tried to write in such a way that any intelligent reader can follow my argument. Specialists will, therefore, encounter explanations of some matters with which they are already familiar. I have also been obliged on occasion to be dogmatic about important details which are still hotly debated in academic circles. I trust that musicologists, classical scholars, and Germanists will tolerate both these features of the book. No other approach would have allowed me to treat adequately, and intelligibly, the issues which are central to this study.

This book could not have been finished without the study leave which was granted to me in 1979 by the Council of the University of Newcastle; my first thanks must go to them for this period of sustained work, during which I was able to complete the research and analysis for the book and write much of the first draft. I also owe thanks to the Department of Drama at the University of Bristol, both for the grant of a Visiting Lectureship and for their congenial hospitality. But I am of course most indebted of all to those who have read and criticized the drafts, and who gave me encouragement and expert advice: in particular to Dr Richard Buxton, to my wife, Dr Jenifer Ewans, and to my editor at Faber and Faber, Patrick Carnegy.

*Newcastle, N.S.W.*
*August 1981*

# Note on References

I have used Denys Page's Oxford Classical Text of Aeschylus (1972). All references to Aeschylus are given by the standard line-numbering, which is used by Page and by most translators. The translations in this book, both from the *Oresteia* and from the *Ring*, are my own.

The best complete translation of the *Oresteia* is that by Richmond Lattimore (*Aeschylus I*, Chicago U.P. 1953), which conveys the feel of the Greek better than any other modern version, and is also remarkably accurate. Its only drawback is that at several points it translates a text which is no longer tenable. Another good version is Robert Fagles's (Penguin, 1977), which is often more imaginative, but also unnecessarily free. Unhelpfully, it does not employ the standard line-numbering. Hugh Lloyd-Jones's annotated translations, with the three plays in separate volumes (Duckworth, 1979), are more prosaic but also far more accurate.

The musical text of Wagner is that of the study scores published by Edition Eulenberg. Since most vocal scores of the *Ring* lack rehearsal figures, and my argument frequently refers to the texture of the orchestration, I have made reference to Wagner's dramas either by act and scene number or, where a more precise indication is necessary, by the page numbering of the Eulenberg study scores.

There are two good modern English versions of the *Ring*: William Mann's translation, published by the Friends of Covent Garden (in the 1973 reprint), and Andrew Porter's singing version (Faber and Faber, 1977).

References to Wagner's prose writings are cited for convenience by the volume and page number of the standard English translation by W. Ashton Ellis (abbreviated as AE). I have, however, provided new English translations for this book, as Ellis's English style is now considerably dated. Wagner's letters are cited by the date of writing, preceded by the initial of the addressee's surname: R (Röckel), L (Liszt), U (Uhlig) and N (Nietzsche). Cosima Wagner's *Diaries* are cited by the letter D followed by the date of the entry. References to all other books are made by the page numbers of the edition or translation which is cited in the bibliography.

# 1
# Wagner and Aeschylus

Wagner never mastered classical Greek. He tells us in his auto-
biography that his love for Greek culture began at the age of six,
when newspaper accounts of the Greek war of independence
were read aloud to him; and he began to study ancient Greek at
the Dresden Kreuzschule, which he attended from nine to four-
teen. In his open letter to Nietzsche (N 12/6/72) Wagner
claimed that at that time: 'no boy could have had greater enthusiasm for classical antiquity than myself; although it was Greek
mythology and history which interested me deeply, I also felt
strongly drawn to the study of the Greek language, to such an
extent, in fact, that I was almost rebellious in my efforts to shirk
my Latin tasks'. In *Mein Leben*, however, he more candidly
admits that Greek mythology was the real attraction: 'in the
matter of the classics, I paid only just as much attention as was
absolutely necessary to enable me to get a grasp of them: for I
was stimulated by the desire to reproduce them to myself dramatically . . . In these circumstances it will be readily understood that the grammar of these languages seemed to me merely
a tiresome obstacle . . .' (p. 15). In spite of this, by 1826 Wagner
had advanced sufficiently far in his study of Greek to make a
German translation of the first three books of the *Odyssey*; and
his master Julius Sillig had sufficient regard for Wagner's aptitude to urge him towards adopting philology as his profession.

The family, however, moved back to Leipzig in 1827, and
Wagner fell behind in his classical studies. He claimed on several
occasions in later life that this was due to the pedantic approach

of the masters at the Leipzig schools; yet it is plain that Wagner's passionate interest in Romantic drama, and his increasing devotion to music, overcame his interest in the Greek world. When he was seventeen, Wagner attempted to resume his classical studies, and to gain a firm grasp of the Greek language, by engaging a private tutor; but this came to nothing. Later—in Paris, between 1839 and 1842—he met the classical scholar Samuel Lehrs and attempted to renew his studies; but he was wisely advised to proceed no further. Lehrs told him that he would need so much time to gain a thorough grounding in the Greek language that it would stand in the way of his work as a composer. Wagner acted on this advice: the classical reading of his later years was done almost entirely in translation, though on one occasion Cosima's diary records that he read Sophocles in Greek with the German version open beside it, comparing the translation with the original (D 18/11/74).

Wagner thrived on his lack of formal knowledge. His mind was not a scholar's, and he drew so much creative gain from his own personal vision of the Greek world precisely because he never submitted to the extremes of formal discipline which were demanded in the higher stages of a classical education in nineteenth-century Germany.

Greek literature first became important to Wagner during the years when he was *Hofkapellmeister* in Dresden (1843–9). He purchased translations of almost all the major authors: Aeschylus, Aristophanes, Aristotle, Demosthenes, Euripides, Herodotus, Homer, Pindar, Plato, Plutarch, Sophocles, Thucydides and Xenophon. He lost all these books to a creditor when he fled from Dresden to avoid arrest for his part in the insurrection of 1849; but he built up an even larger collection in later life.

After 1845, the example of Greek culture was almost constantly before Wagner's eyes. It forms the point of departure for his own aesthetic ideals from the opening pages of *Art and Revolution* (1849) to his last major essay, *Religion and Art* (1880). Cosima's diaries record many occasions on which Wagner read or discussed Greek literature, both during the Tribschen years (when Nietzsche, who had not yet given up his chair of classical philology, was a frequent guest) and at Wahnfried.

Wagner did not exaggerate when he claimed in the open letter to Nietzsche that: 'Again and again, amid the most absorbing tasks of a life entirely removed from these [classical] studies, the only way by which I seemed to be able to gain a breath of freedom was by plunging into this ancient world, however much I was now handicapped by having well-nigh forgotten the language.'

He 'plunged' in particular into the dramas of Aeschylus, returning to them many times. In 1880 Wagner read the three plays of the *Oresteia* aloud, and Cosima wrote: 'I feel as if I have never before seen him like this, transfigured, inspired, completely at one with what he is reading.' (D 23/6/80) And Wagner said of Aeschylus on the last day of his life that: my admiration for him never ceases to grow'.

That admiration had begun over thirty years earlier, in 1847, at the time when Wagner was finishing the orchestration of *Lohengrin*. He records in *Mein Leben* that he then 'for the first time . . . mastered Aeschylus with real feeling and understanding', and goes on to say that the impact on him of the Orestes trilogy was so great that:

> I could see the *Oresteia* with my mind's eye, as though it were actually being performed; and its effect on me was indescribable. Nothing could equal the sublime emotion with which the *Agamemnon* inspired me, and to the last word of the *Eumenides* I remained in an atmosphere so far removed from the present day that I have never since been really able to reconcile myself with modern literature. My ideas about the whole significance of the drama and of the theatre were, without a doubt, moulded by these impressions . . . (p. 415)

The *Oresteia* released Wagner from the artistic impasse which he had reached with the completion of *Lohengrin*; and, as he implies in this passage, Aeschylus' trilogy decisively influenced the form and content of all Wagner's subsequent dramas—and in particular those of the *Ring*.

Aeschylus was born into a noble Athenian family between 525 and 510 BC. He grew up during the last years of Athens' rule by tyrants, came to maturity during the first years of democracy, and fought for his country against the Persian invasions led by Dareios and Xerxes, taking part in the victories of Marathon (490 BC) and Salamis (480 BC).

The most important performances of tragedy at Athens were those given at the spring festival of the god Dionysus. Each year, three playwrights were selected and invited to produce tragedies on successive days, in competition with each other; their entries took the form of three tragic dramas followed by a 'satyr-play', a short, farcical afterpiece.

Aeschylus is the earliest Greek playwright by whom a complete work survives today. He began to enter plays for the tragic competitions in 490—some 30 or 40 years after the first performances of tragedy at Athens, said to have been given by the historically shadowy Thespis. Aeschylus exhibited tragedies in at least twenty festivals; he won the prize for the first time in 484. Only six of his plays survive; except for the earliest (*The Persians*, 472), which dramatizes the impact in the Persian capital of Xerxes' defeat at Salamis, all are based on traditional myths. The other extant plays are *Seven against Thebes* (467), the third play of a Theban trilogy concerned with the quarrel for the throne between Oedipus' sons Eteokles and Polyneikes and their death in single combat; *The Suppliant Maidens* (? 463); and the *Oresteia* itself (458). (*Prometheus Bound*, which is found together with these six plays in the manuscripts of Aeschylus, bears many signs of later authorship and is now generally suspected to be by another hand.) Aeschylus died in 456, two years after producing the *Oresteia*.

Aeschylus and his contemporaries competed annually for a token prize, and for the honour of presenting their plays for one performance at one festival. There was no prospect of revival in Athens, or of a widespread subsequent readership. Yet the audience was vast—the seating capacity of the open-air theatre of Dionysus has been estimated at around 17,000; it comprised every class of Athenian citizen—men gathered together from the city and from the countryside of Attica, bringing with them their wives and families—and also a small number of resident aliens and distinguished foreign guests. For over a century the dramatists of Athens presented this audience with tragedies whose surviving texts have always been envied for their rich poetic invention, their depth of human insight and their intense seriousness. These plays present an almost intolerable challenge to any subsequent dramatist; for—as Wagner well knew—such uncompromising works have never since proved capable of holding the attention of a mass audience in the west.

The plays offered by each competitor at the festival were not normally related to each other. Aeschylus is the only Athenian dramatist whom we know regularly chose to weld his three tragedies together into a trilogy, a sequence of plays which dramatize successive phases of one continuous story; and even he did not do this on more than five or six occasions. The *Oresteia* was his most famous trilogy, and almost certainly his greatest; it is the only one to have survived intact—though the accompanying satyr play, *Proteus*, is lost.

The *Oresteia* follows the fortunes of the legendary royal house of Atreus and of its city, which in Aeschylus' version of the story is Argos. The first play, *Agamemnon*, is set in front of the palace immediately after the fall of Troy; it shows the homecoming of Atreus' son, king Agamemnon, the victorious leader of the Trojan expedition. His wife Klytaimestra is determined to murder him in revenge for the sacrifice of their daughter Iphigeneia, whom Agamemnon had slaughtered at the demand of the goddess Artemis, as the price for being allowed to depart for Troy.

The play begins when the watchman, who is stationed on the roof of the palace, catches sight of a flaring beacon—the last of a relay which Klytaimestra has had posted to bring her the news that Troy has fallen. As the drama moves towards Agamemnon's return, the chorus of Argive elders meditate on the sacrifice of Iphigeneia, the abduction of Helen by Paris and its consequences—the costly, ten-year war, and the eventual fall of Troy.

All these events have implications which make the chorus increasingly apprehensive about Agamemnon's own fate. They have observed the ever-rising, 'unwomanly' power of Klytaimestra; it fills them with caution, even though they cannot sense her full purpose. And then Agamemnon arrives—not in unqualified triumph but alone (except for his prize and concubine, the Trojan prophetess Kassandra). The gods have scattered the Greek fleet during its return voyage, in punishment for their sacrilege in destroying the altars and temples of the gods during the sack of Troy. Klytaimestra hails him in a grotesque, hypocritical speech, and then lures him into walking into his house over a sea of finely woven tapestries, to ensure that the jealousy of the gods—who alone had the right to such an extravagant honour—will help her.

Klytaimestra fails, however, when she attempts to persuade Kassandra to enter the house. Before Kassandra, of her own accord, goes in to meet her death, her prophetic visions bring in front of the audience Klytaimestra's preparations for the murder of Agamemnon, and the sinister lurking presence of Aigisthos. He is the only surviving son of Thyestes, whose other children Atreus had butchered to punish Thyestes for committing adultery with his wife. Aigisthos has now become Klytaimestra's lover and accomplice in order to exact his own vengeance for this from the son of Atreus—Agamemnon. So at the end of the play, when Klytaimestra has murdered Agamemnon and Kassandra, Aigisthos cows the elders by the threat of force, and usurps the throne of Argos, with Klytaimestra as his consort. But Kassandra has prophesied that she and Agamemnon will not die unavenged. Agamemnon's son Orestes will return to exact the price for their deaths.

Klytaimestra sent Orestes into exile as a boy; and the second play begins at the moment when he has come of age and returns to his homeland to avenge the murder of his father. Klytaimestra killed Agamemnon herself, in Aeschylus' version of the story, and Orestes is, therefore, bound to commit matricide. The intense power of the second play, *Choephoroi* ('Libation-Bearers'), lies almost entirely in the implications of this one fact. It opens at Agamemnon's grave, where Orestes has returned to pray, committed to take his vengeance and regain the throne of his father. There too, on this same day, Klytaimestra has sent her daughter Elektra and her Trojan slave-women with libations to appease the shade of Agamemnon; for the gods have given her an ominous dream, in which she saw a snake suckling at her breast and drawing blood. But Elektra does not pray to her father on Klytaimestra's behalf; instead she begs Agamemnon to bring her the help she needs, so that his murder may be avenged and the usurpers defeated. Brother and sister are then united, and together they summon the power of Agamemnon and of the gods—both the Olympians and the gods of Hades below—whom they will need if their attempt is to succeed.

In the second half of the play, Orestes arrives at the palace and gains admission by deceit. With the help of the chorus, Aigisthos is lured into coming alone, without his bodyguard, and is killed by Orestes. At the climax of the play Orestes, drawn sword in hand, confronts his mother and finds the strength to exact the penalty of death from her as well.

In the first play, Kassandra's prophetic vision evoked the sight of the Erinyes or Furies created by the death of Thyestes' children haunting the house of Atreus. In Greek belief, the Furies, goddesses of the underworld, rise from the blood of a slain man or woman and cry out for vengeance. At the end of *Choephoroi*, as Orestes stands over the corpses of his victims and speaks out to justify his deed (just as Klytaimestra did in the first play), her Furies, unseen by the audience, approach Orestes. They madden him, and drive him from the stage.

Aeschylus' third play, *Eumenides*, is dominated by the Furies and by the god Apollo—who commanded Orestes to do the deed, promising that he would be safe if he then sought sanctuary at Apollo's shrine in Delphi. The final drama opens there, and both the god and the Furies now take the stage in visible form. The healing rituals of Delphi have not been enough to rid Orestes of his mother's Furies; Apollo promises Orestes final salvation, if he can evade them and make his way to Athens. There he seeks the protection of the city's tutelary goddess, Athena.

In doing so, however, he places Athena and her citizens in a deep dilemma. She cannot cast out her suppliant; yet the Furies also have a strong case against Orestes, and they will let loose their destructive powers on Athens, if it protects him from their wrath. Athena seeks to resolve her dilemma by assembling a number of her citizens, and joining with them to try Orestes. In doing so, she founds Athens' first homicide court, the Areopagos.

They hear both sides, with Apollo acting as Orestes' advocate. But the arguments are inconclusive—who *could* decide
whether a son owes more devotion to his father or to his
mother?—and the jurors' votes are evenly divided. The Athenian custom in such a case was to give the benefit of the deadlock
to the defendant; and so Orestes is released.

The Furies now turn on Athens, determined to take revenge
on the city for failing to give them their due. But Athena
promises to make up for the slight which they feel, by offering
them a permanent home in Athens. She accepts their view that
both individuals and cities need 'an element of fear' as their
sanction against lawlessness, tyranny and anarchy; she asks
them to fulfil that role in Athens. Eventually, Athena succeeds
in mollifying the Furies, and the trilogy ends as they leave,
escorted by the people of Athens, to take up an honoured residence there. Referred to by the euphemistic title of Eumenides
('Kindly Ones'), they will remain in the city, demanding revenge for the crime of murder, deterring the Athenians from
civil strife, and guaranteeing justice to the future proceedings of
the Areopagos; for the court will sit in judgment on the hill
beneath which they are going to live.

The word 'trilogy' is often loosely applied to almost any work
of drama or prose fiction which consists of one story together
with two sequels which continue its narrative further. The
*Oresteia* of course includes this basic design; but Aeschylus goes
much further, and his more ambitious design is shared by the
*Ring*. All three plays move singlemindedly from the opening
situation towards one main event which occurs two-thirds of the
way through the play; the remaining third of each drama is then
devoted to exploring the consequences of that event, and its
implications for the future of the protagonist.

The effect is that each of the first two plays is very closely
linked to the events which open the action of its successor.
Furthermore, *Choephoroi* and *Eumenides* are not just sequels
which explore the consequences of the events of *Agamemnon*:
they are also parallel to it in action and in structure. The whole
sequence is set in motion by Agamemnon's act at Aulis, which
the elders describe in the first ode of *Agamemnon*. At Aulis,

Agamemnon finds himself faced with a choice which is, from another perspective, no choice at all. He must lead the expedition against Troy, since he goes as the agent of Zeus to avenge the abduction by Paris of Menelaos' wife Helen. That act violated the ties of *xenia* (hospitality) which bound host and guest— bonds which were enforced by Zeus, the most powerful of the Greek gods. But, in sacking Troy to avenge Paris' false 'marriage' to Helen, the Greeks, whom Agamemnon commands, will destroy many innocent lives; for that action the goddess Artemis, protectress of the young and innocent, demands her price. Agamemnon, who will become a sacker of cities and the slaughterer of many, must sacrifice to her his own innocent daughter—and by doing so he will bring about his own death.

Agamemnon's action at Aulis is the paradigmatic situation which underlies the action of the rest of the *Oresteia*. The climaxes of the three plays (the murder of Agamemnon, the death of Klytaimestra, and the acquittal of Orestes) are to be seen in parallel as well as in sequence. Klytaimestra when she murders her husband, Orestes when he kills his mother and the Athenians when they judge Orestes are all, so to speak, 'remaking' Agamemnon's traumatic moment of decision and attempting to purge the world of its consequences. The pattern of the whole trilogy is conveyed through this parallelism: from the rich canvas of *Agamemnon*, the fortunes of the characters are locked into the narrow dark world of the second play, but eventually emerge into the new and different richness of *Eumenides*, where the Athenians find the power to avoid the threatened reprisal for their actions. This finally breaks the chain of violence, and they are then able to create a perpetual bond of mutual renewal with the Furies.

The reasons why the Athenians can escape are central to the meaning of Aeschylus' trilogy. Although Agamemnon's predicament at Aulis is intolerable, and all moral judgment on him at that time is balked, we come increasingly to realize, as *Agamemnon* unfolds, that in retrospect he deserves his death. He receives it at the hands of his wife Klytaimestra, and she is the protagonist in the main action of the first part of the trilogy. Yet, for all the emotional force of her motivation, in the closing third of *Agamemnon* we see her threatened with inevitable retribution for the reckless exultation with which she executed the will of Zeus.

Orestes is different. He approaches calmly, and the will of the gods has been expressed to him overtly, as a clear command from Apollo. He chooses to kill Klytaimestra, not recklessly, but knowing that he, too, does wrong. And so, in the closing third of the second play, the consequences that threaten him for his act of matricide are balanced by an equal hope for his release.

Just as it takes most of *Choephoroi* for the consequences of Klytaimestra's deed to overtake her, so too in the third and final play with Orestes. The first two-thirds of *Eumenides* are devoted to exploring ever more deeply what his fate should be; in the outcome, in the same way that Klytaimestra receives the full retribution which was threatened at the close of *Agamemnon*, Orestes, at his trial, likewise receives the equal balance which the end of *Choephoroi* foretold.

Now it is the turn of the Athenians to receive their deserts. But *Eumenides*, with its tense contest of fluctuating fortunes between Apollo and the Furies, lacks the inexorable development towards one goal which is displayed in the first two plays: its structure is more flexible, and it unfolds towards its climax without the total parallelism of plot and situation which bound together the first two plays—and the fates of their principal characters. This foreshadows a different kind of outcome; in the closing scene of *Eumenides* the Athenians escape totally from the retribution with which they were threatened.

The main action of the *Oresteia* portrays three different agents in parallel dilemmas, all of whom come to find, like Agamemnon at Aulis, that they have to choose between two alternatives. Either choice threatens disastrous consequences; but Aeschylus shows in each case that only one of the alternatives is truly possible. And it is their degree of insight into past and future, their moral stance as they embrace the decision which they must inevitably make, which determines what will ultimately happen to them.

Klytaimestra slaughters her husband recklessly, regardless of the consequences; that is why she dies. Orestes' predicament is more evenly balanced. He chooses a deed so terrible that the case against him is immensely strong, but he chooses it at the explicit command of the god of prophecy; his father's Furies will pursue him if he fails to avenge Agamemnon, and he is fully aware that what he does is itself wrong and that he will deservedly suffer for it. He therefore receives an evenly balanced fate: he is eventually relieved from further torment, but the trial does not grant him vindication.

The Athenians complete Aeschylus' pattern. They act in equal partnership with their tutelary goddess, listening fully to both sides of the question before them and absorbing all its implications. They have played no part in the violence of the trilogy, and choose the only verdict that is fair to both parties. The Athenians deserve release from all retribution—and they obtain it. Having found the 'right' moral stance, they receive in return not simply release from affliction, but positive blessing. The trilogy then closes in lyric splendour, affirming and celebrating the power of the reciprocal benefits granted to each other by the Athenians and the Eumenides.

Aeschylus unfolds a vision of our world as a place where every act has its inevitable, far-reaching consequences, and everyone ultimately receives his deserts—a fate which is the exact due consequence of what he has done. He offers us a fierce, tragic but ultimately affirmative view of mankind, and of the limits which have been set upon our actions by higher powers working within and around us.

The influence of Greek art and literature on the German writers of the eighteenth and nineteenth centuries was so great that E. M. Butler could fairly term it a 'tyranny' in the title of her famous pioneering study. Aeschylus, however, made for a long time less impression than either of the other two great tragic poets. Goethe admired Euripides' clarity of style, and laid down a challenge to his whole vision of human ethics in *Iphigeneia among the Taurians*, the greatest drama of German neoclassicism. Schiller, during his first, relatively brief period of deep admiration for Greek tragedy, translated Euripides, and when he returned at the end of his life to the Greeks, he attempted (in *The Bride of Messina*) to transfer the feeling and the theatrical form of Sophocles' Theban plays to mediaeval Sicily. It was Sophocles whom Hölderlin re-created into German in his astonishing translations, and it was Sophocles' *Antigone* that Hegel placed at the centre of his theory of art, declaring the play to be 'the most accomplished of all aesthetic works of the human spirit'.

Comparable admiration came more slowly to Aeschylus. As Walter Nestle rightly noted: 'his larger than life, monumental characters, his archaic austerity and his intellectually profound piety were fundamentally inaccessible to the generation whose feelings and opinions had been moulded by the Enlightenment and the Rococo' in Droysen *Aischylos*, p. x. Schiller once contemplated translating *Agamemnon* 'because this play is one of the most beautiful ever to have come from a poet's head'; but Goethe's reaction on first reading the *Oresteia* (in 1816, in Wilhelm von Humboldt's translation) was far more typical, and indeed set the tone for the nineteenth-century view of Aeschylean drama: 'a primaevally gigantic form, of monstrous shape, which shocks and overwhelms us . . .' Nestle, Droysen op. cit., p. ix.

Throughout the century Aeschylus was seen as a Gothic or Romantic artist, a poet of rugged, awe-inspiring grandeur and of bold theatrical effects. Only one work from the Aeschylean canon made a powerful appeal to the Romantic imagination, *Prometheus Bound*. (Ironically, this play is itself now felt by many scholars to be spurious, an imitation of what was then seen as the grandiloquent manner of Aeschylus by an author writing later in the fifth century.) *Prometheus* appealed not simply because of its bold theatrical extravagance but also because of its theme—the humanitarian defiance of a tyrannical god. Byron claimed that it had influenced all his work; it became the favourite drama of men as diverse as Shelley and Marx; it inspired the austere, enigmatic but noble fragments of Hölderlin's two Empedokles dramas. Wagner once referred to it, in a phrase from Droysen's introduction to his translation of the play, as the 'most profound of all Greek tragedies' (AE 1.34).

The other six Aeschylean plays, however, were neglected in

comparison with the attention paid to Sophocles and Euripides. Among the prominent creative artists of the nineteenth century, only one poet shared Wagner's intense admiration for the *Oresteia*: Swinburne, who termed it 'the greatest spiritual work of man'. In Germany, the neglect was partly due to Humboldt, who had been all too successful in his professed aim of preserving a feeling of distance between the present and the long departed glories of classical Greece. His translation was stilted, and did less than justice to the plays. In consequence, for many years real understanding of Aeschylus was confined to those who could read him in the original Greek.

The situation changed only with the appearance of the new translation by Johann Gustav Droysen (1808–84). This was the version that revealed the power of the *Oresteia* to Wagner: thanks to Droysen, Wagner became the first German Hellenist to see Aeschylus' surviving trilogy as the central Greek achievement in drama.

In later life Wagner confessed (D 27/6/80) that he followed his own guidance in the pursuit of classical literature—as in his musical education; it is almost certain that Droysen's introduction and notes were his only reading on Aeschylus, apart from the translation itself. For this reason the characteristics of Droysen's translation, and the view of Aeschylus which he presents in his introduction, are very important if we are to understand Wagner's reading of Aeschylus.

Droysen, who was later to become a distinguished classical scholar and historian, translated the works of Aeschylus in 1832, when he was still a student, fired with the ideals of German Romanticism, and especially inspired by Schiller's neo-classical poetry. Droysen's translation was a conscious attempt to make Aeschylus' tragedies accessible to 'all cultured and impressionable minds'. His aims were high:

> The translator must seek to render faithfully the content of the original—and even more truly the impression which the form bestows upon the content; in everything else he must work as a scholar, but in this one respect as an artist. He must know how to think himself into the soul, the spirit and the

character of the poet, so as to find, among the unavoidable approximations forced on him by the differences between languages, the right and beautiful solution . . . We have accustomed ourselves, in translations of classical authors, to take clumsiness for accuracy, and sheer crudity for a sign of archaic flavour. The first consideration is that beautiful poetry should be translated into beautiful poetry; an inappropriate sound, a mutilated word, a dislocated sentence are far more offensively false to the original than a word too many or too few . . . (pp. 7–8)

Droysen was remarkably successful, given that the sheer range of Aeschylus' poetry, from colloquial idiom to recondite neologisms, from the most delicate textures to a trenchant directness of expression, creates formidable problems for the translator. Indeed, there are many passages in which Droysen rises to an eloquence fully worthy of his original—as here, in Kassandra's farewell to life:

> Einmal noch sagen will ich letzten Spruch und Gram,
> Den eignen meinen; Dich beschwör ich, Helios,
> Beim letzten Lichte, fordern müsse, wer mich rächt,
> Von meinen Feinden, meinen Mördern gleichen Tod,
> Wie mich, die Sklavin, ihre Hand behend erschlug!—
> O dieses Menschenleben!—wenn es glücklich ist,
> Ein Schatten kann es wandeln; ist's voll Leid, so tilgt
> Ein feuchter Schwamm dies Bild hinweg; vergessen ist's;
> Und mehr denn jenes schmerzt mich dies vergessen sein!
> (= *Agamemnon* 1321ff.)

The translation often re-creates the beauty of Aeschylus' verse, and only rarely lapses into empty rhetoric. Furthermore, Droysen is conscious of the importance of preserving Aeschylus' complex patterns of interrelated imagery by adopting the same rendering where key words recur.

In one important respect his translation was far ahead of its time. Droysen is willing to risk obscurity to do full justice to the meaning and the feeling of difficult sections of his original. Free paraphrase into 'high' poetic styles became the normal way of translating Greek tragedy later in the nineteenth century, and Louis MacNeice's *Agamemnon* of 1926 is the first new version in either English or German to stand comparison with Droysen's translation, which rapidly became popular. Revised to take account of modern textual scholarship, it rightly remains in print in Germany today.

Wagner, therefore, read Aeschylus in a version which conveyed much of the power and the poetry of his dramas. But there were two important biases in Droysen's view of Aeschylus, and they both had significant effects on Wagner's reading of the *Oresteia* and his own conception of the *Ring*.

Modern classical studies lay much stress on the differences between the values, and the patterns of belief, of ancient Greece and our own. These differences are especially important for the *Oresteia* concerning questions of responsibility and justice. In Aeschylus' world, human beings are always absolutely responsible for the consequences of their actions, regardless of the strength of the motivation which has impelled them; the overtones of the Greek work *Dikē* are normally far closer to the idea of a fair or customary recompense than to a justice which is morally right.

These differences, however, were not appreciated in the middle of the nineteenth century. (Hegel's penetrating commentary on Orestes and the Furies, *Aesthetics* pp. 278–9, did not appear until 1835 and even then was long disregarded.) Droysen, like all his contemporaries, consistently construes responsibility as moral. The principals of the *Oresteia* are in his version guilty of their actions, and suffer moral retribution for sin. The man whose home 'teems excessively with wealth/more than what is best', in a literal translation of *Agamemnon* (377–8), is, for Droysen, *im Übermass schuldig*—'guilty in his excess'. *Hubris* (the normal Greek word for overbearing violence) is translated unequivocally as guilt, and its product is 'guilty crime/which wakes up to breed new sins' in Droysen's version of the famous choral meditation at *Agamemnon* 758ff. (cf. Chapter 4, pp. 136–7). Similarly, his preferred rendering of *Dikē* is simply *Das Recht*, with all its implications of legal and moral rightness; only in a few rare instances does he employ a translation for this word which conveys the ideas which are central to Aeschylus' conception.

This false emphasis is compounded. One of the most original features of Aeschylus' Orestes trilogy is that he refuses to bind it together by the traditional motif of an accursed, doom-laden house condemned by its distant past to inevitable self-destructive violence (cf. Chapter 3, pp. 81ff.). Droysen entirely misses this underemphasis. In the interchange between Klytaimestra and the chorus over the body of Agamemnon, the *alastor* or spirit of vengeance in the house of Atreus (1501) becomes, unequivocally, the 'never-forgetting Curse of vengeance for crimes of old'—by which Droysen intends a reference to the Thyestean banquet. Similarly, at the end of the scene, the 'seed of vengeance' in the house of Atreus (1565) has become *des Fluches Reiss*, the offshoot of the curse. *Blutschuld*, bloodguilt, is the theme of Droysen's *Choephoroi*: his *Oresteia* is the saga of a curse-ridden house, doomed to crime and punishment, guilt and expiation.

Wagner adopted this reading whole-heartedly. Reflecting on the *Oresteia* in 1866, he described *Agamemnon* as the play of 'complete human error—crime—desire', *Choephoroi* as 'revenge—expiation—punishment'; in 1880 he referred to Agamemnon's death as 'expiation for his father's crimes'. Earlier, this conception of the *Oresteia* had profoundly influenced the *Ring*. Alberich's curse and Wotan's guilt, together with the need for Siegfried to throw off the doom on the Volsung race which had struck down his father, are at the centre of the final text for Wagner's own trilogy.

Droysen's other bias had an equal but less lasting influence on Wagner. He was by temperament and specialization a historian, and was fired by the cause of German nationalism, as well as by the military strengths of his native Prussia. His introduction paints Aeschylus in a similar light: as an elder, a conservative citizen who was one of the generation which had twice repelled a Persian invasion and was fully conscious that his nation's freedom had been hard won. For Droysen, all of Aeschylus' plays are responses to the political situation of their times, commentaries and declarations on matters of public policy in the spirit of those passages in *The Persians* which celebrate the role of Athenian ingenuity and courage in the battle of Salamis.

In this way, the *Oresteia* is seen in a historical perspective, almost to the total exclusion of all other aspects. Droysen's Aeschylus is responding to the military crisis which was to lead a year later to the battle of Tanagra, and to the domestic upheavals created by the murder of Ephialtes, the radical reformer who in 462 had successfully reduced the powers of the Areopagos. The playwright is, on this reading, far from neutral in that dispute:

> Aeschylus has in his trilogy composed as it were a ceremony of expiation for the blood-guilt still present in the land, and at the same time a reconciliation between the savage parties which threatened to destroy the state, those who all ought to be of one mind in order to ward off the enemy at hand. But he finds the one true safety in the resurrection of the overthrown Areopagos . . . (p. 34)

Droysen sees the trilogy as the final, solemn plea of a patriotic Athenian who was fully conscious of the weight of his experience and his authority. Aeschylus is entreating the newly victorious democrats to pursue and punish Ephialtes' murderers—but also to be reconciled with the exiled oligarchs, and to unite once more in the spirit of Marathon to face the danger now confronting Athens from Sparta and her allies. Class discord must give way to the virtues of justice and moderation: 'Then the old, newly embellished Areopagos will guard the people's peace in the manner of the heroic days of Marathon, will curb their violence, and will promote every honourable cause, exalted by the blessing of the gods.' (p. 36)

Such, for Droysen, was Aeschylus' dramatic aim. His reading treats the fabric of Athenian politics with reckless anachronism, as if it were totally akin to the situation in contemporary Germany. And it presses our scanty evidence for the actual events of the years around 458 far too hard. Furthermore, Droysen's quest for historical and political relevance seems to deny any universal significance to the subject-matter of Aeschylus' trilogy. However, this one-sided reading appealed powerfully to Wagner in 1847: his own infatuation with German nationalist and revolutionary politics was then growing strongly. Droysen's picture of Aeschylus—the dramatic poet gathering up into his works the spirit of his nation's struggle for freedom, preserving it for all time, and instructing the citizens in the route to future wisdom—raised a powerful echo for Wagner of his own view of the artist's place in society. Alone among German admirers of the Greeks, Wagner held that the decline of Greek tragedy began not with Euripides and the rise of the sophists, but with the first victories of Sophocles. 'The deposition of Aeschylus was the first downward step from the height of Greek tragedy, the beginning of the dissolution of Athenian society.' (*Art and Revolution*, 1849; AE 1.52) For Wagner, the 'conservative' unity of Aeschylus' political and social vision corresponded exactly with the role which he hoped he himself could play when the German people attained unity, after the revolution which he then saw as imminent.

At the time when he read Droysen's translation of Aeschylus, Wagner was considering two possible subjects for his next work: an opera with the subject to be taken from myth, which would be based on the legends surrounding the figure of Siegfried, and a spoken verse drama, *Frederick Barbarossa* whose subject would be drawn from history. His first work in 1 8, after completing the orchestration of *Lohengrin*, was a ne  sketch towards the projected drama on Barbarossa, which was to be concerned with his struggle to achieve a supreme power based on the support of the common people of Germany. But he soon put this aside, and wrote instead an essay on the origins, history and fate of the German nation, centred on the Ghibelline dynasty and entitled (by a fanciful etymology designed to relate them to the mythical Nibelungs) 'The Wibelungen; world-history out of saga'.

In this essay Wagner's view of history, and of legend, fluctuates uneasily. On the one hand he emphasizes the poet's direct relevance to his times in the manner of Droysen, when he reads the legendary hoard of Siegfried as the lost treasure of the ancient German kings, to be won afresh only by a force and courage which contemporary Germany ha t. This is myth as political allegory; but there are other passa n which Wagner

shows that he was becoming aware of the real significance that
Aeschylus' art bore for him—the way in which myth can be used
as the vehicle for deeper truths:

> Bare history in itself scarcely ever offers us, and always
> incompletely, the material for a judgment of the inmost (as it
> were, the instinctive) motives of the ceaseless struggles of
> whole peoples and races; that we must seek in religion and
> saga . . . [they] are the fruit-bearing products of the com-
> munity's manner of insight into the nature of things and men
> . . . The gods and heroes of its religion and saga are the
> concrete personal ties in which the spirit of the community
> portrays its essence to itself; however sharp the individuality
> of these personages, their content is of the most universal,
> all-embracing type . . .                          (AE 7.266)

Wagner had been deeply inspired by Norse and German
mythology, and especially by the story of Siegfried, ever since
he had first read Jacob Grimm's pioneering book *Teutonic Mythology* in 1843. He devoured enthusiastically every other book he
could find on the subject. Yet, as he explained in his 'Communication to my friends' (1851), his vision had long been
hampered by the *Nibelungenlied*. The great epic poem of
mediaeval Germany in which the ideals of courtly romance and
the background of Christianity have drastically altered the character of the story, had prevented Wagner from seeing Siegfried
as a possible dramatic subject. But in 1847 he finally read the
Eddas, and the earlier Norse and German sagas (which were now
attracting increased attention in German cultural circles); and
their intense, pagan vision of the Siegfried story now opened up
this possibility. Although the revolutionary political climate of
1848 inclined Wagner for a while back to his Barbarossa project,
he soon abandoned it for good. He found that he could not
reduce the complex social forces of Barbarossa's life and times to
dramatic form, and could not impose his own impulse towards
universal statement on the historical subject-matter. He returned to Greek tragedy: 'and here, again, I was pointed at the
last *to myth*, in which alone I could touch the ground of even
these relationships but in that myth, these social relations were

drawn in lines as simple, plastic and distinct as those through which I had earlier recognized in it the human shape itself'. (AE 1.358)

Aeschylus exercised no 'tyranny' over Wagner. Apart from his brief notes in 1849, jotting down the themes for a possible *Achilleus* play, Wagner never seriously considered writing on a Greek legend or in close imitation of the style and forms of Greek tragedy. In 1850, he totally rejected both the approach of Racine's neo-classical tragedies, and also Schiller's attempt in *The Bride of Messina* to achieve on stage that union between a modern German content and a classical Greek form which Goethe symbolized in the marriage of Faust and Helen, in *Faust II*, Act 3 (AE 2.130–48). Of all neo-classical dramas, only Goethe's *Iphigeneia among the Taurians* attracted Wagner's unqualified admiration (as we shall see, it was to play a part in the formation of *Die Walküre* Act 3); and in *Opera and Drama* he forbore even to comment on such experiments as Grillparzer's *Golden Fleece* 'trilogy'—his low opinion of which in later life can be seen from Cosima's *Diaries*, D 25/8/72 and 17/2/81.

His relationship with Aeschylus was very different from neo-classicism. By an inspired coincidence, the *Oresteia* made a profound impression on Wagner at exactly the time when he was reading the Eddas and sagas: Aeschylus' procedures showed him the way out of his doubts about handling the myths of his own race on stage. Aeschylus chose to stage only a single, isolated sequence of actions in each play, selecting from the body of myths available to him and creating his own version of the incidents, using a limited number of characters and scenes and evoking the surrounding penumbra of related past or present events only by allusion. This simple, direct method showed Wagner how traditional legends from his own culture could be dramatized; and it influenced him decisively. His choice now went to Siegfried, and he proceeded to outline in a prose sketch his own version of the Nibelungen legends—the story of Siegfried's fate and its mythical background. The sequence of events which he outlined now, in 1848, was to become in three years' time, with only a few modifications, the plot of the four dramas of the *Ring*.

This firm commitment to material drawn entirely from myth was the first stage of an extended rethinking by Wagner of his aims and methods. He did not compose again for nearly five years, and during that time the influence of the *Oresteia* is prominent in all his thoughts.

Wagner needed to reconsider the nature of his art on a number of different levels. Two of his first three mature operas—*The Flying Dutchman, Tannhäuser* and *Lohengrin*—blend history and myth. The story of the Dutchman is a folk legend; but in Wagner's opera its mythical hero makes his appearance in a human action taking place in a particular country. Senta, Erik and Daland are almost entirely created from Wagner's imagination, and the period of the action is not specified; but *Tannhäuser* and *Lohengrin* raise far more serious problems. In these operas historically real figures from the German middle ages take the stage alongside characters drawn from myth (Venus in *Tannhäuser*, and Lohengrin himself) who symbolize forces from the invisible world beyond our immediate apprehension. The antithesis between the aura of the 'other world' and the human figures set firmly in the pageantry of mediaeval life is crucial to the meaning of the operas; but it presented (and still presents) considerable problems in production, and it also led Wagner into stylistic difficulties as he composed. The ethereal music of the Grail in *Lohengrin*, and the astonishing sounds which Wagner created in his Paris revision of *Tannhäuser* to give full musical expression to the delights of the Venusberg, are wonderfully evocative; but they are both fundamentally incompatible with the more conventional, extrovert style of the rest of their respective operas.

Wagner had also fully explored one particular vein in his writing. *Tannhäuser* and *Lohengrin* present exactly the same conflict between sensuality and spirituality, with spirituality gaining the victory after protracted struggles. Both texts offer a subjectively portrayed contest between Romanticism and an ascetic, Christian element. We are invited to be partisans—to give all our favour to the good characters and to abhor those who have evil, seductive powers. But this intention is undermined by Wagner's music. *Lohengrin* in particular, with its powerful characterization of Ortrud and its moments of full sympathy for Friedrich von Brabant, shows that the composer was beginning to feel a need to analyse the forces of darkness more deeply—and more objectively.

Wagner's impasse after *Lohengrin* was not confined to the content of his work. Over the last few years his dissatisfaction with everything to do with opera houses, both the expectations of the audiences and the practices of singers and managements, had mounted to a point where he could hardly contemplate a repertory production of any of his operas without horror. This feeling was partly due, of course, to his appalling experiences whenever one of his operas was produced; but it was also due to a rising discontent with the medium.

Traditional operatic forms had become increasingly incompatible with Wagner's artistic aims. Although the action is continuous and the text lacks formal divisions, *The Flying Dutchman, Tannhäuser* and *Lohengrin* all contain recognizable arias, ensembles and choruses separated by recitative-like passages which carry the bulk of the action. The detailed musical structure is highly regular: long passages are built up in simple groups of four or eight bars. By 1848, Wagner was increasingly preoccupied with exploring in depth the character and psychology of an individual within a developing situation, and he needed to modify his musical idiom drastically in order to do this. He could not develop the use of significant recurring motifs any further within the musical language which he was then using—but he could not advance to a more developed musical language until he could adopt a more profound relationship between music and text. The answer was to lie partly in language, in replacing the flowing verse periods of his earlier libretti by *Stabreim*, a flexible, clipped form of alliterative verse; but also in a complete revision of his idea of dramatic form and his manner of building up scenes.

Wagner's reading of the *Oresteia*, as he reflected in exile on the meaning of Aeschylus' achievement, provided him with solutions to all of these problems. He brooded on the high seriousness of Aeschylus' dramaturgy, the religious intensity of the vast and diverse audience at the festival of Dionysus and the direct communication which Aeschylus had achieved with every member of that audience through the use of known, traditional myths and the union of poetry, music, dance and spectacle into 'the one, the truly great Artwork'. Wagner gained from this the courage to withdraw entirely from any hope of producing his subsequent works in the conditions of a normal German stage. He came to realize that his Nibelung material could not be effectively handled within the compass of one drama, as he had originally intended. In the autumn of 1851 Wagner resolved to follow Aeschylus' example and write a trilogy. His planned new dramatic cycle thereby developed a profound relationship with Aeschylus' *Oresteia*. This relationship influenced the formal construction of the texts, the role of the orchestra, and the whole conception of fate, inevitability and expectation in the *Ring*.

# 2

# The *Oresteia* and the Creation of the *Ring*

Wagner's first attempt to dramatize the Nibelung story was the poem for a 'grand heroic opera' entitled *Siegfried's Death* (AE 8.1f), which was written in October 1848. In phrases influenced by Ludwig Feuerbach's philosophical writings, Wagner expressed the hope that Siegfried would incarnate his revolutionary ideal, 'the human being in the most natural and carefree fullness of his sensual vigour', untrammelled by any conventions and true to his instincts even in the face of death (AE 1.375). Siegfried was to be the new man, who would rise to power after the oppressive forces of capitalism had brought about their own destruction. His tragedy was to be 'the feast of all mankind; in it free, strong and beautiful man will celebrate the joys and pains of his love, and will achieve, exalted and fulfilled, the great love-offering of his death' (AE 1.58). The opera was to embody Feuerbach's visionary philosophy of a life which could place all its trust in the instincts and be committed to 'joyfully and consciously recognizing the truth of sensuousness'.

The actual text makes a rather different impression. *Siegfried's Death* is a drama of human ambitions, intrigues, deception and betrayal. The plot, treatment and structure are firmly in the tradition of German Romantic drama, and the apotheosis of Brünnhilde and Siegfried, who rise at the end from their funeral pyre to join Wotan in Valhalla, simply restates the ideal of redemption in death through love which Wagner had already placed at the close of his last three operas. There is little here in common with Aeschylus apart from the use of legendary subject-matter and a few details of form. Indeed, this text needed several major modifications, and all the musical powers which Wagner had developed some twenty years later, before it could become (under the new name of *Götterdämmerung*) an adequate vehicle for the closing stages of the trilogy which Wagner eventually resolved to write.

The events of 1849, and his own prominent (though futile) role in the Dresden insurrection, forced Wagner to leave Germany in haste. Meanwhile he had already felt the constrictions of his proposed new operatic text. He toyed with two ideas for verse dramas—on Jesus, and on Achilleus. Both would have involved abandoning music, and Teutonic myth. Once again Wagner was at a crossroads.

When he had settled in Zurich, Wagner did not immediately attempt to compose the music for *Siegfried's Death*. Instead he wrote three prose treatises, in and through which he completely re-examined his aims and methods as an artist. They are *Art and Revolution*, *The Art-work of the Future*, and *Opera and Drama*. They occupied Wagner throughout the second part of 1849 and the whole of 1850. During this time he composed no music, apart from attempting a sketch for the first scene of *Siegfried's Death*.

Wagner was the first to admit that he was not comfortable as an essayist; and many parts of his prose treatises make difficult reading. But they shed a wealth of light on the musical and dramatic practice of the *Ring* and of *Tristan und Isolde*; and their importance to Wagner at the time was immeasurable. When he had finished them, he returned to his Nibelung material with his conception of what a drama based on mythical material should be very much enhanced, and in the course of 1851 he totally modified his plan. He expanded the proposed work of art from a single opera about Siegfried to a trilogy covering the entire Nibelung story as he had originally outlined it in his sketch; and he renounced the conventional idea of opera altogether. The musical riches of the *Ring* are entirely directed towards the illumination of the action. Wagner marked this new dramatic orientation, and the cycle's formal affinity with the Orestes trilogy, by the subtitles which he gave to its component parts. The *Ring* is a sequence of three 'stage festival plays' preceded by a 'preliminary evening'.

In the three prose works, Wagner evolves his conception of the 'art-work of the future' by a wide-ranging consideration of aspects of Greek tragedy. The new drama is to be not a simple imitation but a re-creation in the deepest sense of the spirit of Greek tragedy, drawing on all the resources of the modern theatre and orchestra to rescue drama from the vices which Wagner diagnosed in the nineteenth-century theatre. As he developed this argument, Wagner's response to Aeschylus evolved far beyond the simple act of abandoning historical material for myth.

*Art and Revolution* opens with the statement that 'in any investigation of the art of today, we cannot take a step without coming face to face with its connection with the art of the Greeks' (AE 1.32). And as the treatise proceeds it becomes plain that the first role of Greek tragedy in Wagner's argument is as the means to register and clarify his fundamental dissatisfaction with the theatre of his own times. Greek tragedy, he argues, was far superior to the art of the present for three reasons: first, the finest minds of the fifth century poured 'the noblest principles of consciousness' into the art of the theatre, whereas in the nineteenth century intelligent people justifiably despised the stage. Second, Greek tragedy was performed at a religious festival, not as an everyday evening's entertainment; Greek cult and Greek drama were united, while Christianity and the contemporary theatre were not. Third, the character of actors and audience was entirely different. The Athenian audience comprised the whole of the *dēmos*, not simply the most affluent members of society; the Athenians themselves acted in their dramas, rather than delegating this task to half-despised members of the lower classes; and their performers worked for nothing or a token reward, rather than being paid professionals.

Wagner argued (correctly) that Greek tragedy only went into

its final decline when, under the acute social and political stresses of the Peloponnesian war, the Athenian audience lost that unity of culture, customs, and religious belief which had given Aeschylus and his audience such a close relationship. 'The flowering of tragedy lasted for just so long as it expressed the spirit of the community, and as this spirit was a truly popular, that is a communal one.' (AE 1.136)

But Wagner's conception of the role of the unified national community in the creation of art goes further. 'Poetry can be made only by the community, or in its footsteps.' (AE 1.134) This view obliged him to ask how and why the products of the community have poetic force—and so to confront, in *Opera and Drama* (2.2), the nature of myth and its role in the dramas of the Greeks.

Myth, he argues, is the basic material of Greek tragedy. It had to be, because no one person alone can fully understand the nature of our world. The community created its gods in an image it could understand, that of man—and so took the first step towards interpreting the world and the place in it of mankind. By its own imaginative powers, the community 'becomes, in myth, the creator of art'. And, since the myths are essentially attempts to achieve a comprehensible portrait of the world as human beings experience it, 'they must necessarily achieve artistic value and form'. The Greek tragedian, on this view, had the role of compressing and distilling such myths into the form which appeals to the imagination of every audience, and so of bringing them from the realm of fantasy to that of reality:

> The form of his artwork, and its unifying features, were already indicated to him in the contours of the myth, which he had only to develop into a living edifice; he was in no way to break them into pieces and fit them together again as an arbitrarily invented artistic building. The tragic poet merely imparted the content and essence of the myth in the most convincing and intelligible manner, and his tragedy is nothing other than the artistic completion of the myth itself; while the myth is the poem of a life-view in common.    (AE 2.156)

Interpreted narrowly, these words would leave the dramatist

with the simple role of a vehicle for rich, ambiguous ideas passed through him from folk-legend to his audience.

Wagner came to take a rather different view of myth. It is of course true that many myths express truths of wide import about the world—even if they do not all necessarily embody timeless or archetypal insights. But this feature, while important, is not central to the impact of Greek myth as it was handled by Aeschylus, Sophocles and Euripides before an Athenian audience. The conflicts and sufferings of the great households of the heroic age mirrored on a large scale, and with exceptional clarity, tensions which could arise in the lives of every member of the audience; and the playwrights used the cultural continuity between the world of Homer and that of the fifth century to present their views on fundamental aspects of human life in an economical, direct medium—that of myth. But for Wagner, in the second half of the nineteenth century, there was no analogous continuity between the German people of his time and the world of his sources. The *Ring*, therefore, had to rely far more on the shaping powers of its creator than this theory of myth would allow. So it is not surprising that, talking to Cosima in 1871, Wagner frankly acknowledged that 'the reason why the Greek legends have made such an impression on you is that they were seized on by such tremendous poets' (D 2/7/71). Myths are the raw material, whose images the poet can employ as the vehicle for his own exploration of the world around him.

Such a position is already implicit in *Opera and Drama.* Just before the final statement quoted above, Wagner writes of the tragic poet's task in very Aeschylean terms: the Greek playwright was to take a far-reaching but compact 'idea' (the content of the myth), and to ensure that this was realized 'with the fullest definition' in one 'inevitable and decisive action'. How was this to be done?

> To bring to understanding the inevitability of the action, by demonstrating the truth of the 'idea'—in this lay the solution of his task.                    (AE 2.156)

The role of necessity and inevitability in drama is the most neglected aspect of Wagner's *Opera and Drama*, even though it is the most fundamental connection between Wagner's dramatic technique in the *Ring* and that of Aeschylus.

Wagner's argument (AE 2.157ff.) turns on the question of man's relationship with nature. The Greeks, by 'an involuntary error', created their gods in man's image. In doing so they endowed everything they saw in nature with human form and an existence like that of human beings. This was their mistake, according to Wagner. Nature for Wagner has her own necessity and logic, which are very different from the reasoning processes of human beings. But it is a mistake which made tragedy possible, as the structures of Christian belief and nineteenth century society did not. For Wagner as for Goethe, modern man lives in exile from nature, divided off from it by his *Kultur*—the artificial world of civilization. We must be able to turn our backs on civilization and cast ourselves once more into the arms of nature. Conceiving nature in man's image gave the Greeks a feeling of affinity with the natural world, and with that an external viewpoint from which they could take comfort in man's own achievements and his ethical conceptions. For them:

> death counted not merely as a natural, but also as an ethical necessity; yet *only as the counterpart of life*, which *in itself* was the real object of all his perceptions, including those of Art. Life itself, by its reality and instinctive necessity, caused the tragic death, which in itself was nothing else but the ending of a life fulfilled by the development of the fullest individuality, a life expended on making this individuality significant. (AE 2.159-60)

And from this perspective, tragedy was possible for the Greeks.

*Opera and Drama* later turns to the needs of the contemporary theatre (II.5), and Wagner argues that here, too, a convincing relationship with nature is essential if tragic sense is to be made of death. The modern dramatist must understand nature to the full, because he can place the human action of his drama in context only by setting an understanding of nature before us, and he can complement this understanding properly only by conveying a feeling for nature. For he must make sense of his action by displaying its inevitability (just like Aeschylus); and he can do this only by relating man to his surroundings, by displaying 'a great coherent group of the phenomena of human life, through which alone their necessity can be grasped' (AE 2.220).

Wagner's argument is an attempt to confront the intense presence of the gods in Aeschylean drama, and to answer the need in the modern theatre for a corresponding vocabulary of the marvellous. It is scarcely an exaggeration to say that in Aeschylus the gods *are* nature. They personify it in all its various aspects and forms, and their activities portray the ways in which the power of natural forces affects the actions of men. It is nature, exhibited in the portent and the hostile winds, that dictates Agamemnon's sacrifice at Aulis; the whole of the first part of *Choephoroi* portrays the process by which Agamemnon's rightful heirs come into full alignment with the forces of nature, while as the play unfolds Klytaimestra and Aigisthos are increasingly seen to be monsters, divorced by their tyranny from all that is fruitful and natural in life. Conversely, the reconciliation of Athens and the Eumenides, at the end of the trilogy, is portrayed almost entirely in the images of mutual increase and regeneration. Just as Klytaimestra almost blasphemously aligns Agamemnon's homecoming and her victory with the cycles of the seasons (*Agamemnon* 966ff. and 1299ff.), so the female fertility, that was blighted in her, is finally restored in the women of Athens. The imagery of nature, fertility and storm is not the most important complex of metaphors in the *Oresteia*; but it is clearly present and significant. In Aeschylus, to be in harmony with nature is to deserve peace and prosperity; and in Aeschylus men inevitably receive, sooner or later, their deserts.

So too in the *Ring*. Wagner's gods do not, with three exceptions, personify aspects of nature; they have other roles to play. But the stage spectacle and rich orchestral palette of the *Ring* cycle are designed among other things to evoke the many moods of the nature which surrounds Wagner's characters; and their aspirations and achievements are measured by the degree to which they match and harmonize with the world around them.

As we shall see, this procedure is even more important in the *Ring*, especially in *Siegfried*, than it is in the *Oresteia*.

Against this deep affinity with Aeschylus, however, there is a crucial difference. Wagner's vision of nature was considerably influenced by that of Feuerbach. For the philosopher as for the composer, nature is human experience—all that shapes man and can influence man. And our sensuality—the interrelation between our experience and our feeling—is central in the development of our understanding of human life. Modern civilization's denial of nature is the principal barrier between humanity and freedom (AE 1.56–7). For Wagner, man himself manifests in his instincts and his impulses the powerful impetus of nature; Wagner is committed to exploring the world of inner feeling in a way which is quite alien to the spirit of Aeschylus. But there are two good reasons for this. First, human life, for Aeschylus and his audience, is constantly surrounded and interpenetrated not merely by the gods themselves, but also by the *daimones*— lesser personified powers such as Persuasion, Blindness, Ruin and Strife. To the early Greeks, the boundaries of the human self and the human psyche are narrow. A mortal's talents and powers, and his physical and mental limitations, are the gift or the infliction of the gods; indeed, only those actions which are performed by the conscious rational mind in full command both of itself and of the limbs are regarded by Homeric man as initiated by 'himself' and as 'his own'. All other actions— especially those, such as a sudden, unexpected change of purpose—which we would ascribe to 'our' sixth sense, instinct or inspiration, are for them *theia* (the Greek word which conveys at once the notions of strange, marvellous and godlike), and were regarded as being the work of the gods—that is, of forces outside the borders of the self—no less than events such as the onset of death or disease, fair weather or foul, of love or war.

The influence of Homer's Olympians extends over almost every area of human experience. They 'give expression to all that is great and vital in the world', as Bruno Snell once wrote. Aeschylus' dramas are less expansive than Homer in their portrayal of the gods; but his human characters are arguably even more surrounded by the presence of the divine; and the gods and *daimones* of Aeschylus are inexorable. In his tragedies their actions portray the working of forces which Wagner, writing in the nineteenth century against a very different conceptual background, was obliged to regard as inside his characters.

Second, Aeschylus placed his characters within the framework of a fully stable political and social world. Wagner, in *Art and Revolution*, regarded this as a 'conservative' artistic stance because Aeschylus' plays do not argue for radical social change. The completed *Ring* trilogy not only abandons this level of simple political dissent but is also a revolutionary work in a far deeper sense. It is set in a shadowy world in which the text only hints at the external appearances of the characters and their surroundings, and is not related to any precise political or social context. One of the most radical features of the *Ring* (and also of *Tristan und Isolde* and *Parsifal*) is that the feature which primarily relates them to our own real world is not anything which is seen on stage, but the intangible sound of the unseen orchestra.

Nature for Wagner includes human nature; the two are interrelated, and man himself in his instincts is one of the highest manifestations of nature. Wagner employs his orchestra both to express the forces of nature as they are seen on the stage and, more importantly, to explore the ways in which nature manifests itself in the human psyche—in the conscious and unconscious feelings of Wagner's characters. This is how, in the *Ring*, the vital impression is created, that what is taking place is inevitable.

Wagner claimed on several occasions that the orchestra plays the same part in his dramas as the chorus in Greek tragedy. The Greek tragic playwrights placed a group of twelve (later of fifteen) singing actors in the *orchēstra*, the circular dance-floor which lay between the spectators and the scene-building in front of which the solo actors played most of their parts. In later antiquity the chorus simply provided lyric interludes between scenes, but in Aeschylus' dramas it is a collective character which participates strongly in the action. Its comments and lyric meditations are interwoven with the rest of the action; they are always directly relevant to the situation and contribute in themselves to the advancement of the plot. Wagner held that in his dramas the Greek chorus was replaced in its emotional effect by the concealed instrumental musicians, who occupy a similar middle position in Wagner's theatre; while in its individual human reality the Greek chorus is replaced by the singing actors of Wagner's stage.

This claim has been too readily dismissed, chiefly because of the wide influence of Schlegel's false doctrine that the chorus played the part of an 'ideal spectator' in Greek tragedy. Wagner had greater understanding. In 1861 he described the Greek chorus, correctly, as constantly 'seeking to understand the motives of the action, and to form from that a judgment on the action', and claimed that in a similar way 'the orchestra of the modern symphonist will take so intimate an interest in the motives of the plot that while, as the embodiment of harmony, it alone allows the melody to make a definite expression, it will also keep the melody in the requisite unceasing flow, and so convincingly impress these motives on the spectators' feeling' (AE 3.338).

Wagner wrote these words after he had composed the music for two thirds of the *Ring* and for *Tristan und Isolde*. And they are an accurate description of the role played by the orchestra in those dramas. Wagner had no desire to locate his central characters and their predicaments firmly in the context of political life, as Aeschylus had done by his use of the chorus. But he *did* need to place them in the context of nature, and to explore their relationship with it. Aeschylus' choruses are groups of people who analyse the situations in which they find themselves—and they do so with obvious intellectual coherence. Wagner's orchestra has a parallel purpose, as he first put it in *The Art-work of the Future*: to make sense of the action for us by relating the actor's surroundings to his inner emotions and 'to enclose the performer with an atmospheric ring of Art and Nature' (AE 1.101). This goal required one difference from Aeschylus' choruses. The intellectual coherence of the orchestral scores—so clear when Wagner's late works are analysed in the study—should not be predominant when they are heard in the theatre. Thought has been converted by the music into emotional understanding; and this matches the difference between Aeschylus' social and political context, with its open processes of reasoning, and Wagner's context of nature, with its direct appeal to instinct and the unconscious mind.

Wagner had fled from Dresden precipitately, and with hardly any personal effects: in exile at Zurich, he was at first without a copy of Aeschylus. If anything this increased the influence of Wagner's conception of Aeschylus' writings on both the prose works and the *Ring*. Wagner's general reflections on tragedy profited by the distance which enabled him to theorize about those aspects of the Greek achievement which were most important to his own artistic needs; and in 1851 his conception of the use to which he would put his Nibelung material altered radically. It evolved into a relationship with the *Oresteia* which was so close that it would have created an impossible pressure on Wagner, had Aeschylus' trilogy actually been at hand as he embarked on creating his own.

Wagner completed *Opera and Drama* in January 1851. Comments in his letters indicate that as late as the beginning of May he still envisaged composing *Siegfried's Death* as a new opera by itself; but as the year continued his intentions changed completely. He first came to realize that many intricacies of motivations and relationships in the projected opera were either loosely suggested, or relayed to the audience in an allusive narrative form more appropriate to epic than to drama; and that since *Siegfried's Death* was 'at present unproduceable and, for the public, incomprehensible', there was nothing to deter him from placing the earlier phases of Siegfried's life on his hypothetical stage as well, in a complementary work to be called *The Young Siegfried*. And the two operas would contrast well with each other. As he wrote to his Dresden friend Theodor Uhlig:

> *The Young Siegfried* has the decided advantage that it presents the important myth in the form of a play to the public, just as a fairy tale is presented to a child. Here everything makes a plastic effect by means of sharp sensuous expressions, here everything is understood at once—and then if the serious *Siegfried's Death* follows, the public knows all which has

there to be presupposed or even only hinted at . . .

(U 16/5/51)

The plan which Wagner envisaged at this stage was for the connection between the two operas to be relatively loose. They were to be given their premières in sequence, but could afterwards be performed separately.

Even while he was still living in Dresden, Wagner had told one of his friends that 'I will write no more grand operas; I will write fairy tales, like the one about the boy who knows no fear.' Wagner—perhaps half-consciously remembering that in the *Volsung Saga* (c. 20), when Odin (Wotan) punished Brünnhilde, she swore an oath that she would marry no man who knew fear—was now stimulated by the idea of grafting this folk story on to Siegfried's early adventures, and he rapidly sketched and versified the text of *The Young Siegfried*. Despite many later alterations of detail, it resembles the final version set to music in all essentials.

One feature of the text whose substance was not subsequently altered was the Wanderer's decision in his dialogue with Erda (Act 3 scene i) to renounce the world and bequeath it to Siegfried. Wagner had rightly become dissatisfied with the end of *Siegfried's Death*, in which Brünnhilde frees the Nibelungs from enslavement to the ring and ascends from the pyre with Siegfried to join Wotan in eternal joy in Valhalla. Already by 1850 he had pencilled in the margin another ending, in which Brünnhilde tells Wotan that his guilt has been purged, redeemed by Siegfried's deed, and bids him:

> pass away in bliss before the deed of a man,
> the hero whom you begat!
> From your anxious fear
> I proclaim to you blessed redemption-in-death!

At one point in his 1848 prose sketch, Wagner had envisaged the possibility that the gods could come to their end: 'it is for the high destiny of expiating their own guilt that the gods now educate mankind; their purpose will have been achieved when they have destroyed themselves in this creation of human beings, namely when they have had to surrender their direct influence, faced with the freedom of the human consciousness' (AE 7.303). And now, as he drafted *The Young Siegfried*, Wagner took up this idea and made a radical alteration in the course of the story. 'Wotan and the Wala; end of the gods. Wotan's resolution' is Wagner's first note for Act 3 scene i. 'Guilt of the gods, and their inevitable decline. Siegfried's destiny [*Bestimmung*], self-annihilation of the gods' was the way in which this idea was to be developed into the second scene.

Wagner's attention came to focus increasingly on Wotan and his predicament, and these scenes now became central to his conception of the meaning of his Nibelung story. As Wagner wrote to August Röckel, Wotan, when he resigns his power before the advent of Siegfried, 'rises to the tragic height of *willing* his own destruction. This is the lesson that we have to learn from the history of mankind; *to will what necessity imposes*, and ourselves to bring it about.' (R 25/1/54)

The *Oresteia* had, in Wagner's reading, presented a world of initial crime and turbulence, which ultimately achieved harmony and reconciliation at Athena's hands, with Zeus, enthroned on high, adding his approval. The original ending to Wagner's own proposed plot mirrored this pattern; but during his years in exile Wagner's attitude changed completely, as his disillusionment with the prospect of revolution—and with all hopes for the advancement of human society—increased. As he embarked on *The Young Siegfried* he began to realize that the true direction of his Nibelung story was towards a complete dissent from Aeschylus' vision. He felt this intuitively, even when he was using this story, in *Siegfried's Death*, as the basis for a socially and historically optimistic work. But this feeling surfaced only now. The project, he later wrote to Röckel:

> had taken form at a time when I had built up in my thought an optimistic world, on Hellenic principles; believing that in order to realize such a world, it was only necessary for men to want it. I ingeniously set aside the problem, why men actually did not want it. I remember that it was with this definite creative purpose that I conceived the personality of Siegfried,

with the desire to represent an existence free from pain. But I meant to express my meaning even more clearly in the presentation of the whole Nibelung myth, by showing how from the first wrong-doing a whole world of evil arose, and consequently fell to pieces— in order to teach us the lesson that we must recognize evil and tear it up by the roots, and establish a just world in its place. I was scarcely aware that in the working out, indeed in the first elaboration of my plan, I was being unconsciously guided by a wholly different, infinitely more profound scheme, and that instead of conceiving a phase in the development of the world, I had grasped the very essence and meaning of the world itself in all its possible phases, and had realized its nothingness; the consequence of which was, that since I was faithful to my living intuitions and not to my abstract ideas in my completed work, something quite different saw the light from what I had originally intended.

(R 23/8/56)

The new conception of the work, however, caused problems in its turn. Once again, as with *Siegfried's Death*, Wagner found that parts of *The Young Siegfried* narrated significant events which needed to be shown on stage to be fully understood. And so, in October 1851, he decided to dramatize the whole of the plot outlined in the 1848 sketch. His dissent from the 'Hellenic optimism' of the *Oresteia* was now to be matched by an assent of form: his Nibelung drama was now to be a trilogy, with the three dramas preceded by what Wagner at first termed a 'grand introductory play', *The Theft of the Rhinegold*.

He had chiefly been led to this point by the decision to change the ending of the drama. The two great confrontations in the Third Act of *The Young Siegfried*, between the Wanderer and Erda, and Brünnhilde and Siegfried, had drawn Wagner's attention increasingly to the tragic predicaments caused earlier by the love of Siegmund and Sieglinde and their flight from Hunding's house—first for Wotan, and then for Brünnhilde. And as he now dramatized these events, in the new first drama *Die Walküre*, Wagner found himself approaching a fundamental question which he had previously neglected.

The three plays of the *Oresteia* are bound together by the relationship between the events which form the climaxes of the successive dramas, and we see these events as parallel and inter-related because we are invited to measure each of them in turn against the sacrifice of Iphigeneia, which is set at the beginning and provides the impetus for the whole triology. Wagner's plan now contained a sequence of loosely related, parallel events in the three main dramas; but it lacked a cogent starting-point. In 1848, the sketch began with Alberich's theft of the Rhinegold from the depths of the river. Only now did Wagner supply that theft with a motive. Drafting the prose outline for the action of *Das Rheingold*, he invented the idea that the gold could be acquired only by renouncing love.

The dramas now achieved unity and completeness. This motif became the connecting theme of the *Ring* and the focal point round which all the subsequent principal characters are mea-sured. In Wagner's writings of this period, the giving of one's self to others in love is central. Again echoing the ideas of Feuerbach, who argued that man's individuality can be perfected only through love and relationships with other people, Wagner maintained that only love for each other can redeem mankind from the tyranny of violence and the suffering caused by human weakness. Wagner further claimed that this universal love of fellow human beings can grow only from the basis of heterosex-ual love; indeed, it is only when man and woman are united that they attain 'the full measure of humanity'. All else is a compro-mise with the world. In the *Ring*, the inescapable tragedy of life is that we must all in some way make such compromises, and sacrifice love to a greater or lesser extent in order to gain power of any kind.

The creation of *Das Rheingold* therefore marks the final shift in the emphasis of Wagner's Nibelung work. Siegfried, the perfect ideal of humanity, still remained important after Wotan's predicament came to the forefront of Wagner's mind; and so, too, Wotan now remains important, as Wagner proceeds to measure him, and all the other main characters of the *Ring*, against the new basis of Alberich's frustration by the daughters of the Rhine, the temptation offered by the Rhinegold, and Alberich's choice (all of which were invented by Wagner).

This idea is developed further after Alberich places a curse on the ring of power in *Das Rhinegold*, scene iv. The curse is a prominent theme in *Die Walküre*, and it is stressed in the two major revisions which Wagner now made to *Siegfried's Death* (which in 1856 he retitled *Götterdämmerung*)—the rewriting of the opening scene for the Norns, so that the curse rises to break their rope, and the new scene (Act 1 scene iii) in which Waltraute unsuccessfully pleads with Brünnhilde to renounce the ring.

The intense importance of these two dramatic motifs was reflected in the music. As we shall see, each climactic moment of the *Ring* is shaped musically in such a way as to establish the moral stance towards love and power of each character in his or her moment of tragic choice. Each such moment is shown (chiefly by the recall of the 'renunciation of love' theme (Ex. 2) in the music) as a 'remake', an attempt to purge the world finally of Alberich's curse and the consequences of his initial decision. Alberich inaugurates the action of his trilogy (Wagner now entitled the cycle *The Nibelung's Ring*) by preferring power to love—just like Agamemnon at Aulis. In the three successive dramas of the main action, first Wotan, then Siegfried and finally Brünnhilde attempt to 're-make' his deed and purge the world of its consequences, as do first Klytaimestra, then Orestes and finally the Athenians in the *Oresteia*. And so Wagner's dramatic concept had come intensely close both in form and content to Aeschylus'.

Wagner now renounced totally the ideal of producing his dramas on the conventional operatic stages of his time. The Nibelung trilogy was to be performed under conditions as near to Aeschylus' as was possible in the nineteenth century, 'at a great festival, to be arranged perhaps specially for the purpose of this performance' (L 20/11/51). Wagner (in two letters) even envisaged presenting his new work for only one performance, after the custom of the fifth-century Athenian playwrights—and then destroying the score and parts!

But Wagner no longer writes of the community and its creative need supplying him with a new, intuitively understanding audience. Just as the *Ring* itself was now far from the ideals of social revolution which lay behind its initial conception, so too Wagner, disillusioned by the failures of the nationalist movement, had abandoned the ideal of a new public for his works, one more popularly based than the traditional class of opera-goers. Foreshadowing his later ideal for Bayreuth, he wrote that:

> As an audience I can only imagine an assembly of friends who have come together for the purpose of knowing my works somewhere or other, best of all in some beautiful solitude, far from the smoke and pestilential business odour of urban civilization.                                           (L 30/1/52)

The *Ring* suffered only one more change while the music was being written. Wagner's mood of withdrawal and isolation from the world deepened over the next two years, until in August 1854, shortly after sketching the music for the famous scene (*Die Walküre* Act 2 scene ii) in which Wotan bitterly and angrily renounces life, he wrote to Liszt: 'let us look upon the world through the medium of contempt alone. It is worth nothing else; to found any hope on it would be deceiving our own hearts . . .' This mood developed to a point at which Wagner found himself forced, in 1857, to abandon the composition of the life-affirming *Siegfried*. *Tristan und Isolde*, which Wagner had first planned in the autumn of 1854, had increasingly come to dominate his thoughts.

In *Tristan und Isolde*, the values of ordinary life are totally inverted. In Act 1, the ship which carries Isolde to her arranged marriage is seen entirely through her eyes, embittered by Tristan's ceremonious care for etiquette and apparent indifference to her love. In Act 2 the day is hateful to the lovers; they would have the night of their ecstatic union stay for ever. And when that ideal passes from their reach they resolve without hesitation to pursue their love beyond our world, united in the endless night of death.

In 1856 Wagner grafted an ending in the same spirit on the close of *Götterdämmerung*. He wrote twenty extra lines of verse for Brünnhilde which reflect the ideas of the writings about Buddhism which he had recently been studying. In them she enters 'the open gates of eternal becoming'. Stricken into insight by the sufferings of her love, she is 'redeemed from rebirth', renounces both Valhalla and our world, and achieves 'the blessed end/of all eternity':

> Deepest suffering
> of grieving love
> opened my eyes;
> I saw the world end.

These lines remained in the text of the *Ring* until Wagner came to compose the music for the final scene, in 1872. Then Cosima, who felt (rightly) that they were rather artificial, persuaded Wagner not to set them to music (D 26/10/71 and 10/1/72). He printed them, however, in a footnote to his final version of the text, claiming that in his role of composer he had had to omit them from the drama as staged, but only because 'their meaning is expressed with the utmost precision in the effect of the drama sounding in the music'.

The concluding music which Wagner actually wrote in 1872 bears little relationship to the spirit of the lines which he had written in a pessimistic frame of mind in the mid-fifties. In the finale of the completed *Götterdämmerung*, Brünnhilde passes not to Nirvana but to glory; and although the gods do come to their end, the world does not. As we shall see in Chapter 6, there are considerable differences between the close of the *Ring* and that of the *Oresteia*. Nevertheless, Wagner extends in the music, as Valhalla blazes, a promise of hope and fruitful increase which is comparable with that which Aeschylus perceives as springing from the closing concord between the Athenians and the Eumenides. Wagner's idea of basing a drama on the story of the Nibelungs began with a superficial debt to the use of myth in Greek tragedy; but by the time the music had been completed the *Ring* had evolved into a close harmony of spirit, form and subject-matter with Aeschylus' trilogy. In the same way, what was originally, in *Art and Revolution*, a simple revolutionary dissent from the 'conservative' character of the *Oresteia* now became, in Wagner's final conclusion to the *Ring*, an act of profound, creative acceptance and qualifying dissent. Wagner assents to Aeschylus' closing assurance of prosperity but disagrees utterly as to how it is to be brought about.

Wagner's *Ring* shows a genuine affinity of feeling with the world of the *Poetic Edda* and the early Norse sagas. This is especially evident in the language of the poem, which ingeniously re-creates in modern German the verse forms and the alliterative style of the *Edda*, and exhibits a kindred fascination with kennings, riddles and etymology. Wagner was also predisposed by his nationalist leanings towards using Teutonic myth for the subject-matter of his most important work. But this material caused several problems, when chosen for the basis of a drama which was to renew the spirit of Aeschylus in the nineteenth century.

Aeschylus wrote for an audience which was closely familiar, perhaps since childhood, with a number of previous versions of the story of the house of Atreus, from the Homeric epics down to recent lyric poems and plays which are now lost to us. Aeschylus did not of course expect them to clear their minds of all memory of those versions while watching the *Oresteia*—this would negate the whole purpose of basing new tragedies on old stories. The audience was to presume, in general, that the 'standard version' of each story was being followed, unless it was specifically contradicted. But the audience had to hold that knowledge in a special relationship to the new dramas. It must not be allowed to rush in actively and fill gaps with incidents deliberately omitted by the playwright; and it must never be allowed to obliterate new variants, even when they departed from central, near-canonical parts of the traditional version. The audience's provisional 'knowledge' of how the story is likely to turn out was a passive field, so to speak, for the Greek dramatist to play on. The audience 'knew' more than the human characters in the plays, who are placed in the normal human situation of having no certain knowledge about the future. With so much of *how* things are to happen supplied by tradition, the Athenian playwrights were largely saved the burden of exposition, and could concentrate their powers primarily on showing the interactions of people and events which explain *why* they happen.

Aeschylus had of course to make plain what is going on where the *Oresteia* innovates—as, for example, with the new reason supplied in *Agamemnon* for the sacrifice of Iphigeneia (in the main tradition, Artemis demanded the sacrifice because Agamemnon had shot a sacred stag, and boasted that 'not even Artemis could shoot so well'). But elsewhere, allusion sufficed to carry even the most central points.

In the *Oresteia*, Aeschylus exploits his audience's partial foreknowledge. He works his innovations gently into the plays, and in general keeps close to the patterns set by previous treatments. Aeschylus does not employ the surprises, and sudden reversals of audience expectation, which play so large a part in Euripides' work, in the late plays of Sophocles and in Aristotle's theory of drama. The climaxes of the three dramas are not surprises: on the contrary, each play leads up to a moment of acute tension whose outcome fulfils the audience's deepest expectations. Agamemnon must and will die; Orestes will succeed in his plan, and must kill Klytaimestra; the Athenians will acquit Orestes and yet escape retribution. The audience's foreknowledge makes each outcome a strong possibility from the earliest moments of the play; and Aeschylus organizes the subsequent action so that this possibility is slowly but inexorably converted into certainty. And so the act of violence at the climax of each of the first two plays is elevated to tragic stature, simply because by the time it takes place Aeschylus has shown it to be inevitable. For all their horror, the deaths of Agamemnon and Klytaimestra brought to the Athenian audience a profound sense of relief.

Wagner was in a very different situation. The poems which he drew on provide far more variants on even the most basic questions about Siegfried's parentage, upbringing and later adventures than the versions of the story of Agamemnon and Orestes that were available to Aeschylus; and Wagner also needed to clarify the antecedents of Siegfried's life, to work out the motivations of his characters right back to the theft by the gods of Andvari's (Alberich's) gold—and, indeed, further, to answer the question of where that gold itself came from. These were matters on which his sources presented no clear or consistent accounts. When Wagner outlined a version of the story for his own use in 1848, he was obliged to perform a quite formidable feat of adaptation, synthesis and creative innovation.

This gave him full creative freedom; but the price was high. Only a few specialist scholars would know these legends in any other form than that which Wagner presents; the rest of the audience, unlike Aeschylus', had no expectations drawn from other previous versions of this story on which Wagner could play. This meant that one of the main resources which the Greek playwrights exploited by dramatizing traditional materials was not available to Wagner, and he was obliged to devise alternative ways of directing the audience's expectations so that the outcome of the dramas fulfils them satisfactorily. Nor could Wagner draw on a knowledge of the basic functions and roles of the gods and goddesses, a shared vision of the disposition of the universe and vocabulary for describing it. The Nordic gods and goddesses were strange to the nineteenth-century audience, and their roles in the *Ring*, like everything else in Wagner's version of the myth, can be apprehended only from the dramas themselves.

In most instances this is possible; the final text of the *Ring* only very rarely makes the mistake of alluding to legends which are neither enacted nor expounded elsewhere in the trilogy. And since, unlike the *Oresteia*, the *Ring* was published in advance and ultimately designed for more than one performance, Wagner could rely on an increasing familiarity with his own version. All Wagner's musical and dramatic powers were, however, still needed to compensate for the audience's lack of any previous knowledge of the mythology used in the *Ring*.

Wagner's choice of material presented a further problem. Classical Greece is exceptional in that the earliest surviving poetic version of its principal myths is immensely sophisticated: all primitive and uncivilized elements have been discreetly eliminated from the accounts in the *Iliad* and *Odyssey* of the deeds of gods and heroes. The two great Homeric epics concentrated on the human interest of their mythical material, suppressing as far as possible all fantastic, magical and barbarous legends. As a result of this emphasis, the fifth-century dramatists could use the myths with few essential alterations, because they were directly related to the world of the audience.

By contrast, the cultural gap between the world of the *Eddas*, *Thidrek's Saga* and the *Volsung Saga* and any audience which Wagner could have hoped to assemble for his dramas in the nineteenth century was immense. The world of the sagas is violently divided between the dwarfs, the trolls, and two groups of gods who are fully their equals in savagery and treachery. It is threatened by monsters—wolves, dragons and the Midgard-serpent. Magic and murder, theriomorphy and cannibalism are recurring motifs in the actions of human beings.

There is, therefore, a total divergence between the values of Wagner's sources and those which he sought to impose on them. In the sagas, Odin (Wotan) frequently intervenes in human affairs for reasons which have nothing whatever to do with love, guilt or self-redemption; and the human world is committed to warrior codes of honour and revenge which were completely alien to Wagner's vision of human motivation. As a result, Wagner had to superimpose the entire ethical structure of the *Ring* on his material. Such central decisions as Alberich's renunciation of love for power, Wotan's act of willing his own destruction, and Brünnhilde's elevation of Siegfried's blind loyalty to the level of heroism are made in the *Ring* for reasons which could not have been understood by the heroes of the original poems and sagas. Even where action and reaction totally coincide in Wagner and his source, as in Brünnhilde's decision to avenge herself upon Siegfried, Wagner had to supply a completely new motivating link.

Despite the fact that his material was unfamiliar, Wagner sought to make the homogeneous, self-contained world of the *Ring* not only credible to the audience but as close, and as direct in its impact, as the world portrayed in Aeschylus' tragedies had been to the Athenians. Like the classical Greek tragedians, he sought to use the ancient myths of his own culture to dramatize contemporary problems. This enterprise raised formidable difficulties.

Wagner's first problem was, of course, the presence of the gods. *Siegfried's Death* alone committed him to little more serious presentation of divine forces than any other nineteenth-century opera. Except in the Valkyries' visit to Brünnhilde's rock, divine powers do not appear on the stage, and the gods are simply unseen forces who are supplicated by the human characters at appropriate moments in the drama. In the 1850s, the time of the rise of Naturalism, this was mere operatic convention; and Wagner rightly came to realize that his trilogy would have to go far further, to present its gods on stage and involve the spectator in their predicaments, if it were to carry any conviction. But this created a further problem. Aeschylus' gods only rarely appeared on stage: when they did appear they created an immediate effect, since the audience believed in them and their functions and powers were all known, basic features of everyone's lives. By contrast Wagner, especially in *Das Rheingold*, was committed by his story to presenting a strange world inhabited by gods who were completely unknown to a majority even of German audiences.

Part of his solution was to raise classical echoes in the spectators' minds. Wagner disregarded the Norse distinction between the Aesir and the Vanir, and united the gods presented in *Das Rheingold* into one group under the command of Wotan, who like Zeus on Olympos is authoritative but not omnipotent. There are clear echoes of Homer's Zeus and Hera in the edgy confrontations between Wotan and Fricka in *Das Rheingold*, scene ii, and *Die Walküre*, Act 2 scene i. The wise prophetess, the Wala of *Voluspa*, has become an earth-goddess of Wagner's invention: Erda's name is taken from Gaia (Earth), the goddess who is called 'the first prophetess' (cf. Wagner's 'Urwala') in the second line of *Eumenides*.

These are examples of obvious, specific debts to the Greeks: ingenious scholars have alleged others, some rather far-fetched. Wotan's subjugation of Erda, so that the Valkyries were created by a union between the father of the gods and the Earth-mother, is a good example; although sometimes claimed to have been inspired by the fragment of Sophocles in which Earth is the mother of the Furies, it was in fact Wagner's own invention—see D 8/5/74. In general the details of mythological parallels are far less important than the characters of the individual gods;

Wagner brings some of the less well defined gods and goddesses of the Nordic pantheon to life by deliberately echoing their counterparts on Olympos. Fricka takes on some of the characteristics of Hera, Freia of Aphrodite, while Loge (though his chief model is the Apollo of the *Oresteia*) has also gained a verbal dexterity akin to that of Prometheus—also, like Loge, the bringer of fire—in addition to the attributes of the Nordic trickster-god Loki.

The *Ring*, nevertheless, needed far more than these simple echoes if it were to attain anything comparable to the rich, direct role that the gods play in Aeschylus. The world of Aeschylus' dramas is solidly anchored in a social hierarchy which ascends from the lowest slaves to the lord of Olympos himself, a hierarchy in which each man and woman, god and goddess has an assigned place, and in which there is danger simply in the act of going beyond that place, regardless of the causes. Perhaps Wagner's greatest single achievement in the *Ring* was to create for himself a credible hierarchy which could match Aeschylus', and provide a background against which equally important aspects of human life could be dramatized.

One of the most striking features of Teutonic mythology is the presence in many of the legends of dwarfs and giants, living in the world alongside men and gods. Eddaic cosmology is notoriously complex, and the disposition of the world which the poems presented to Wagner is quite beyond dramatic representation. Nor did their difficult, three-dimensional picture of the universe provide a clear hierarchy which could replace Aeschylus' perfect ordering of powers.

Aeschylean man lives on earth between the gods of Olympos above him and the shadowy underworld of Hades. Shakespeare's tragedies and Goethe's *Faust* present an even more pronounced version of the same vertical division into three: their stage, like that of the mediaeval mystery plays, is a precarious platform suspended, as it were, between heaven and hell. Wagner organized the *Ring* in the same manner. As the Wanderer tells Mime in *Siegfried* Act 1 scene ii, their world is divided between the gods' high abode, Valhalla; the earth, lived on by men but dominated by giants; and the depths of

Nibelheim, home of the dwarfs, the spirits of darkness. And throughout the trilogy the music reinforces this division: the inhabitants of each region are distinguished from each other by music of sharply characterized harmony, rhythm and orchestration.

Vertical division is also employed in the first three dramas of the *Ring* to organize the scenes and arrange them in a symbolic relationship with each other. Man is absent from *Das Rheingold*, and the earth on which he is to move later in the trilogy is replaced as the middle level by the Rhine. The drama moves vertically from the initial position at the centre, which is occupied by the Rhinegold. First we ascend to the environs of Valhalla, then descend below the Rhine to visit the depths to which Alberich has taken his prize; we are taken up again for the final scene to Valhalla, from whose radiant heights Wotan feels able to look down—both literally and metaphorically—on the laments, 'in the depths' from his point of view, of the daughters of the Rhine.

Wagner takes pains in *Das Rheingold* to establish the symbolic force of these vertical movements. The prelude itself is an ascent from the opening E flat in the basses. Then Alberich arrives on the scene from below the bed of the Rhine, and the Rhine-daughters incite him coquettishly by falling near to and rising out of his reach. He must climb up in order to take the gold, and they feel its loss so keenly because he takes it down into his darkness. In scene iii, Alberich's ambition is to advance with his army to the heights, rising up to conquer the gods and rape the goddesses; while the pathos of his position in scene iv is expressed by his being forced to command his Nibelungs to make the same ascent simply to deposit his treasure at Wotan's feet.

The music at each of these points, and that of the interludes during the three scenic transformations in *Das Rheingold*, is designed to reinforce these metaphors, and they are continued in *Die Walküre* and *Siegfried*. Until Fafner is dead, the earth remains the province of the giants, and the gods and dwarfs venture there from the heights and depths only because they are drawn by the lure of the ring. Meanwhile, the success of

Wotan's two consecutive attempts to remake Alberich's theft, and atone for his own brief tenure of the ring, is chronicled by the gradual ascent through the action of each of these two dramas. *Die Walküre* begins on earth in Hunding's hut, then rises in Act 2 via the slope on the mountains to the summit on which Brünnhilde is confined in Act 3. In his own drama, Siegfried remakes that ascent, passing from Mime's underground cave via the surface of the earth—which he clears of its last giant and so makes safe for mankind—to the heights. He alone has the power to climb to Brünnhilde against the barrier which Wotan has placed. These two slow but steady ascents ensure the fullest pathos at the end of the first act of *Götterdämmerung*, where the traumatic rape of Brünnhilde by 'Gunther' drags the trilogy down for good from the heights to the ground level of human intrigue.

Wagner also sought to bring the *Ring* close to Aeschylus' structural methods. Only a certain amount could be done with *Siegfried's Death*, which was written before Wagner's ideals for the *Ring* were fully formed. It still contained extensive passages for the operatic chorus, all but one of which were cut from *Götterdämmerung*, and a number of areas of interest which is quite un-Aeschylean. But *Opera and Drama* firmly proclaims the virtues of dramatic economy, continuity, and unity of texture. Each phase of the action, Wagner writes (AE 2.215), must be shaped towards a single point, a 'moment' into which as much 'life-energy' as possible is concentrated. And the number of such 'moments' in a drama must be limited, so that each may be adequately motivated. Incidental, complex side-motives must be subordinated to this design, so that the causes of these decisive 'moments' are fully intelligible to the audience.

This is simply the Aeschylean ideal of an action shaped so as to culminate in the illumination of one central event, rephrased into Wagnerian terms. And it is followed absolutely in the first three dramas of the *Ring*—and also, incidentally, in *Tristan und Isolde*. Each act, and in *Das Rheingold* each scene, is completely shaped so as to lead up to one central event or decisive 'moment', which occurs just before the end:

*Das Rheingold*
Scene i  Alberich takes the Rhinegold
Scene ii  Wotan resolves to take the gold from Alberich
Scene iii  Wotan and Loge capture Alberich
Scene iv  The gods take possession of Valhalla

*Die Walküre*
Act 1  Siegmund and Sieglinde unite in love
Act 2  Wotan kills Siegmund
Act 3  Wotan renounces Brünnhilde to Siegfried

*Siegfried*
Act 1  Siegfried forges Notung
Act 2  Siegfried learns that he can win Brünnhilde
Act 3  Siegfried and Brünnhilde abandon themselves to mutual love

Although the form is rather more discursive, a parallel pattern may tentatively be traded in *Götterdämmerung*:

*Götterdämmerung*
Act 1  'Gunther' overpowers Brünnhilde
Act 2  Brünnhilde, Gunther and Hagen resolve to murder Siegfried
Act 3  Brünnhilde renounces the ring and immolates herself

In Acts 1 and 2 of each drama, these climaxes are followed by a brief but trenchant coda. With another act to follow, which will itself develop the full implications of what has just happened, there is no place for an extended closing section establishing the consequences. But in each case Act 3 is different. Wagner, like Aeschylus, was aware that the conclusion of each work must establish precisely the implications of the main event and crystallize the moral stances of the agents, in order to generate the next drama of the trilogy. The final scene of each of the four *Ring* dramas does this as carefully as the closing third of each of the three plays of the *Oresteia*.

*Das Rheingold* corresponds to the first, extended choral ode of *Agamemnon*: it expounds the preliminaries necessary to the understanding of the main action of the trilogy. The end of

Aeschylus' ode is a shifting web of suggestion, in which the positive aspects of Agamemnon's expedition are undermined; Wagner closes his 'preliminary evening' with a similar crystallization, as the magnificent tableau of the rainbow bridge and the grandiose orchestral music to which the gods attain their entry into Valhalla are undercut by the laments of the daughters of the Rhine and by Loge's ironic commentary.

The conclusion to each of the three main dramas is equally precise. The complex pattern established in the orchestra, as Wotan departs leaving Brünnhilde on her rock, presents a balance of aspirations, hopes and fears which draws out all the implications for the future of his act; the extended duet at the end of *Siegfried* closes with an abandoned exultation in present joy, carefully undercut by premonitions for the future. And the orchestral conclusion to *Götterdämmerung*, with its complex interplay and counterpoint between all the relevant main motifs of the trilogy, is a lyric coda to the entire work which is truly parallel to the lyric concord of the last pages of *Eumenides*.

This Aeschylean organization is matched by an Aeschylean economy. With the exception of the 'ride of the Valkyries', *Die Walküre* and *Siegfried* both obey the Greek rule that no more than three principal actors should ever be on stage together. *Siegfried* indeed is even more classical in its economy: if the three animals are counted as supernumeraries, it is a two-actor drama like the earliest plays of Aeschylus. But Wagner's achievement in *Die Walküre* is perhaps even more notable, since its plot is adapted from a section of the *Volsung Saga* which teems with characters and incidents. Wagner compressed his material into three acts of formidable economy which profit considerably from the small number of characters. Aeschylus would have recognized and admired the way in which Act 1 crystallizes round the triangle of Siegmund, Sieglinde and Hunding; and the confrontations in Act 2 between Fricka and Wotan, Brünnhilde and Siegmund, and the scene (Act 2 scene v) where Sieglinde awakes alone and sees in a vision her husband's imminent death, are no less Aeschylean in spirit. Wagner had begun to move towards this kind of economy in *Tannhäuser* and *Lohengrin*; but it is not fully practised in either, since the requirements of the plot made him frequently resort to operatic forms—arias, choruses and elaborate ensembles. In such passages the words of the drama frequently overlap and, therefore, text to become inaudible—a vice which the Greek tragedians constantly avoided, and which Wagner did not permit himself in the *Ring* before the closing duet of *Siegfried*. The new economy of staging is matched by the measured, ordered pace of the *Ring*, and the way in which dialogues and monologues of controlled passion issue into decisive moments of action. These techniques, which were to be developed even further in *Tristan und Isolde*, are the most overt mark of Wagner's debt to Aeschylus.

They would not, however, have been possible without the entirely new role which music takes in the *Ring*. Aeschylus' gods are the forces of nature; Wagner's (with the exception of Erda, Donner and Froh) are not, and the burden of providing the *Ring* with an equivalent to Aeschylean man's rich relationship with nature falls almost entirely on the orchestra. The principal reason why the *Ring* sounds radically different from Wagner's earlier operas is this new purpose to which the orchestra is applied. It envelops the characters of the trilogy in a seamless web of sound, a lyric cosmos which creates the illusion that they and their actions are permanently surrounded and placed in the context of nature—even in the many passages where the orchestration is restrained and almost of chamber-music texture.

Much of the most obviously spectacular orchestral music in the *Ring* is directed towards this end—one need think only of the preludes to *Das Rheingold* and *Die Walküre*, the 'forest murmurs' of *Siegfried* Act 2 scene ii or the three dawns of *Götterdämmerung*; but the relationship goes far deeper than this. In scenes ii and iv of *Das Rheingold*, the fortunes of the gods are measured not simply by the way in which their strength fades when Freia is taken away as a hostage—although this is itself a powerful indication of their loss—but also by the density of the mist on stage. As she is taken away, a thin mist advances on the gods; it begins to disperse when Wotan acquires the ring and Freia is brought back by the giants, but it is finally cleared by Donner only when Freia is redeemed and the gold has passed entirely from Wotan's possession. Each of these sequences on stage is carefully matched by orchestral music which finely evokes the changing situation, so that music and stage-image together measure and illuminate the moral stance of the characters. Syntheses of this closeness are not practised continuously throughout the *Ring*, any more than nature-imagery obtrudes itself throughout the *Oresteia*; but Wagner, just like Aeschylus, employs harmony with nature as a measure of the characters' aspirations and deserts at every decisive moment in his cycle, and the orchestra plays an essential part in communicating this and binding the characters' inner psychic states to the nature which surrounds them.

The 'forest murmurs' themselves, and Siegfried's two great meditations under the linden tree are a crucial part of the process by which Siegfried gradually comes to attain a harmony with nature which makes him worthy to break the Wanderer's spear and pass through the fire to Brünnhilde; and the measure of how much better his fortunes are than his father's is that Siegmund, in contrast, is relatively unable to harmonize his perceptions with nature. Siegmund and Sieglinde do attain a joyous union with nature in *Die Walküre* Act 1 scene iii, when the great door flies open and spring replaces the winter storms at the moment when their mutual love displaces their long loneliness and suffering; but they maintain it only briefly. The storm is back in earnest as Act 2 begins.

Harmony with nature is one of the main axes of the meaning of the *Ring*. And so the characters' attempts to dominate nature by force and impose their will are equally important. Four obtrusive means to power—the ring and the Tarnhelm, Wotan's spear and the sword Notung—play a prominent part in the drama.

Although they are very rich in metaphorical images, the dramas of Aeschylus are not allegorical and almost never employ symbolism. The boundaries of the self in the fifth century are so narrowly drawn that the objects employed by the characters of the *Oresteia*—Klytaimestra's tapestry and net, the offerings at Agamemnon's grave, the sword of Aigisthos and the tokens of purification which Orestes takes on at Delphi—have unequivocal force, being clearly real and 'outside' the person who wields them. Indeed, Aeschylus consistently sees unity where we would make a distinction between the material and the spiritual. The *miasma* ('pollution') which Kassandra detects in the house of Atreus is presented by the play as a real, literal defilement, even though to us what she sees is a psychic phenomenon—the presence in the house of the Furies, crying out for vengeance for blood shed in the past—added to a material one—Klytaimestra's preparations for the murder of Agamemnon. And when, at the end of *Eumenides*, the Furies feel that the Athenians have wounded them by freeing Orestes, they make no distinction between their (to us, abstract) loss of prestige and the concrete denial of their place and role in life. The pressures and motivations which we categorize as social or moral, psychological, legal or religious are all homogeneous for Aeschylus, since all are portrayed as the interventions of gods. He employs a 'vocabulary of the marvellous' which is also direct and literally true.

The *Ring* is in a more equivocal position. Wagner must create his 'marvels' for us out of myths with which we are not familiar, and our modern minds have no choice but to read them symbolically. This necessarily makes the question of their reality ambiguous. Is Wotan's spear just a symbol of the will to power, or has it some independent literal force?

The orchestra guarantees the independence of these instruments of power. It is Wagner's intermediary between the inner world of the characters' minds and the outer world which surrounds them; and just as the sumptuous textures of the 'forest murmurs' establish a reciprocal relationship between the forest which surrounds Siegfried and the thoughts which stir within him as he rests in its shade, so too the orchestra relates the inner ambitions of Wotan, Alberich and others to the four instruments of power which they wield on the stage. The themes associated with these four objects are not simply static, pictorial descriptions but mesmeric, dynamic realizations in music of the effect which they have when they are used. They guarantee that the objects do not appear simply as metaphorical extensions of the personalities of their bearers. They symbolize four of man's chief means of acquiring power over nature and over other living creatures; their musical treatment shows that it is as important for the characters of the *Ring* to achieve an adequate relationship with them as with their surroundings.

Nowhere, perhaps, is this more evident than at the start of *Die Walküre* Act 1 scene iii. Siegmund, left alone in Hunding's hut, gives expression to the desires which Sieglinde's 'fixed, eloquent look' has implanted in him. His feelings rise to an intense passion in which he cries out for his father's sword; and it is partially revealed to him, embedded in the central tree. Throughout the monologue Siegmund's aspirations rise and fall both with the surrounding web of orchestral sound and the images presented on the stage, since the light of the fire in the hearth behaves in a most unnaturalistic fashion. As the scene evolves, it rises as if in answer to his call from a tiny glimmer to a flare which almost reveals to him the sword which he needs; but it is not quite revealed, because his perception and his love are not yet great enough for nature to yield him this as his deserved prize.

Ex. 1

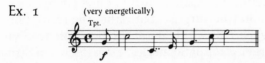

Wagner uses the orchestra to establish a total congruence between Siegmund's inner thoughts and his surroundings: the interplay of motifs, the varied recurrences of Ex.1 and the rise and fall of the musical tension support the imagery of the text, binding together the blaze of the fire and the gleam in Sieglinde's eye so that her piercing gaze at the end of the last scene is now matched and answered by the sudden flaring of the fire; and the orchestral fabric binds together the rise and fall of Siegmund's aspirations both with the gleam of the fire which is the work of nature, and that of the sword which is the instrument of power bequeathed to him by a god. In such scenes as this Wagner's ideal of integrating the resources of music, acting and stage-picture is fully achieved; so too is the promise of his theoretical works, that in his new dramas the orchestra would establish his characters' inner thoughts in a firm relationship to the world around them.

The scene is also one to which expectation and fulfilment, hopes and fears are central. The memory of Sieglinde torments Sieg-mund and assails his heart with 'enchanting fear'. His hope and apprehension mount until he gains the courage to cry out in a prayer for his sword; and that prayer is answered. But the firelight blinds him, and he cannot see clearly what it is. Gently, as the fire dies down, the glare of the hilt and the penetrating gaze of Sieglinde fuse in his memory, and he falls back into the comfort of serene expectancy:

> The shadow of darkness
> closes around me;
> in the inmost depths of my heart
> still glows this invisible fire. (112)

His hopes and his prayers, for both the woman and the sword, are answered at once with the return of Sieglinde.

The *Ring* is the fullest attempt in modern drama to re-create the sense of gathering anticipation, and fulfilment in release by a 'surprise' that is no true surprise, but rather the realization of what is deeply expected, which are at the heart of Aeschylus' work and the earlier plays of Sophocles. Even Ibsen and Strind-berg did not disdain the techniques of Scribe: melodramatic intrigue, intense surprise and the sudden reversal of the aud-ience's expectations. Indeed, they positively exploited them. But Wagner had begun to turn his back on such methods after *Rienzi*. The quasi-mythical quality of *The Flying Dutchman*, and the way it moves steadily towards the feeling that Senta *is* the woman who will end his wandering by sacrificing herself, are an even more decisive break from the general direction of nineteenth-century theatrical practice than the opera's overall economy and its innovations in musical language and form. To create in the *Ring* a trilogy based entirely on mythical materials, Wagner had now to abandon melodramatic surprise almost completely.

He had already shown that he was aware of this, in a powerful passage of *Opera and Drama*. He argues that foreboding or presentiment will be an essential part of the drama of the future, and assigns the main burden of awakening it to the orchestra:

in the evocation of moods such as the poet must awake in us, if he is to procure our indispensable assistance, absolute instrumental speech has already proved itself all-powerful; since precisely the arousing of indefinite feelings of foreboding has been its most characteristic effect; but this aptitude could only become a weakness wherever it also wanted to give a definite shape to the emotions it had roused. Now if we apply to the 'moments' of the drama this extraordinary, unique enabling aptitude of instrumental speech; if we entrust it to the poet, to be used to further a definite aim in a real situation, then we must try to agree on the source from which this language has to derive the sensuous moments of expression in which it is to clothe itself . . .                    (AE 2.331)

Wagner does not describe that source fully or satisfactorily in *Opera and Drama*. But in the *Ring*, the text is organized so as to create sequences of expectations which arouse the probability that they will be fulfilled; and Wagner's orchestral music elevates that probability into a feeling of necessity.

One of the most obvious of the textual devices is the way in which Wagner grafts familiar elements from fairy tale on the myths used in the *Ring*. Siegfried's early adventures are fused with the motif of the boy who had to learn to fear: Loge captures Alberich, in the third scene of *Das Rheingold*, by a trick borrowed from Perrault's *Puss in Boots*; and the variant traditional versions of Siegfried's first encounter with Brünnhilde are synthesized with the help of deliberate echoes of the story of Sleeping Beauty. In each case Wagner relies on the fact that his plot is close to the pattern of a well-known story to help the spectator to anticipate a particular outcome—the outcome which in fact occurs, in all three cases.

The other way in which the text is organized is by adopting a fundamental pattern found in western folk stories. It has often been observed that western European myths and folk tales tend to be organized with three as the unit of satisfaction and narrative completeness. Paris must honour one of three goddesses, and chooses the gift of the third. Thor is set three tests by the giant Utgard-Loki, and acknowledges defeat when he has been unable to succeed fully at any of the three. Fate is personified by three Moirai in popular Greek belief, three Norns in Germanic. A very large number of parallels could be cited.

Wagner imposed organization by threes at several significant points on the stories used for the text of the *Ring* (which is of course a trilogy of three-act dramas). In Wagner's dramatization, the Rhine has three daughters; only when Alberich has courted, and failed with all three is it poetically appropriate and satisfying that he should renounce love for gold and power. The Nibelung treasure, when forged, has three parts: the solid gold, the Tarnhelm and the ring. They are of progressively greater importance, and it is only when all three have been wrested one by one from Alberich that we sense his defeat by Wotan as total. This makes the extent and bitterness of his curse dramatically right; and it also prepares for the ransoming of Freia, who is freed by precisely the same sequence of three progressively harder exactions, this time from Wotan himself.

In *Siegfried,* important information comes in threes on two occasions. Mime asks the Wanderer three questions, spanning the three levels of the known world; the Wanderer counters with three also, spanning past, present and future. With his failure at the third Mime's life is forfeit. Similarly, the woodbird has three pieces of advice to give Siegfried, and there, too, the third is the most important and the one that leads to decisive action. The sequence of the woodbird's advice is restated in Siegfried's narrative of his youth in *Götterdämmerung* Act 3 scene i—and it imparts a chilling impetus to the movement towards the third revelation. For again the third is decisive; the simple pattern of three gives all the necessary finality to Hagen's revenge.

The *Ring* also engages the problems of expectation and fulfilment on a far deeper level than this. Foreknowledge and prophecy play a decisive part at several principal moments in the trilogy. Wagner intends his audience to take Sieglinde's visions in *Die Walküre* Act 2 as seriously as their counterpart, Kassandra's prophetic agony in *Agamemnon,* was taken by Aeschylus'. Erda and the woodbird are to be no less authoritative in their advice than Aeschylus' Apollo.

This would have been impossible in the nineteenth century without the use of music to reinforce Wagner's vision of destiny, and large-scale musical designs are used to make his dramatic strategy carry conviction. Two decisive moments in *Das Rheingold* are made to overshadow the remainder of the action of the trilogy: Alberich's renunciation of love, and his curse upon the ring.

Musical recalls of the theme (Ex.2) to which Alberich renounces love for power set in perspective three decisive choices in *Die Walküre*: Siegmund's taking of Notung, the sword of

Ex. 2

need—and also of misery—by whose power alone he can defend his love, Sieglinde's resignation in Act 3 from a life without Siegmund, and the climactic moment at which Wotan renounces all his love for Brünnhilde and bequeathes her to Siegfried. The theme is absent from *Siegfried*, whose hero, because of his 'innocence', is not faced with this choice; but it returns with terrible force in *Götterdämmerung*, where it chronicles the baleful rise of Hagen, and is also heard in all its power at the crucial moment where Brünnhilde rejects Waltraute's plea, clinging to 'Siegfried's ring' whose allure is about to destroy her marriage (469-70). Wagner remarked when composing this scene: 'when the ring was snatched from her I thought of Alberich; the noblest character suffers the same as the ignoble, in every creature the will is identical' (D 4/6/70).

Alberich pronounces his curse in *Das Rheingold* scene iv to an equally trenchant thematic phrase, Ex. 3. Throughout the trilogy its recurrence reinforces and chronicles the rising

Ex. 3

power of fate, the strength with which Alberich's curse constricts the characters and limits their choice, until the climactic moments, near the end of *Götterdämmerung*, during which the Rhinedaughters drag Hagen away from the ring, and the motif is graphically snapped in mid-utterance (1333).

In the *Ring*, these fateful products of 'male' ferocity are surrounded by a gentler fate which is, in Wagner's vision, of female origin and is even more inexorable. As Erda appears in *Das Rheingold* a simple ascending sequence of chords (Ex.4c) is heard—it is a development of the arpeggio, Ex.4a, which is the first evocation of the Rhine and its daughters. And as she prophesies that the gods will come to their downfall even if Wotan takes her advice to flee the ring, this theme becomes joined for the first time with the corresponding, symmetrical descent (Ex.5), which completes the pattern. The conjunction of Ex.4c with 5 is almost magical in its calm authority, and imparts a new hope at once to the world of the *Ring* when it returns to herald the Wanderer's colloquy with Erda in *Siegfried* Act 3 scene i. Later still, returning even more calmly than before when Brünnhilde enters the hall in the final scene of *Götterdämmerung*, it prepares the audience for the feeling that the end of the gods is now utterly right.

These are principal motifs of the *Ring*. But the transformations and recurrences of all the major themes of the work are similarly designed to shape our expectations over a wide span of the action. One of the most notable examples is the use of Ex.6 in *Siegfried*. It first appears in *Die Walküre* Act 3 scene iii, at the moment (955-6) when Brünnhilde first begs that, if Wotan is to leave her asleep on the rock, she may at least be protected by a terrifying barrier, so that only a fearless and free hero may find her there. And it returns with overwhelming force in the last pages of the drama, in such a way that it becomes totally associated with Brünnhilde.

Ex.6

This motif first occurs in *Siegfried* when Mime tries to persuade Siegfried that he needs to learn fear (276ff.). Mime expects him to do this by fighting Fafner. But the association of Ex.6 with Brünnhilde at the end of *Die Walküre* undermines this expectation of Mime's in the audience's eyes from the start; while the recurrence of this motif later in *Siegfried*, almost every time learning fear is mentioned in the text, powerfully increases the expectation that Siegfried will learn fear only when he finally confronts Brünnhilde. This expectation is abundantly fulfilled in the last scene of the drama (991–2).

These are examples of large-scale, obvious effects, analogous to that of the two principal motifs, 'he who does, shall suffer' and its counterbalancing hope 'yet may good prevail', against whose dialogue the rich canvas of the *Oresteia* unfolds. There is of course a wealth of supporting detail. It is so richly and rigorously conceived that in this respect Wagner is convincingly Aeschylean. The *Ring* unfolds a world in which expectations *are* fulfilled, at the widest and most satisfying levels. Just as in Aeschylus, almost all the characters eventually receive their deserts. And the one exception, as we shall see, lies at the heart of the difference between Wagner's vision of the world and Aeschylus'.

It was never Wagner's aim, even in the first enthusiasm of *Art and Revolution*, to imitate the achievements of the Greeks in the manner of neo-classicism. Revolution, not restoration, was his aim then; and the trilogy which he eventually composed achieved it. The *Ring* is, in Wolfgang Schadewaldt's gnomic but accurate paradox, an *Urschopfung aus Vorgeformten*—an original creation from previously formed elements. Wagner has adapted the ancient legends of the north to express his own personal vision of the world. But the patterns which he imposed in order to organize his material are either adapted from, or designed to replace, those used by Aeschylus in his tragic dramas. It was perhaps sheer coincidence that Wagner read the earliest surviving versions of the Nibelung and Sigurd myths with the example of the *Oresteia* before him; but that coincidence began the process which led to the conception and creation of the *Ring*.

The *Ring* is so closely related in procedure to the *Oresteia* that it may be said without exaggeration to be in a constant dialogue with it. This dialogue extends to every aspect of Wagner's conception of his trilogy, from the use of myth as the material for drama through the surface level of overall organization, to the most profound affinities between the Greek chorus and the modern orchestra—between Aeschylus' methods of creating and satisfying expectation and Wagner's own. And it also extends to the plots and subject-matter of the two trilogies.

# 3

# *Das Rheingold*

## GODS AND HEROES

During his days on the Dresden barricades in 1849, Wagner made jottings for a possible drama on the subject of Achilleus. One of his notes read:

> Man is the perfection of God. The immortal gods are the elements, which only beget mankind. In Man creation accordingly achieves its end. Achilleus is higher and more complete than the element-power Thetis. (AE 8.367-8)

The idea that man is superior to the gods was soon transferred from the Greek world to that of the Nibelungs. Already in the prose sketch of 1848, Wagner notes that his gods will have achieved their end 'when they annihilate themselves by the creation of men'; and it is fundamental to the plot of the final version of the *Ring* that Wotan, simply by having possessed the ring, has been tainted himself and must therefore resign his power to mortal men.

In the *Oresteia* the gods, far from yielding their place to mankind, consolidate their power at the close of the cycle. Zeus is revealed, in the trial-scene of *Eumenides*, as the ultimate power behind all the dilemmas of the trilogy (616ff.). And Athena can draw on his authority to the full, as she settles the differences between the Furies and her city (797, 826ff. and 1046-7). Indeed, the belief that the gods could come to an end at all was unknown to the classical Greeks. Precisely *the* main difference between gods and men was that gods are immortal.

The characters who do go down to their end in the *Oresteia* are the 'heroes'. From a political point of view, Priam and Paris, Agamemnon, Klytaimestra and Aigisthos are the murderously violent autocrats of the now vanished 'Homeric' epoch. They are succeeded first by the calmer, more self-disciplined Orestes and then by the citizens of Athens, a developed city-state in which there is a full respect for the law.

This sequence of events is paralleled in the *Ring*. The gods, giants and dwarfs of *Das Rheingold*, with their superhuman powers and failings, correspond to the grand but violent autocrats of *Agamemnon*. Both groups must eventually be defeated and superseded. As Shaw stated:

> the dwarves, giants and gods are dramatizations of the three main orders of men; to wit, the instinctive, predatory, lustful, greedy people; the patient, toiling , stupid, respectful, money-worshipping people, and the intellectual, moral, talented people who devise and administer States and Churches. History shows us only one order higher than the highest of these; namely, the order of Heroes. (p. 29)

From one point of view, the *Ring* is an allegory which embodies Wagner's dream of the 1840s, the downfall of Germany's established political and economic order, and its replacement by an age of heroism and love.

There are, however, other levels of meaning to Aeschylus' trilogy; it does not simply proceed from a violent past to a tranquil vision of the Athenian present. John Jones has rightly insisted (p. 112) that Aeschylus 'is not looking down from a position of superior enlightenment on the urgencies of the *Oresteia*'. The savageries that afflict the characters of *Agamemnon* and *Choephoroi* are not confined to a distant past era. Athenian generals fought protracted wars at as much risk, and for as slight a cause, as Agamemnon; the pressures imposed by a woman's expected role in the household had not changed since Klytaimestra's time; and the duty to seek vengeance in person for his father's death would have lain as firmly on any young man in

Aeschylus' audience as on his mythical Orestes. The development of the city-state and its law-courts had not solved any of these moral dilemmas.

Agamemnon's deed at Aulis, therefore, does not only stand at the outset of the Oresteia to explain his fate. Aeschylus creates out of the sacrifice of Iphigeneia a paradigmatic tragic situation, an archetypal act which is the basis for his trilogy. First Klytaimestra, and then Orestes and finally the Athenians will attempt to purge the world of its consequences; but in doing so each is also remaking the moment in a new way, and it is only at the third 'remake' that freedom is completely achieved. The death of Iphigeneia is portrayed in depth because it is the model for what follows—both the place from which the action of the trilogy starts and the measure against which we must judge the three further central actions which follow from it, and lie parallel to it.

Wagner broadened his conception of the Ring until it came to display a pattern of parallel, universally significant actions like the Oresteia. For the completed Ring cycle does not simply unfold as a chronological narrative, passing from a violent past to a hoped-for, tranquil future. Das Rheingold does indeed portray the 'buried past' of the main action. It shows the beginning of the downfall of the three races who will be defeated by the hero Siegfried, and then extinguished together with him at the close of Götterdämmerung. But Das Rheingold also lays down a paradigm, a pattern of action whose sequence of events is true for all time. The dilemmas of Das Rheingold recur to dominate the situations of the characters in the main action of the trilogy, just like that of Agamemnon at Aulis, in the Oresteia.

But Wagner's design developed to a point where the crux which opens his cycle could not be handled by a narrative alone, even by one as powerful as Wotan's in Die Walküre Act 2 scene ii. As the classical scholar Walther Kranz remarked in Stasimon (a major study of Greek choral lyric), the first ode of Agamemnon provides the fundamental basis of the trilogy, 'just as the prologue to the Nibelung trilogy is the sea of sound, out of which the giant work rises up'.

By the 'prologue', Kranz meant *Das Rheingold* as a whole. In this drama we come to realize that the dilemmas which begin the *Ring* are even more extensive than those in the *Oresteia*. Aeschylus' Agamemnon is not alone in his predicament: as *Agamemnon* develops, it becomes plain that the blindness which led Paris to abduct Helen, (so causing the Trojan War), is parallel to that which led Agamemnon to kill his daughter and so doom himself. But at least there is the possibility of escape: the old are helpless, but their old age does free them from the hazards which may afflict the 'sacker of cities' (471ff.).

Wagner's vision is even more severe. In *Das Rheingold* all three of the races who inhabit the world are corrupted by the pursuit of the gold; no one can escape its influence. *Das Rheingold* exhibits not one paradigm but two: first Alberich, the power of darkness, and then Wotan, ruler of the realm of light (he is later to style himself 'Licht-Alberich'). He finds himself trapped in a situation parallel to Alberich's, and is propelled by Alberich's curse and Erda's warning into the actions which generate the remainder of the *Ring*.

The first character to pursue the gold is a dwarf; and to be a giant or a dwarf is an obvious deformity (Wagner points the parallel with his music, in the kinship of the two obsessive ostinato motifs Exx.7 and 8). It will emerge that in Wagner's

Ex.7    (Very heavy and holding back on the tempo)

Ex.8    (Very fast)

vision to be a god is also, if more subtly, a weakness. Scene ii takes us to the heights; we learn there that the gods, for all their radiance and intelligence, have likewise been obliged to barter love for security and power. And by the end of *Das Rheingold*, *any* use of power, even in the quest for security and survival, amounts to a renunciation of love. The road is clear for heroes, long before heroes independent enough to attempt to survive have even been foreshadowed. The closing dilemma is the one which underlies Aeschylus' trilogy: power must be pursued; everyone must to some degree renounce 'love, and woman's worth'—but at what cost?

In the Greek theatre of the fifth century, only the predicaments of men and women of royal rank were felt to be suitable material for tragedy. All the members of Aeschylus' audience, whatever their own station in life, were required by the convention of their theatre to apprehend his meaning from the actions of characters more exalted than themselves: it was assumed that the situations and dilemmas of the heroic age would throw a powerful light upon the audience's own contemporary problems, by analogy from the greater to the lesser.

His intense involvement with the class discords of the 1840s obliged Wagner to take a different path in the *Ring*. He was determined to demonstrate, through the behaviour of his allegorical dwarfs, giants and gods, that in the society of his own time the basic dilemma, which the beginning of his trilogy shares with that of Aeschylus', extends to every class and type of human being. All three races are vulnerable to the temptation symbolized by the lure of the gold; and as *Das Rheingold* unfolds, we come to see that all three have tried, and failed, to avoid making some sacrifice of love for power. In order to show this, Wagner needed to compose a lengthy one-act preliminary drama, where Aeschylus was able simply to devote one choral ode—admittedly a complex one—to Agamemnon's dilemma at the beginning of the *Oresteia*.

## AGAMEMNON AT AULIS

In some traditional Greek accounts, the misdeeds of the royal house of Argos extended back far beyond Agamemnon himself and his father Atreus. The story could include the treachery and murder committed by Agamemnon's grandfather Pelops, or even the insatiable aspirations of *his* father Tantalos. For his own purposes Aeschylus rejected this vision of the family as accursed and doomed to disaster, and at the outset of the *Oresteia* the primary cause of Agamemnon's death is located firmly in a personal action of his own. The longest choral ode in any surviving Greek tragedy evokes the way in which Agamemnon became compelled to sacrifice his own daughter Iphigeneia, as the price of leading the expedition against Troy; and in the course of the ode it is hinted that Agamemnon's wife has gained a murderous resolve from the desire to avenge her child. As a result, the extra dimension of past violence in this house plays a subordinate role, when it appears later in *Agamemnon*. Klytaimestra's 'unwomanly' resolve, her patient planning and her ever-increasing power over the male characters are the main threads that Aeschylus develops in the scenes leading up to the king's murder; for this reason alone the sacrifice of Iphigeneia needs to be described as early as possible. In a real sense her death, rather than the beacon which heralds the fall of Troy, is the play's opening; it is the motive for Agamemnon's death.

As they enter the *orchēstra* the elders of Argos recall the time when the expedition set out. At first, they see it as unequivocally good: an act of heroic retribution sent against Troy by Zeus himself, in his capacity as *Xenios*, protector of the rights of guests and hosts (40-63). But this confident focus is undercut almost at once. The war is being fought 'for one promiscuous woman', and its sufferings bear as hard on the Greeks as on the Trojans (61ff.). The chorus find no relief from the burden of the unseen, but inevitable future, so they fall back into apprehension.

To ease their fears they begin again, and attempt to remake their account of the events of Aulis (104ff.). However, this plunges them into a darker vision. The Trojan expedition is not now sent on its way by Zeus, but by an obscure portent, hard to interpret. And as they describe and explain the portent it reveals a new perspective from which the expedition is unequivocally wrong.

In their second account, the expedition encounters a 'wild bird omen': two eagles devouring a pregnant hare. The seer Kalchas interprets this: the eagles stand for the sons of Atreus, and the portent confirms that in time the expedition will capture Troy. But Kalchas fears that divine anger may darken the army's course:

> . . . for in her pity Artemis the pure is angry
> with the winged hounds of her father
> who sacrificed the wretched cowering thing, with
> its young, before birth;
> and she hates the eagles' feast. (134ff.)

Artemis, he explains, is the goddess who protects the young of all creatures; to follow Wagner's interpretation: 'she appears as the protectress of animals and of peace, in opposition to the god of war' (D 11/10/79). The portent means that she is angered by the sacrifice of innocent lives which the sack of Troy is going to involve. The expedition now no longer seems so totally right. 'The visions are favourable, but yet full of evil' (145). Kalchas looks into the future, and fears that Artemis will delay the expedition with contrary winds:

> . . . in her eagerness for another, lawless sacrifice
> that is no feast,
> an innate builder of feuds that fears no man; for
> a terrible craft remains at home to rise again,
> a remembering Wrath that will avenge her child.
> (150ff.)

These words are half obscure, as befits a prophecy; but they are of great importance. They point far into the future, going beyond the half-envisaged, monstrous sacrifice of Iphigeneia to hint at the consequences which Artemis creates by her exaction: the feuds, the craft that will destroy Agamemnon when he returns to his home are Klytaimestra's.

In the dramatic present, only part of Kalchas' prophecy has been fulfilled. And the chorus, anxious about the outcome, turn to Zeus. But they find no comfort there. Zeus' powers are great, but not so great as to release mankind, even in sleep, from the steady drip of the pain of memory. The favour of the gods is always accompanied in some way by violence (182).

Their illustration is Agamemnon, to whom the gods had

granted the favour of sacking Troy. Aeschylus' narrative returns to him, and to his predicament at Aulis. For the winds have
arrived, and waste away his ships and men. Now that the first
part of his prophecy has been fulfilled, Kalchas can see more
clearly into the future. He tells the remedy that Artemis re-
quires, to stay the winds:

> The elder king spoke, and said this;
> 'Heavy my fate to disobey,
> but heavy if I
> slaughter my child, the ornament of my house,
> polluting with streams of virgin blood
> my hands, a father's, near the altar.
> Which of these things is without evils?
> How can I become a deserter
> abandoning the expedition?
> For her to demand
> a sacrifice to stop the winds
> and the blood of a virgin
> with an anger beyond all anger—
> it is right. May all be well.' (205ff.)

The Trojan expedition began as an act of legal right, a retribution sent by the most powerful of the gods, Zeus *xenios*. It would
have been unthinkable for Agamemnon not to exact vengeance
from Paris, who had broken a law fundamental to the organization of Greek society when he abducted Helen. Furthermore,
Kalchas explicitly states (156) that the expedition will bring great
prosperity in its wake; and the pursuit of material prosperity
through warfare is central to traditional Greek values.

This perspective has not been removed. It has, however, been
completely qualified, first by the chorus's own misgivings, and
then by the portent which indicates that the Trojan war will also
be a hateful massacre of innocents, for which Agamemnon must
pay a price.

But who is demanding that price? The Greek is ambiguous on
this central point. In line 216, Agamemnon says that it is right
either for 'them' (Agamemnon's fellow-chieftains) or for 'her'
(Artemis) to demand this sacrifice 'with an anger beyond all

anger'. Droysen preserved this ambiguity as far as was possible in German, by writing *sie*; nevertheless, the verb forms in his version show that ultimately he followed the majority of scholars, and took the view that Agamemnon is pressed by the feelings of his fellow-leaders into sacrificing his daughter.

I have argued in my article, 'Agamemnon at Aulis', that this is unlikely to be right. If Agamemnon killed Iphigeneia simply because he was urged to do so by other men, his own fate would cease to be tragic: Klytaimestra would merely be meting out his fair punishment when she kills him. Both Wagner's comments on the scene, and the actual dilemmas which he created for Alberich and Wotan in *Das Rheingold*, show that he was alert to the alternative possibility—that the demand was Artemis' and that Agamemnon's chosen course, though terrible, is necessary. Agamemnon decides to sacrifice Iphigeneia only when he recognizes that Artemis is right to demand this price from him for his promised achievement.

His situation is complex, and invested with paradox. Agamemnon clearly chooses between two real alternatives; but as his speech develops, it becomes obvious that only one is possible. The chorus describe the situation correctly as they begin the next stanza; 'so he put on the harness of necessity'. The choice is at the same time both inevitable, and freely taken.

This double perspective is reinforced. The development up to this point has been clear and steady. The chorus's own doubts, the portent and its interpretation, Artemis' anger and the coming of the winds have all intruded on the expedition in a measured and perfectly lucid way; to match this, the speech in which Agamemnon reaches his decision is a rational, logical one. Looked at in relation to preceding events, Artemis' demand is right and Agamemnon *must* perform the sacrifice. In this perspective, Iphigeneia is less a living girl than an object, seen in terms of her status, 'the ornament of my house'.

As soon as he is resolved, however, the chorus change their focus completely. Looked at with hindsight, the demand is horrible and the king's decision appears insane; they attempt to explain it by describing how extreme daring can sometimes be associated with a man's first crime. Then they launch into an almost unbearable account of the struggles of Iphigeneia, in which her humanity, her femininity and her youth are fully exploited. By the time this narrative breaks off, Agamemnon is seen as a man who *chose* to do something utterly mad:

> . . .to become the butcher
> of his daughter, to help a war
> fought to avenge one woman. (224ff.)

Choice and no choice; utterly right and absolutely outrageous; rational and insane; a completely disastrous act which yet breaks a total deadlock. All these tensions are in the text; and Aeschylus' vision here is so difficult that we all instinctively take sides, to ease the paradoxes and resolve the morality of the situation. If only we can make the text say clearly that Agamemnon was—or was not—justified, compelled, insane . . .

This instinct must be resisted. The doubleness of vision is deliberately designed, to balk any attempt at moral judgment on Agamemnon. This emotional and moral crux is the point of departure for the *Oresteia*. Agamemnon, by going to war over the body of his daughter, accepts violence now as the price for later prosperity and power; and in doing so he lays down the theme of Aeschylus' trilogy. For the same choice (though in different terms) will confront Klytaimestra, Orestes, and the Athenians.


## ALBERICH AND THE RHINEGOLD

Wagner's thoughts returned many times to this ode; indeed, the portent of the eagle and the hare was the passage from Aeschylus which he recalled, with deep admiration, on the last day of his life. And the *Ring* opens with the same concern as the *Oresteia*. Alberich gains the gold which will give him power by committing an act of violence against love; and Wagner begins, like Aeschylus, by asking how such things can happen at all, why men are forced to commit acts of such folly.

No element of mystery, magic or evanescence intrudes into

the severe, anxious beginnings of Aeschylus' trilogy. Though drawn with extreme power, Aeschylus' evocation of Iphigeneia (243ff.) is strictly confined in scope. She is portrayed simply as Agamemnon's virgin daughter, 'the ornament of my house' as he has termed her. Aeschylus avoids emotional side-issues: against Agamemnon's duty to take revenge he sets nothing but the affection, and the obligation to sustain her life, which he owes to his daughter as a member of his household, one of the closest to him in blood. The elusive, beckoning powers of femininity do not appear in the *Oresteia* until, in the second ode of *Agamemnon*, Aeschylus comes to portray Helen and her momentous departure for Troy (403ff.). The *Ring*, by contrast, begins in a world almost reminiscent of fairy-tale; Wagner portrays the waters of the Rhine as an idyllic world, a 'garden of Eden' upon which Alberich intrudes and whose peace he disrupts.

The prelude to *Das Rheingold* takes us out of our own world, into one where our perception of time will be totally dictated by Wagner; and the opening E flat pedal remains alone for so long, before the horns begin to introduce the first theme of the work, that during it we lose our sense of time completely. The *Ring*'s opening image is that of a timeless world, a paradigm of peace.

The second image develops this picture, without disturbing it. With the tempo remaining 'a quiet, serene motion', the orchestral movement becomes ever more vigorous and playful, until the curtain rises to reveal a stage 'filled with swirling waters that flow ceaselessly from right to left'. The Rhine represents a world of stability in flux. The perpetual horizontal motion of the waves is a powerful symbol, precisely opposed to the aggressive vertical movements which will chronicle the aspirations of those who seek power in the *Ring*.

The music complements this stage-picture. Throughout the prelude, it remains stable and diatonic; and this stability remains, when the musical materials of the prelude reappear to accompany the games of the three nymphs of the river. But these are not innocent games. In Wagner's Eden, all three Eves have already tasted of the apple.

English usage has canonized Woglinde and her sisters as the 'Rhinemaidens'. But the mistranslation obscures Wagner's

meaning even today, when the word maiden no longer automatically carries the implication of virginity. They are the
*Rheintöchter*, the daughters of the Rhine; and as Fricka makes
plain in scene ii (310–11), they are anything but virginal. Wagner deliberately offsets their provocative sexuality against the
name of the river; in the text of the *Ring*, where alliteration,
assonance and other forms of word-play are constantly present
and important, 'Rheingold' irresistibly suggests 'Reines Gold'
('pure gold') even in the first scene, long before the point is made
explicit in the lament with which the Rhine-daughters conclude
the drama.

This paradox is reinforced as scene i proceeds. The music
associates chromaticism with the intrusion of Alberich, whose
musical materials develop to reflect his ever-increasing frustration. The melodies associated with the Rhine-daughters, by
contrast, do not develop. They are flowing, strophic and repeti-
tive; and they are consistently diatonic. There is a deliberate
tension between the innocence of the Rhine-daughters' music
and the three progressively more unpleasant games—adult,
sexual games—which they play on Alberich.

For he, surprisingly, is the true innocent in scene i. Alberich is
not initially characterized either by the text or the music as a
figure of evil. Being a dwarf may make his desire to share in their
game absurd; but he is not morally corrupt. On the contrary, it
is his naivety which allows the Rhine-daughters to tempt him.
The three successive torments increase his frustration to break-
ing-point; and this is because they encompass symbolically
every possible way in which woman may tempt man to feel
desire. Woglinde, the first, simply eludes Alberich by her
physical agility and distance, while Wellgunde provokes him
further by allowing him to come physically close to her and then
rebutting him with pointed, but open words. Only one form
of deception remains—and Flosshilde uses it. She actually
embraces Alberich, and her words seem to make love to him; but
they really reject him totally, through covert irony and sarcasm.
After his education at the hands of the other two nymphs,
Alberich comes to understand this only too well. He then
embarks on a furious, desperate pursuit.

This game, and its outcome, are the starting-point of the *Ring*. The Rhine-daughters, like the river itself, are both stable and elusive, both placid and frustrating in their beckoning allure; and they drive Alberich first to desperation and then to violence. The reason for this is simply that they are female.

Wagner was obliged by German grammar to leave *Der Rhein* technically in the male gender, and Flosshilde alludes once to 'their father's ' admonition to them to guard the treasure; but everything else heard so far in the music and text has been designed to establish an opening polarity between male and female; and as the cycle unfolds every aspect of the Rhine and its music, from the start of the orchestral prelude, will turn out to have specifically female associations. The figurations of the prelude will return only once in the score of *Das Rheingold*—at the moment when Loge tells the astonished gods and goddesses that no one will give up the joy of woman's love (273ff.); and the opening theme (Ex.4a) will be unforgettably associated with the feminine by its powerful transformation, as Ex.4c, to underlie Erda's prophecies.

The opposition between male and female values and expectations is, of course, a fundamental theme of the *Oresteia*. Agamemnon sacrifices Iphigeneia at the demand of the goddess Artemis; he is trapped when Artemis places the grievances of femininity and outraged nature (symbolized by the pregnant hare) in opposition to the two male eagles, Agamemnon and Menelaos, who will fulfil the will of Zeus by sacking Troy. By killing his daughter, Agamemnon initiates an implacable contest between male and female power. For him, at his moment of choice, she was simply 'the ornament of my house' (208); but Klytaimestra, justifying to the elders the murder of her husband, bitterly scorns him as the man who could kill 'the dearest fruit/of my labour pangs, to charm away the winds from Thrace' (1417–18). This opposition remains: throughout the main action of the trilogy male strength contends with female (and one woman, Klytaimestra, takes on the powers of a man); the fundamental conflict between the sexes is resolved only at the close of *Eumenides*. There, the representative of Zeus (Apollo) argues that the supreme god has backed Orestes' cause, responding to and defending the basic social and religious organization of Greek society, in which primacy went automatically to the male; but at the end, in the concord between Athena and the Eumenides, the values, and the creative power, of femininity at last receive their due.

In order to establish his vision of the importance of love and the power of womanhood, Wagner pursues this theme even further than Aeschylus. In the *Ring*, though there are gods as well as goddesses, nature is female. Her deep riches and her wisdom are guarded, with stable and seductive power, by female creatures: the Rhine-daughters, Erda, the woodbird, and the Norns. The power of the male characters, though more dynamic, is also more limited, and is frequently dependent on the female world which surrounds them. The two male gods who have natural powers (Donner and Froh) are confined to spectacular display; and even Loge, although he shares the splendid sophistry of Aeschylus' Apollo, does not possess his degree of prophetic insight. Wotan is bound by his treaties, and will need Erda's intervention to free him from the fatal step of keeping the ring. Siegmund arrives at Hunding's hut alone, wounded and unarmed, and it is Sieglinde who rescues him, guiding him to the sword which will defend their love and inspiring the harmony with nature which gives them strength. Siegfried achieves his deserts only when he begins to attune himself, in his turn, to the rhythms of the *Wald* that surrounds him, which is personified by the (female) woodbird. It is only at the decisive climax of the *Ring* (*Siegfried*, Act 3 scenes i–ii) that Erda is overcome by the 'greater wisdom' which the Wanderer has learnt from his experiences. The males of Wagner's universe are alone and poor by birth; and they are forced to violence by the beckoning riches of nature's 'female' passivity, for they may acquire power only by that violence against nature.

Scene i establishes the paradigm which explains each of these 'moments'. After outwitting Alberich, the three nymphs tempt him into trying to chase them. Despite his knowledge that they find him ridiculous, Alberich still makes frantic attempts to capture one of them; the music now contrasts the serene movements by which they once more evade him with the mounting desperation of Alberich's endeavours. 'At last he stops, foaming with rage and breathless, and shakes his clenched fist up at the girls.' As soon as he does this, and, 'hardly in control of himself', utters his threat, the Rhinegold appears to him. Why?

Femininity, as it appears in the form of the Rhine-daughters, is both desirable, and infinitely frustrating. Alberich has tried his persuasive charms on all three nymphs, and has failed with them all. It is only when he turns from persuasion to the threat of violence that the Rhinegold appears, and provides him with an alternative goal.

At this point the texture and tempo of the music change completely. Although the gold is guarded by the daughters of the Rhine, it has a theme quite unlike any of their melodies: played on horns or trumpets, Ex.9 is angular, sharp and therefore, in Wagner's musical symbolism, male (cf. Exx. 1 and 30). There is a basic contrast, as the scene develops, between the warmth and radiance of the gold as it is now, the object of the girls' play in their hymn to the pure and unspoilt 'Rheingold' (Ex.10), and the potential for male power implicit in the angular thematic phrase (Ex.9). Alberich's willingness to use force has exposed him as corruptible: at the sight of the gold, he becomes 'attracted and spellbound', while the horns and the trumpet beckon him with Ex.9 against a shimmering background of *divisi* violins. Like Aeschylus' Paris at *Agamemnon* 385ff., Alberich turns out, when he is tested, to 'have blackness fixed in him'—to be vulnerable to temptation. He now forgets the girls' attractions.

Ex.9

Ex.10

Alberich's situation has now been fully revealed—just like Agamemnon's, after Kalchas has been able to read the full meaning of the portent. The ambiguity of the Rhine-daughters—are they true seductresses, or do they tease only to reject their suitors?—has disappeared; they *are* faithful, but only to those who can catch them. By turning to violence, Alberich has revealed that he lacks the will to persist in that pursuit; for him, as for Agamemnon and Wotan, the beauty of women is, ultimately, secondary to the allure of achievement.

For these reasons, therefore, the gold appears. Alberich, like Agamemnon, is now faced with a 'choice' which from another perspective is no choice at all; an act which is both inevitable, and freely chosen:

> Only he who curses
> all love's power,
> only he who drives out
> the joys of love,
> only he will master the magic
> to forge a ring from the gold. (140–2)

Robert Donington was right to insist that Ex. 2 expresses not resignation but acceptance. Throughout the trilogy this motif is sounded when characters accept that they must pay the price of future torment for the gains they are making now. Alberich is not resigned; he accepts the full horror of the consequences of what he must do; and the music responds, by increasing the dissonance almost unbearably as he accepts the price and moves towards the gold, releasing us only at the moment when Alberich has seized it. This, too, like Agamemnon's situation at Aulis, is a moment of paradox, a moral crux in which all judgment is balked. Until Alberich decides to climb towards the gold, the scene has developed with great psychological plausibility: the musical inventions have chronicled his ever-increasing frustration, and they explain fully why he becomes capable of accepting the gold despite the terrible exaction which is demanded of its possessor. But from another point of view, now, 'the dwarf has gone mad . . . /Love has cost him his wits' (160–1). And the music supports this perspective as well. There is nothing *ambiguous* about this scene: as in Aeschylus, we are offered two contrary perspectives in unresolved opposition, and we cannot tell which is right. It is the heart of Wagner's intention here to balk all judgment on Alberich.

The character of Alberich, however, is not analogous with that of Agamemnon. This would have been impossible; Aeschylus' Agamemnon is a real character, a very powerful king: he 'sacrifices love for power' literally, and the murder of his virgin daughter, conveyed in narrative form, withholds nothing of the emotional force of this action. Alberich by contrast is only a dwarf, in a symbolist drama; he does no actual violence in scene i, and the love he rejects is only that of three water-nymphs. It is as if Aeschylus had depicted at the start of the *Oresteia* the inner weakness of Priam's youngest, over-favoured son, Paris, and the susceptibilities which led him to fall so completely under the strange, intangible fascination of Helen. By electing to start with Alberich—the representative of our darker side—and to place him in confrontation with such elusive representatives of 'woman's beauty and worth' as the Rhine-daughters, Wagner begins the *Ring* obliquely, and arouses expectations which he only fulfils in scene ii, by introducing Wotan and Freia.

## WOTAN AND FREIA

The symbolism of our ascent is obvious. Alberich is too lowly to stand for all of us. Aeschylus presents us first with a great king, and only undermines his greatness later, when he brings out in the second and third odes the parallels between Agamemnon and Paris. Wagner reverses the process, inducing us to expect, as we arrive for scene ii in the dazzling light of an alpine landscape, that the gods who live there should be assailed by subtler temptations, and more capable of resisting them.

Wagner then undermines both these expectations. In scene i, Wellgunde describes for Alberich the power that the gold confers: he who can forge it into a ring will inherit the world (136-7). A new theme (Ex.11) is heard here, and recurs in the critical moments when Alberich begins to move towards the gold; it gives eloquent expression to the ring's power to corrupt.

Towards the end of the interlude, this theme returns and then

Ex.11 Ob., E.H.

Ex.12 (Calm tempo, very gentle)

Wagner Tubas

becomes, by a slight transformation, Ex. 12, the musical portrait of Wotan's grandiose dreams. The parallel with Alberich is implied at once; and just like Agamemnon, 'yielding to the sudden blasts of fortune', in the moments before Artemis' demand is fully revealed (*Agamemnon* 186), Wotan first appears to us as a complacent dreamer, sleeping as if already secure in the shelter of his new fortress.

Ex. 12 will become totally associated, during *Das Rheingold*, with Wotan's fortress, which he names at the close as Valhalla. On a purely political reading, Wotan is the representative of the nineteenth-century aristocracy in their decline, and Valhalla is the symbol of their civilization, on the point of disruption. There is no doubt that when the Nibelung story originally took shape in Wagner's mind, this was his conception; in the 1848 sketch Wotan needed the castle as a base from which the gods 'could possess the power to organize the world in safety and rule over it'; but the completed work is far more profound and wide-ranging in its implications. Wotan does not now stand for an infamous aristocracy, clinging to a power which it no longer deserves. Like Agamemnon, he represents any man of success and prosperity, forced by circumstances into a crisis.

Wotan, like Agamemnon, has been morally judged too often. For Valhalla is not a luxury. Wotan is under as much pressure as was Agamemnon, when he became the appointed instrument of Zeus *xenios*. In his dreams, Wotan does indeed look forward to using Valhalla as the base from which to acquire 'endless fame', in language much like Agamemnon's on his return from Troy; but his chief purpose in acquiring it is to achieve security. This becomes explicit in the famous moments in scene iv where he salutes the fortress:

The night is near:
from its dangers
this offers us refuge now.
So do I greet the fortress,
safe from terror and dread.          (714–16)

The quest for 'release from toil' is a significant but minor
theme of the *Oresteia*. In the Greek world, where inaction was in
itself shameful and the noble was expected to take every oppor-
tunity to increase his standing at the expense of others, such
security was normally to be acquired not by passive self-defence
but by going out to attack his enemies and destroy their city.
Wagner adopts a different focus, one which reflects nineteenth-
century conditions. The aspirations of the Greek noble are
assigned in the *Ring* to the 'have-not' Alberich, who threatens in
scene iii to storm Valhalla, enslave the gods and rape the goddesses. Wotan, by contrast, is intent on material possession;
Valhalla is to be a secure refuge, from which he will go out only
on brief excursions to maintain his power over the outside
world. (Fafner simply takes this 'fortress ethic' to its logical
conclusion when, *als Wurm*, he makes Neidhöle into a minia-
ture stronghold and refuses to leave it except for food and drink.)
   One method may be creative, the other destructive; but
neither offers true security. Valhalla is seen first as a literal
dream, and Alberich's megalomaniac ambitions in scene iii will
be seen as a metaphorical one. Like the recurrent, ever-
dwindling hopes of the characters in *Agamemnon*, dreams are
intangible:

It is not the repulse of Alberich by the Rhine-daughters—the
repulse was inevitable owing to their nature—that was the
cause of all the mischief. Alberich and his ring would have
been powerless to harm the gods, had they not themselves
been susceptible to evil.                          (R 25/1/54)

The gods are 'susceptible to evil' because their predicament is far
more extreme than it appears at first sight. Freia does not appear
in the 1848 sketch—her role was created only when Wagner

drafted the text for *Das Rheingold*; that is, at the same time that
the idea of renouncing love was first added to the *Ring* cycle.

'Whatever lives, wants to love' sings Wellgunde; and in
bartering Freia, Wotan risks renouncing more than Alberich.
Freia is the goddess of love, and as such she inspires the heart-
felt devotion of the simple giant Fasolt; but Wagner also gave
her the stewardship of the apples (belonging in traditional
mythology to the goddess Idunn) which confer eternal youth on
the gods. And so the gods' lives—not simply their happiness—
depend on possessing love. It is possible for the lower, less
sensitive creatures, the dwarfs and the giants, to renounce love;
both Alberich and Fafner actually do so. But the god cannot
(even though he needs to)—precisely because he rules, as
Fasolt reminds him in this scene, *durch Schönheit*.

Loge's narrative (*'Immer ist Undank/Loge's Lohn . . .'*) is
the turning point. As Loge pretends that he could find nothing
which anyone would accept in place of 'woman's beauty and
worth', the first part of Freia's theme (Ex.13a) sounds out,
clothed with almost magical harmonies and evolving out of
string arpeggios which rise gently upwards over a ground bass
(273ff.). This is an unmistakable recall of the opening bars of the
drama, and it completes the parallel between Freia and the
Rhine-daughters; *mutatis mutandis*, the outrage to nature,
when Wotan promised Freia to the giants, is parallel to that
when Alberich turned from the Rhine-daughters to the pursuit
of power.

Ex.13   (fairly animated)

All males may need the love of woman; no less fundamentally, they also seek power. When Loge concludes by telling the
gods and the giants about the theft of the Rhinegold, they react
in the same way as Alberich. The lure of the gold now spreads.
The giants, being the most naive of the characters now on stage,
are the first to succumb; indeed Fasolt, who was originally the
more rapturous admirer of Freia, is the first to voice jealousy of

Alberich. Fricka sees that the gold has potential in a wife's hands, to help her retain her husband's fidelity; and she turns all her feminine charm on Wotan to persuade him to get it. The god responds with a masterly understatement:

> To gain possession of this ring
> appears to me to be a sensible action.   (298–9)

But the music belies the diplomatic neutrality of Wotan's language. Ex. 11 is heard in harmonies which imply that corruption is working subtly yet undeniably on him as well.

The giants now fall fastest; it is no time at all before jealousy and greed lure Fafner into the fatal delusion that possessing the gold will give them eternal youth just as surely as possessing Freia. In the music, a dark cello variant of Ex. 13 undermines this hope; and the lure of the gold brings Fasolt round, against his will, to his brother's point of view (313–4). Just as in Aeschylus, 'old violence is apt to breed a younger violence' (*Agamemnon* 763–4), so also in the *Ring*, all three races have been corrupted by the lure of the Rhinegold.

Wagner develops the situation in an equally Aeschylean manner. Gods, dwarfs and giants all eventually receive their deserts— deserts which are in proportion to their nature. The gods, being the most sensitive creatures in Wagner's world, suffer most severely at first. But they are also the most intelligent—and this gives them a greater chance of survival. Wotan *knows* that he must redeem Freia at all costs. Loge is right, as always:

> But you staked everything
> on the youth-giving fruit;
> that the giants knew well;
> they took their aim
> at your lives;
> now work out, how to keep them!
> Without the apples,
> ancient and grey,
> morose and old,
> withered, the joke of the world,
> the race of gods will die.   (341–5)

We are immersed in the gods' immediate predicament, both by the text and by the intense, plangent music that Wagner writes here; but Loge's words also point forward—to Erda's prophecy, to Wotan's resignation in *Die Walküre* Act 2, and even beyond that, to Waltraute's narrative in *Götterdämmerung*, Act 1 scene iii. The speech plays the same role as the prophecy of Kalchas, who—even as the vision of the necessity of sacrificing Iphigeneia came upon him in all its horror—could still see dimly beyond, into the future and to the fate that awaited Agamemnon on his return:

> . . . a terrible
> craft remains at home to rise again,
> a remembering Wrath that will avenge her child.
> (*Agamemnon* 153ff.)

Wotan does not, ultimately, have to sacrifice Freia. Wagner's central dissent from Aeschylus in *Das Rheingold* is that Wotan, by his intelligence, Loge's cunning, and Erda's intervention, manages by the end of *Das Rheingold* to redeem his pledge, escape possession of the ring and enter Valhalla in triumph. But Wagner's god pays as high a price for this romantic freedom as Aeschylus' king paid for his submission to the demand of Artemis.

Agamemnon was not corrupt when he set out for Troy; but when he resolved to sacrifice Iphigeneia, and (as the chorus sing) 'put on the harness of Necessity', then:

> the breath from his heart veered round, became impious
> bitter and unholy; and from then on
> he was warped, and his thoughts stopped at nothing.
> For men are given boldness by the wretched
> false-counselling madness of their first crime . . .
> (*Agamemnon* 218ff.)

Wotan, too, has suffered corruption simply because of the tensions, and the pressures, which have increased as his situation develops. His choice, like those of Agamemnon and Alberich, turns out to be no choice at all: he must take the gold from Alberich for his own survival. Loge is morally right to remind him of the complaint of the Rhinedaughters; they have appealed to Wotan, as the highest power in their world, to see that their gold is returned to them. But Wotan ignores him; the gods cannot respond to this appeal without causing their own destruction.

Wotan must gain Valhalla; but he can do so only at the cost of sharp practice, treachery, and deceit. Already at the end of *Das Rheingold* scene ii, the action implies that the 'pure' world of the opening can be regained only when Valhalla is destroyed. Neither Valhalla nor the ring will free its owner from fear. Hence the strange blend of underlying hope and continued apprehension which the music expresses as Wotan and Loge set out for Nibelheim. It is parallel to the apprehension that colours the chorus's first, optimistic account of the setting out of Agamemnon and Menelaos for Troy (*Agamemnon* 60ff.).

## ALBERICH AND HIS RING

The orchestral interlude which accompanies the descent to Nibelheim is one of the most powerful and terrifying passages in the whole of Wagner's music. Increasingly plaintive harmonizations of Ex.2 emerge from the chromatic opening figurations; and the despairing, falling minor seconds which follow evolve without rest into an animated, furious distortion of Freia's motif (Ex.13b; 358ff.). Then, with the tempo remaining very fast, an almost demonic, *forte* intrusion of Ex.9 (361ff.) generates the first entry of the ferocious ostinato (Ex.8) which depicts and introduces us to Alberich's kingdom.

The symbolism of the first part of this sequence is plain from what we have seen already. By the end of scene ii, all three races have shown their desire and need to accept the loss of love in return for power. What is surprising, or at least perhaps expected only on an unconscious level, is the sheer horror explicit in the first appearance of Ex.8. This motif *can* sound harmless, if a context demands it; in Mime's narrative (402ff.), played softly and 'in a very leisurely tempo', it depicts perfectly the age of innocence in which the Nibelungs were 'carefree smiths' before

Alberich gained the gold. But we hear it first in a form which conveys the images of obsessive labour and of pain. The dwarfs were once honest, patient workers; now they have been forced to never-ceasing labour as Alberich's slaves. Ex.9, as it sounds out so clearly and brutally, both shows where the power to drive the dwarfs has come from, and lays down the subject for scene iii—the corruption which the gold has worked on Alberich. Wagner's strategy is as remorseless as Aeschylus'; first the deed, and then its inexorable consequences.

The thought of Alberich and of his gold diverted Fasolt with alarmingly little difficulty from his simple desire for a beautiful woman to share his dwelling, as the payment for his work in building Valhalla; and later, when Fafner murders him, we will hear the theme which depicts the giants' labours (Ex.7) as corrupted as we now hear that of the dwarfs. But the beckoning lure with which Ex.9 sounded, as Fafner won Fasolt over to the idea of accepting the gold in place of Freia (314), is as nothing when compared to the power with which it now heralds the enslavement of the dwarfs. As the smallest (though not the least intelligent) members of Wagner's universe, they have virtually no resistance to the gold and its effects.

As the sheer violence of the interlude proclaims, these effects have been extensive. Deception and treachery now take on, in Nibelheim, the tangible physical form of the Tarnhelm. In the music, its associated motif does not simply evoke the idea of transformation: the chromatic motion carries an eerie undertone of malevolence, which is fully justified by the use which Alberich makes of the helmet. This scene shows us how the first lord of the ring proposes to use what he has forged. With the Tarnhelm to guard him and give him the power to oversee his underlings without their knowledge, Alberich's empire is complete; and as he leaves after tormenting Mime (384ff.), both music and text bring out the terrifying degree to which he has been corrupted. The dwarf who evoked considerable sympathy from us, when the Rhine-daughters tormented him in scene i, has now become a sadistic tyrant.

Wagner completes this picture when Alberich returns, driving his labourers before him. His brutality, his contempt for the other dwarfs, and his cruelty grow throughout the scene and become totally explicit in the final *rallentando*:

> Are you still skulking?
> Lingering still?

(he draws the ring from his finger, kisses it and holds it out menacingly)

> Tremble and quake,
> you wretched slaves:
> quickly obey
> the lord of the ring!　　　(433–4)

As Alberich extends the ring, a cymbal sounds alone, lightly beaten with a drumstick; and this extraordinary effect, which expresses perfectly the horrific menace of Alberich's power, leads into Ex.14, a new, distorted version of Ex.10.

Ex.14

This expresses both the perversion which Alberich has inflicted upon the pure gold, by forging the ring of power from it, and the sinister, almost demented nature of the power which the gold has conferred on him.

But this is not all. Alberich's first sight of the strangers who have come to visit Nibelheim makes him immediately suspicious; and to his fear and his sadism he now adds megalomania. This impressive treasure, he informs Loge, is just 'a miserable little pile for today' (446). As he declares this a new motif

(Ex. 15) enters the score, and its recurrent rising sequence gives musical expression to the limitless range of Alberich's ambition, as the scene develops. Wotan's further questions elicit a diatribe

Ex. 15     (Very animated)

in which Alberich's near-insanity, his envy and his jealousy are fully revealed. Ex. 13a sounds, the original fine textures now reduced to obsessive repetition on one solo violin, as Alberich reveals his hatred for the gods 'living, laughing and making love' on the heights above; and it is then no surprise that his ambition at the end, when he has subdued them by the power of the ring, is to force himself on their 'lovely women'. Since he has re-nounced love, all other creatures must do likewise.

These vast ambitions reveal that for all the apparent strength which he has gained from the ring, Alberich has in fact become weaker under the corrupting influence of its power. Alberich is *not* a naturally stupid creature, and in the final moments of the scene he is overcome simply because of the megalomania in-duced in him by possessing the ring. Alberich can think of nothing more impressive to do to display the powers of the Tarnhelm than turning himself into a giant dragon. Unlike Fafner, who will prove unable to think of a use, either construc-tive or destructive, for his power, Alberich ought to know better. Yet Loge easily outmanoeuvres him and brings him to defeat.

Wotan has not yet been termed 'Licht-Alberich', by himself or anyone else in the *Ring*; but after the transformation of Ex. 11 into Ex. 12 in the first interlude, and the parallels of situation between Alberich and Wotan which have been completed by the end of scene ii, the way in which Alberich falls in scene iii raises direct questions about Wotan himself. To own the ring, it is now clear, is to go beyond the limits of safe conduct and to be exposed to risk—in much the same way as do those in the *Oresteia* who wield power and commit excessive violence. No matter how necessary their cause, 'the gods do not fail to mark/those who have killed many'. And the Furies destroy the man who is 'successful beyond due measure' (*Agamemnon* 461–2, 464). Wagner is creating the expectation that, when he wins the ring, Wotan will be endangered in a similar way to Alberich.

The dramatic technique here is closely parallel to Aeschylus' in the first half of *Agamemnon*. At first sight, the conqueror of Troy and the defeated Paris would seem to have nothing in common—a great king, and a younger son who could be tempted by Helen's beauty into precipitating a disastrous war; but as Aeschylus' drama develops, their situations come to be more and more comparable, and the threat of disaster comes to hang over Agamemnon as much as it had done over Paris. So too in Wagner. The third interlude begins with a triumphant celebration of the victory of Wotan and of Loge's rhetoric; but after we have passed the forges of Nibelheim and draw increasingly nearer to the environs of Valhalla, the music is pervaded by an ever-intensifying harshness and savagery. Can Wotan survive the possession of the ring? Or will he also become tyrannical, and be brought down in his turn?

## ALBERICH'S CURSE AND ERDA'S WARNING

On his return to the heights, Wotan progressively exacts the gold, the Tarnhelm and the ring from his prisoner. Then, once he is freed, Alberich lays an extended and powerful curse on the ring. For Bernard Shaw this curse was a lurid relic of nineteenth-century operatic stagecraft, which 'is superfluous and confusing, as the ruin to which the pursuit of riches leads needs no curse to explain it' (p. 31). A more recent commentator has elaborated this criticism: 'Wielders of tyrannical power have always been quite liable to come to a sticky end; and it is a truism that tyrannical power brings no joy to its possessor, because he must constantly guard against being eliminated by one of the envious who covet it.' (Cooke, p. 224)

These are serious objections; but it is quite clear that Wagner was prepared to risk such criticism. In his sources, the dwarf Andvari proclaimed, when the gods took the gold from him, that 'the ring should cost everyone who possessed it thereafter his life'. Wagner echoed this straightforward phrasing in the 1848 sketch. But in the final text for *Das Rheingold*, the curse is considerably more important. Alberich pronounces his actual curse to a theme of intense power and awesome symmetry (Ex. 3), which becomes of focal importance later in the cycle; and he then elaborates its implications in eloquent detail. The curse is soon shown to be effective: when they have obtained the ring, the giants quarrel over it and Fafner murders Fasolt. At this point Ex. 3 is enunciated *forte* by all three trombones, soli over a timpani pedal (653); and Wotan comments, 'shattered'; 'Now I see/the terrible power of the curse'. Is this just melodrama?

Wagner conceived the project for the *Ring* at a time when he was prepared to risk his life to bring down an entrenched monarchy by armed revolt, and he completed the actual text for *Das Rheingold* at a time when he regarded the whole of our world as so corrupted and worthless that men like himself and Liszt should abandon it to Alberich (L –/8/54); it is unlikely that he shared at either period the comforting liberal humanist belief that 'tyrannical power brings no joy to its possessor'. As yet we have seen nothing which could prevent Wotan, entrenched in Valhalla and equipped with the Tarnhelm to provide his security, from successfully ruling the world for ever, now that he has gained possession of the ring of power. Alberich's curse is therefore dramatically necessary; it is the decisive factor which Erda uses, to persuade Wotan to overcome the lure of the ring and surrender it to the giants.

From his reading of Droysen's translation Wagner was under the impression that the *Oresteia*, like Sophocles' Oedipus plays, used the motif of an inherited curse to bind together the successive parts of the cycle. In *Opera and Drama* he objected to the role played by inherited curses in Greek tragedy; his view was that such curses were society's excuse for failing to recognize its own ills, and that those called accursed, men such as Laios and Oedipus, were scapegoats:

> this curse, which is represented in the myth as the divine punishment for an ancient crime, and as clinging to one

particular family until its downfall, is in reality nothing more than an embodiment of the power of instinct working in the unconscious actions of the individual in a way which, due to Nature, is inevitable. (AE 2.180)

But his own trilogy, like Aeschylus', needed to create a pressure from the past on the characters of each new drama, to provide structural unity and continuity. The form which he finally gave to Alberich's curse provides a further thematic parallel between the *Ring* and the *Oresteia*.

Just before the return of their king, the chorus of *Agamemnon* draw out, in a justly famous meditation, the implications of their reflections on the news that Troy has fallen (750ff.). They dispute a proverbial Greek saying, that great prosperity of itself ultimately creates its own inevitable destruction. It is lack of awe for the gods, they argue, which breeds and reproduces itself. One act of *hubris* (violence) sooner or later creates further violence, and breeds the *daimōn* Destruction. Equity pays respect only to those who live within their appointed lot in life; she deserts the rich and successful once the pollution of violence has soiled them, 'paying no respect to the might of wealth/that is stamped with false praise' (779–80).

In context, this has the most direct and ominous relevance to the position of Agamemnon, whose success has been founded on the sacrifice of his daughter and the brutal destruction of a city. Both are acts which exceed the normal limits of human conduct, and come near to the scale of violence which, for Aeschylus, is the privilege of the gods alone.

Aeschylus' diagnosis of Agamemnon's position is brief. He could afford to be elliptical, because the idea of 'tainted wealth', and of danger lying in the pursuit of extensive power on a scale near to the preserves of the gods, was a frequent motif in contemporary Greek thought, which the poet could evoke by the faintest of echoes. Wagner had to establish this idea, since it was not so familiar to his nineteenth-century audience. Alberich's curse taints the Rhinegold, and will become central to the *Ring*. The fate which Alberich now lays on the ring, in twenty-five lines of explicit denunciation, will underlie the entire action of Wagner's trilogy.

The scene draws out an idea which was only implicit in scene i. The gold appeared to Alberich when he threatened the Rhine-daughters with force. But at least he acquired it by fulfilling the condition on which it was to be gained—he could not, otherwise, have wrested it from its rock. Wotan, however, has stolen it, by violence. And it is, therefore, now tainted wealth, like that acquired 'beyond their due' by Paris, and by Agamemnon. That is why Alberich curses it, and why his curse is effective.

The ransoming of Freia is a moral outrage. Donner, Froh and Loge 'hasten to end Freia's shame' by piling up the gold. This visual image is almost as powerful in its context as the tapestry-scene in *Agamemnon*. The giants, now totally corrupted by the lure of the treasure, force the gods to show that the goddess of love is, almost literally, 'worth her weight in gold'.

Wotan finds this process merely distasteful. Nevertheless, he too will be obliged to undergo the same sequence of three exactions that he himself made from Alberich. Being a god, he can realize the potential of the ring far more than Alberich—and it is, therefore, far more difficult for him to part with the ring. So difficult, indeed, that he refuses to give way, even in the face of pressing appeals from the other gods. But none dare oppose him. The giants sense the urgency, and the crisis; 'Fafner stops Fasolt from hurrying away. They all stand perplexed.' And Wotan refuses yet again.

This impasse is answered by the finest *coup de théâtre* in *Das Rheingold*. Erda appears, heralded by a *fortissimo* C sharp blast from the trombones in octaves, out of which there gradually arises a new theme (Ex.4c). This patently lies in the closest relationship to the opening phrase which began the entire work, (Ex.4a).

In Teutonic mythology, the principal form of wisdom provided by a seer was knowledge of one's own imminent destruction. It is that power which Wagner's Erda now brings to Wotan.

Wotan's seer names herself not only 'Urwala', the world's archetypal prophetess (Wala was Jacob Grimm's conjectural Old

High German equivalent for the Old Norse word Völva) but also 'Erda'. This name reflects both her role—*Udr* is the Eddaic word for fate—and her origin—*Erde* is the German word for the earth. By bestowing this name of his own invention on his seer, Wagner ensured that her status is explicit. She is the fundamental nature-goddess of the *Ring*. Her appearance at this point, to save Wotan, shows that the gods, simply by their position and strength, have the potential of access to a deeper wisdom; the wisdom of nature, which only manifested itself to Alberich in the form of three flirting temptresses, appears in a more substantial and intensely impressive form to Wotan. Loge's intelligence, sophistry and deceptive powers have helped Wotan immensely, but they are not enough to save him now. Erda can. Her wisdom and her femininity tempt Wotan so strongly that he attempts pursuit even as she disappears from the scene. And after she has gone, Ex.4c rises in the Wagner tubas (639–40) to mark the fact that Wotan's decision to let the ring go, taken 'after a few moments of deep thought', is made only by absorbing Erda's advice.

In the first draft of *Das Rheingold*, the format of Erda's warning was essentially Greek. In classical Greek belief, destiny was not omnipotent, and *moira* (fate) usually manifested its decrees in the form of conditional clauses, which allow some possibility of evasion. Achilleus in the *Iliad* (18.95) is fated to die himself soon after Hektor—*if* he kills Hektor. In *Prometheus Bound*, Zeus will fall if he makes love to Thetis, for there is a prophecy that if she bears a son to anyone, that son will be mightier than his father. In *Agamemnon*, the Greeks will return home safely from Troy only if in sacking the city they leave untouched the temples and altars of the gods (338ff.). Wagner originally conceived Erda's warning in exactly this spirit. Her words were to be:

> A dark day is dawning for the gods;
> your noble race will end in shame,
> if you do not surrender the ring!

But with the final text, Wagner made his first major dissent in the *Ring* from Aeschylus' vision of the world. Erda now prophesies that:

> All that is, will perish.
> A dark day
> dawns for the gods;
> I advise you, yield up the ring!     (631–3)

As she utters these words, Ex.4c is answered for the first time, *immer pp*, by its inversion, Ex.5. The gentle rise and fall of the completed melody indicate Erda's total acceptance of destiny. The musical polarity between the placid but inexorable movement of these motifs and the sharp-edged melodies which are associated in the *Ring* with male power indicates that this destiny is inevitable regardless of Wotan's decision. The gods will, finally, be destroyed anyway. Wagner puns in the third line on *Dämmerung*, the German word which indicates both the half light of dawn and that of dusk: that which in this prophecy will 'dawn' is the *Götterdämmerung*, the twilight of the gods.

The effect is that Wotan's apparent escape now from the dilemma of Agamemnon at Aulis is, in the long run, no escape at all. Freia is freed, not sacrificed for Valhalla; but Alberich's curse touches all who possess the ring, for however short a time; and Erda's warning has foretold Wotan's destruction. Because he has possessed the ring, Wotan will be forced progressively, as the next two dramas unfold, into greater and greater renunciations, until he willingly accepts his own destruction and the end of the gods.

Not only is Wotan far more confined in his actions than the characters of the *Oresteia*; he now knows it, almost at the start of the trilogy. Agamemnon, Klytaimestra, Orestes and the Athenians are of course forced to make similar 'impossible' choices, and at the moments when they commit their climactic deeds these are fraught with inevitable consequences which, though they are not fully known then, are bound to emerge sooner or later. They are not, however, overborne at the time with the knowledge of their certain destruction; and while all of them do what they must with an apprehension natural in such fraught situations, they are not paralysed by fear.

For Wagner, by contrast, at the time when he created the text for *Das Rheingold*, it was fear that paralysed all human action—in particular the fear of death, which he saw as 'the source of all lovelessness'. As he wrote to Röckel (R 26/1/54):'the development of the whole poem sets out the necessity of recognizing and yielding to the change, the many-sidedness, the multiplicity, the eternal renewing of reality and life'. For Wagner, this could be achieved only by transcending the fear of death. By introducing, at this stage, the vision of a fate which, though destructive, is gentle, natural and even seductive, Wagner is already preparing his Wotan for the marvellous paradox of *Siegfried* Act 3 scene i. Having created in Erda a destiny more implacable than any that Aeschylus could conceive, he later extends to us the possibility of a triumph over that destiny to be made simply through the act of accepting its supremacy and abjuring all material values.

## VALHALLA

In the immediate context, however, the principal function of Erda's warning is to undermine the glory of Valhalla, even before Wotan has taken possession of his fortress. He has finally achieved his original aim of paying the giants for their work without either breaking his contract or losing Freia. The music is, therefore, suitably jubilant when she is finally freed, and returns to be embraced by the gods (642–4). But this mood lasts only for three pages of full score; and the next spectacle to confront us is the quarrel between the giants, which ends in the brutal murder of Fasolt. This shatters Wotan, impresses on him the power of Alberich's curse, and fills him with a new fear which—he now knows—will need a deeper wisdom than his own, and a securer bastion than Valhalla, to dispel it.

Nonetheless, Valhalla *is* a real and splendid objective, a beautiful fortress which beckons enticingly to its owner. Wagner, therefore, proceeds to impress on us the full extent of Wotan's achievement. In a scene of spectacular scenic and musical grandeur, Donner dispels the mists—at once the literal mists which threatened the gods with imminent decline, while

Freia was the giants' hostage, and the metaphorical mists which Alberich's curse, and the murder of Fasolt for the gold, have cast over Wotan's success. When Donner summons and orders the clouds, and Froh creates the rainbow bridge, the orchestral textures are rich in the extreme—the upper strings are divided into many individual parts, and no fewer than six harps are added to the textures for the depiction of the rainbow bridge, for the short scene in which Wotan hails and names the fortress ('*Abendlich strahlt . . .*' 703ff.), and for the tutti which concludes the whole drama. All this conveys that the gods have achieved at last that harmony with nature which in the *Ring* is the central measure of achievement. But will it last?

Erda's warning and Fafner's fulfilment of the curse are inauspicious enough in themselves; and the closing pages are designed to undercut Wotan's achievement at least as much as they exalt it. Fasolt's corpse remains on stage right to the end, and no amount of harmony between the gods and the upper atmosphere can dispel the effect of its mute and ominous presence.

Furthermore, from the moment at which Wotan fearfully recognizes in Fasolt's murder the power of Alberich's curse, Loge turns against the gods the irony which earlier he had so successfully used in their service. His first comments may sound favourable, but by the time when Wotan begins to form the gods into a procession to cross the bridge into Valhalla, Loge has dissociated himself totally from them:

> They are hastening to their end,
> they who pretend that they're so strong and enduring.
> I'm almost ashamed
> to share in their doings.
> To transform myself back
> into flickering flame
> I'm strongly tempted . . .                    (702ff.)

Wagner rightly claimed (R 26/1/54) that Loge here 'only gives utterance to our own conviction; for anyone who has followed the Preliminary Evening sympathetically, and not in a hypercritical, cavilling spirit, but abandoning himself to his impressions and feelings, will entirely agree with Loge'.

If all this were not enough to undermine the ideal of Valhalla, Wagner arrests Wotan's triumphal progress with the *Klage*, the ritual lament of the Rhine-daughters. The gods laugh at them, and Loge attempts to quieten them, on Wotan's behalf, with the reassuring news that:

> Even though the gold
> doesn't shine on you girls any more,
> In the new splendour of the gods
> you can sun yourselves happily from now on!
>
> (732–3)

But this does not silence the daughters of the Rhine. Their lament continues, and it takes all the force of the radiant music of Valhalla, as the curtain falls, to crush their plaintive cries. It is sublime and splendid music—but its main component, Froh's rainbow bridge motif, is a circular theme of hollow grandeur which does not reappear in the *Ring*. The optimism and security of the closing moments are already being clearly seen to be impermanent:

> Tenderness and trust
> are only in the depths;
> false and cowardly
> are those who enjoy themselves up there!   (736–9)

These words, sung by the Rhine-daughters, are the last to be heard in this drama. They look forward to the end of *Götterdämmerung*; the world of the *Ring* has suffered corruption so intense that it will indeed know no permanent 'tenderness and trust' until Brünnhilde returns their gold to them.

By this point the parallel with Aeschylus' account of Agamemnon at Aulis is complete. At the end of the ode, the great expedition has set off on its way. Its success is guaranteed, but at a hideous price; and the elders close in apprehension, almost recklessly trying to ignore the implications of the story which they have told:

> The scale of Retribution falls, and some men learn
>     from their experience. As for the future—
> you'll hear about it when it comes. Until then,
>     let it go;
> it's just like weeping in advance;
> for all will come clear with the rays of the dawn.
> At any rate, may all this have a good outcome,
> as we desire . . .                    (*Agamemnon* 250ff.)

That hope has been totally undermined by the sheer power and horror of the description of the sacrifice of Iphigeneia. Such cautious hope may be the only possible position—but it is futile.

The last image which *Das Rheingold* leaves with us is the triumphant music for the gods' entry into Valhalla; but Wotan's situation is no better than Agamemnon's, despite the confidence with which he shrugs off the complaint of the Rhine-daughters. By the end of the 'preliminary evening' in the *Ring*, the prospective glory of his triumph has been qualified as decisively as has that of the Trojan expedition, by the end of Aeschylus' choral ode.

Nonetheless—for all the ominous prospects—the immediate gains are considerable. Agamemnon *has* acquired the means to sack Troy; Wotan *has* acquired the fortress from whose security he can rule the world. These are not illusory achievements—but they will prove to be impermanent ones. That is why so much time passes before the action resumes; ten years in the *Oresteia*; around twenty in the *Ring*. Aeschylus and Wagner both pause now, and each begins the main action of his trilogy when the moment, at which the achievement seen in the preliminary work will be undermined, has become imminent.

# 4

## *Die Walküre*

### *DIE WALKÜRE* AND *AGAMEMNON*

Wagner always regarded *Die Walküre* as the darkest section of his trilogy, and he declared it to be 'the most *tragic* work which I have ever conceived' (L 13/12/55). Its composition caused him intense suffering and nervous exhaustion; he once remarked to Cosima, after playing over to her the first two scenes of Act 2: 'you can understand that I felt the need, after writing these parts of the *Nibelungen*, to leave this element of dreadfulness and to write *Tristan und Isolde*, which was, so to speak, just a love scene' (D 8/3/70). Audiences have invariably shared the composer's own response to this drama. Even at the moments where their actions fill us with the greatest horror, Wagner compels us to understand and sympathize with the central characters of *Die Walküre*.

Each act moves gradually and inexorably to a single climactic situation—and each of the three climaxes is more severe than the one before. The first traumatic moment of tragic choice confronts Siegmund, who embodies Wotan's first attempt to create that 'other' than himself who may retrieve the ring: he can defend his love only by accepting the power of the sword Notung. The second and third confront Wotan himself, who is obliged in Act 2 to renounce his love for Siegmund and kill him, and in Act 3 to renounce his love for Brünnhilde and part from her for ever. By the time at which these choices are made, we have come to realize that both Siegmund and Wotan undertake what they do out of necessity—also that they do it only at great immediate cost, and that by their action they are consigning themselves to future oblivion.

There is no question in *Die Walküre* of voluntary renunciation. *Das Rheingold* has foreshadowed a vision of our world in which everyone must renounce love to some extent in return for power. At the outset of the main action, both Siegmund and Wotan are compelled to use their power. And so, they are obliged to sacrifice their love. They both attempt to live with love *and* power; their tragedy lies in the fact that they fail. Although Wotan now embarks on the first attempt to 'remake' Alberich's deed and remove its effects from the world, he has himself been so closely involved in theft, deceit and violence that he cannot escape their consequences.

Nor can his agent. The love of Siegmund and Sieglinde brings to the trilogy a warmth and musical richness which at once distinguishes human beings from the corrupted *mores* of the other three races. With this a hope for the distant future enters the cycle; but their love is incestuous, and Wotan's attempt to break free of the restraints of morality collapses. Fricka successfully upholds moral convention, and insists that Siegmund must die at Hunding's hand.

Wotan's predicament is central to *Die Walküre*. In the final version, he is absent from the action of the first act; but he initiated it, and his absence serves only to intensify his situation in Act 2, when he has to accept the full responsibility. Although Alberich began the action of the trilogy, and it is entitled *The Nibelung's Ring*, the primary focus is now on Wotan. As Wagner wrote to Röckel:

> Wotan rises to the tragic height of *willing* his own destruction. This is the lesson that we have to learn from the history of mankind; *to will what necessity imposes*, and ourselves to bring it about.  (R 25/1/54)

But he does not reach that stage in *Die Walküre*. In this drama he finds himself obliged to accept ever greater sacrifices, until finally he must not only lose Brünnhilde as well as Siegmund, but must bequeath her to Siegfried—'the creative product of this supreme, self-destroying will, its victorious achievement; a fearless human being, one who never ceases to love'.

Wotan's position in *Die Walküre* is parallel to that of Klytaimestra in *Agamemnon*. Each is the central figure, dominating the first drama of the main action by their towering stature, tragic predicament and underlying nobility. Despite this, neither is granted the honour of the title; Aeschylus and Wagner give to their first dramas the name of the character on whom Klytaimestra and Wotan take vengeance, but whose memory remains to bring back—in the second drama—the heir who will destroy them and claim his inheritance.

Klytaimestra and Wotan both go beyond accepted limits; they attempt to gain their freedom by establishing an indefensible 'new law' which strikes at the bases of the structure of their society. Klytaimestra pursues her vengeance to the point of killing the legitimate king and accepting into her bed—and thus placing on the throne—his hereditary enemy Aigisthos. Wotan takes *his* plans even further, not merely committing adultery himself but also promoting incest between his two human offspring. Both attempts, though powerfully motivated, are too one-sided in their purpose to survive; and both fail. Klytaimestra has been forced to lose Iphigeneia, and will alienate both Orestes and Elektra; Wotan is forced to lose both Siegmund and Brünnhilde. And at the end of the first drama, both Klytaimestra and Wotan lie under the unequivocal threat of vengeance in the next generation. We recognize that both will ultimately suffer defeat at the hands of a returning hero, their victim's son. The law which they invoke to justify their own deeds will bring them down in their turn. Neither Klytaimestra nor Wotan has succeeded in 'remaking' the original disastrous acts of Agamemnon and Alberich; on the contrary, what they have done now, in their attempt to do so, creates instead an attitude in their children which will destroy them in the second drama of the trilogy.

These resemblances are so central that they quite outweigh the obvious differences between Aeschylus' calculating murderess and Wagner's tormented god. And, as if to mark clearly the relationship between *Die Walküre* and *Agamemnon*, Wagner begins the main action with the same concern as Aeschylus

—the act of hospitality and its abuse; conducts a moral debate in Act 2 whose principal issues are closely related to those at the heart of *Agamemnon;* and makes extensive and varied use, during Acts 2 and 3, of a scene in *Agamemnon* (that between Kassandra and the chorus) which is among the richest and most striking in all surviving Greek drama.

The most important parallel between *Die Walküre* and *Agamemnon* lies in the way in which, though Klytaimestra and Wotan grow constantly in stature, their plans and hopes are ultimately undermined. Both characters are confronted by a formidable opposition whose case against them is unanswerable, and vigorously argued. In Aeschylus, the elders confront Klytaimestra after the murder of Agamemnon, and reduce her from exultant defiance to a pathetic hope that she will evade the destructive *daimōn* of the house of Atreus. Wagner, characteristically, doubled the exaction from his Wotan. First Fricka in Act 2, and then Brünnhilde in the final scene, reduce Wotan— who begins by being firmly resolved to oppose each of them—to compliance with their wishes.

There is a deeper aspect to this correspondence. At the end of Act 2 Wotan takes action, killing Siegmund and resolving that Brünnhilde must be punished. And this has consequences which, although he has not anticipated them, are deeply expected by the audience. Wagner undermines his character's expectations in a manner which is exactly Aeschylean. The lustrous music given to Sieglinde in Acts 1 and 2 prepares us for a possibility which never occurs to Wotan himself—the height of understanding, and of love, to which a woman can rise. Sieglinde's depth of feeling prepares us for Brünnhilde's development. In the last act she gains a full female nobility which inspires Wotan to accept his greatest sacrifice; for by creating the magic guardian fire, he guarantees that only Siegfried can free her and thereby ensures that in the next drama he himself must yield to Siegfried. So too, in *Agamemnon*, Kassandra has the power to balk Klytaimestra—even if only temporarily; and her prophecies undermine in advance the glory of revenge and release which Klytaimestra hoped to obtain from the murder of Agamemnon. At the end of both first dramas, the hope which shone out at the beginning—in the news of Agamemnon's imminent return, and in the creation and coming together of the Volsung twins—has been irrevocably overcast. Both Klytaimestra and Wotan must finally accept the prospect of an exaction from them, in the next generation, which will be far more severe than anything they could have predicted, when they took the steps which set the main action of the *Oresteia* and the *Ring* in motion.

Having established these fundamental similarities. Wagner is now able to register his second major dissent from Aeschylus' vision of the world. The audience is strongly encouraged to sympathize with Siegmund's hostility to, and rejection of, society, and his incestuous union with Sieglinde. Wotan's promotion of this liaison, and indeed all of his actions so far, are therefore also viewed sympathetically. And Wotan is of course forced to act against his will, when he kills Siegmund, and when he renounces Brünnhilde.

Aeschylus presents Klytaimestra in a much less sympathetic light; she defies the norms of Greek society and strikes them at the heart, killing her husband (the king and the legitimate head of both the household and the city) voluntarily and exultantly. The snarling, bitter close of *Agamemnon* is unique among the surviving Greek dramas. It is designed to foreshadow the blight which her action, and the establishment of the usurper Aigisthos on the throne, will cast over the opening stages of *Choephoroi*.

So there is a total contrast at the end. After killing Agamemnon, Klytaimestra begins by releasing all her exultant joy, as she emerges from the palace to glory in her deed: but she is then forced in the final scenes towards a passive, weary resignation. Wotan by contrast ended Act 2, after killing Siegmund, in a mood of sad and bitter fury. He enters in Act 3 to the same music, but then moves during the course of the great final scene to an exultant acceptance of his fate, which gives him *his* release as he glories in his resignation from power and from life.

Wagner therefore precisely inverted Aeschylus' closing pattern. We shall see Wotan and Klytaimestra move together again, as their position develops in *Choephoroi* and *Siegfried;* for the moment, at the end of the first drama, Wagner places

Wotan's hope in deliberate opposition to the fears of Aeschylus' Klytaimestra. By doing this he brings out his absolute conviction of the necessity of 'recognizing and yielding to the change, the many-sidedness, the multiplicity, the eternal renewing of reality and of life' (R 25/1/54).

## SIEGMUND AND SIEGLINDE

In the first scene of *Die Walküre*, Wagner explores the gradual growth first of the sense of affinity, and then of love, between Siegmund and Sieglinde. With the sheer intensity of this human love, we are taken away, at once and decisively, from the terms of cynicism and self-preservation on which the affairs of *Das Rheingold* were conducted. The music flowers with a sustained richness, and we find ourselves in a new world, with new hopes and expectations—just as we do in the parallel moments in *Agamemnon*, when Klytaimestra embarks on her narrative of the flaring of the beacons. But the events portrayed in *Das Rheingold* will undermine the love of Siegmund and Sieglinde as decisively as the sacrifice of Iphigeneia overshadows the homecoming of Agamemnon.

In scene i, their gradual growth towards love is portrayed with intense care, both in the stage action and in the music. Each act of compassion which Sieglinde bestows on her unknown guest (first the gift of pure water, and a little later the rich mead which, at his insistence, she touches first to her lips) evokes from Siegmund a greater intensity of emotion—carefully prescribed in the stage directions, and reflected by the ever-greater richness of the orchestral response in the moments when both are silent, moved by his acceptance of each of her gifts (24–5 and 33–5). The process is completed when he reveals the depth of his misfortune, and forces a personal admission for the first time from her:

> Sieglinde (calls after him with violent abandon)
>     Then stay here!
> You bring no misfortune here,
> for it lives in this house already! (39)

And this revelation, that she too is suffering, evokes an even longer and more passionate response from the orchestra; a passage which proceeds to such heights of poignant emotion, as Siegmund resolves that he will stay and wait for Hunding, that it seems already to anticipate the moment of decision, at the end of the next scene, in which Sieglinde resolves to drug Hunding's night-drink (40–1). Ex.16 plays a central role in these three orchestral passages, expressing the gradual development of their feelings for each other; and Ex.17, flowering from it and gradually developing in itself, portrays their affinity and the beginnings of their love.

The love of Siegmund and Sieglinde grows from a gradual mutual awareness of their loneliness and suffering, as well as from their capacity for compassion. Sieglinde's first reaction on seeing Siegmund is one of sympathy; her concern is immediate when he admits that he is wounded; and gradually, during the scene, *his* compassion develops into a selfless determination that he should not bring his misfortunes to rest upon her too. She is 'the sunlight, smiling on me again' after the darkness of the storm (31), and this Aeschylean image, of light after darkness, will be used again when Siegmund lies alone by the fire at the start of scene iii.

The image is not gratuitously chosen. For there Siegmund likens the gleam of the sword-hilt in the firelight to 'the glance/ of that radiant woman'. He is recalling the glance with which Sieglinde indicated that same place on the trunk to him, before Hunding drove her from the room. The light that is in Sieglinde shines from her *eyes*.

The three passages in scene i during which the voices are silent lead up to this, for here Wagner's stage directions carefully instruct the two players in the use of their eyes. As Siegmund takes the water, his eyes are to fasten on Sieglinde's face 'with growing sympathy'. As he puts down the horn, after drinking the mead, he is to look at her again, 'while the expression on his face shows that he is powerfully moved'. At the end of the scene, after her outcry, he gazes at her 'with calm and steady sympathy'. At first, embarrassed and sad, she lowers her eyes; but finally, during the last moments of the scene, in its final 'long silence', she raises her eyes to meet his and their gaze becomes reciprocal for the first time.

The ability to look each other in the eye is Wagner's token not simply of the growing love between Siegmund and Sieglinde but of their affinity and of their honesty. The contrast with *Das Rheingold* is absolute; there deception, deceit and treachery dominated the action, and nobody looks anyone else sincerely in the eye throughout the entire Preliminary Evening.

There is a close parallel in the *Oresteia*; Aeschylus twice speaks in *Agamemnon* of the shaft of light which darts from the eyes of a woman. The image first occurs in the two horrific stanzas in which the elders describe Iphigeneia's last moments. Her mouth was gagged to prevent her from making any sound which might be a curse on the house, and Iphigeneia's eyes then 'cast on each of her slaughterers/a shaft imploring pity' (*Agamemnon* 240–1). The poet does not need to tell us that each of them avoided her look.

Hypocrisy and dishonesty, however, are not driven out of either trilogy at the preliminary stage. If a married woman's eyes gaze with sincerity on a man other than her husband, that husband is being deceived. Such is the gaze of Sieglinde's counterpart in *Agamemnon*, Helen, as it fell on Paris; 'a soft shaft from her eyes/a flower of love that pierces the heart' (742–3). And Wagner uses this motif from the corresponding part of the *Oresteia* to give theatrical form to the betrayal of Hunding— who correctly suspects that Siegmund is as likely to deceive him as Sieglinde, and speaks of the 'glittering snake' that gleams from the eyes of both his wife and his guest. The metaphor comes from Aeschylus, whose Orestes explicitly recognizes that he and his helpers must put on the manner of the snake— deception—in order to defeat Klytaimestra and Aigisthos, the usurpers who have used deception in their turn (*Choephoroi* 549–59).

Klytaimestra did at least succeed at the time in carrying through her deception of the elders and, on his return, of Agamemnon. But Wotan does not. In Act 2 of *Die Walküre*, Fricka, correctly suspecting that Wotan is trying to evade her, forces him to look her in the eye. He can then no longer deny that he was attempting to leave Brünnhilde free to defend Siegmund against Hunding, by simply promising that he himself would not do so.

But this new focus has not yet entered the drama in scene i. Here the Volsung twins introduce a sincerity, and a potential for closeness, which are new to the world of the *Ring* and hold out at once, even at this early stage, the promise that human heroes may indeed turn out to be in some way better than the gods. Their deep emotion on seeing each other is transformed into love and recognition by the oppression of the world in which they live.

The music of the orchestral prelude makes plain that part of this oppression is Wotan's contrivance, designed to bring Siegmund to the place where he will need the sword which the god has placed in the tree. As the storm rages Ex.18 blazes in the brass instruments. But this music, which was first heard in the last scene of *Das Rheingold* as a glorious motif, while Donner cleared away the clouds, now signifies only persecution. And the

Ex.18

persecution is Wotan's. The ostinato which proceeds relentlessly almost throughout the prelude, and which returns in scene
ii when Siegmund describes how the storm pursued him(48),
is clearly reminiscent of the motifs associated with the power
of Wotan's spear (Ex.25, see p. 149).

Their abandonment as children by Wotan, and his persecution
now is only one source by which the Volsungs are oppressed.
The other is the work of darker forces. As scene ii proceeds, it
becomes clear that the human society from which Siegmund has
been outcast is a violent and primitive one. Siegmund tells of the
death of his mother and the loss of his sister taken by 'a cruel
gang of vicious men'—and Hunding's sinister motif (Ex.19)
sounds clearly in the horns at this point (58), to associate him as
soon as possible with the ideas of force and oppression.

Ex.19        (moderately slow)

Society rejected Siegmund, because 'whatever I thought was
right/to others that seemed bad' (65–6). And the final part of his
narrative supplies a specific and highly relevant example. Siegmund had attempted to rescue a girl who—like Sieglinde—was
being forced by her relatives into a loveless marriage. This
society respects the claims of *Sippe*, kinship and family, above
those of love, and will use any force it can to impose those
claims. Hunding is its representative in *Die Walküre*—for the
girl's relatives were his as well. Therefore he will fight Siegmund to avenge their deaths.

But not until the morning. For there is one other code that
Hunding observes, beside the claims of kinship. Welcoming
Siegmund to his house, after questioning Sieglinde in a way
which makes it obvious to Siegmund that he suspects her
already, Hunding declaims, forcefully and unaccompanied:

> Sacred is my hearth:
> treat my house as sacred too!                    (44)

The meaning, in the context, cannot be doubted. In scene i,

Sieglinde told the stranger despairingly that 'this house and this woman/belong to Hunding' (27–8). Hunding is now warning his guest against any attempt to seduce the wife who is his property; and, more specifically, against seducing her in his house. Having offered the hospitality of his hearth to Siegmund, Hunding feels bound to give him shelter for the night, even after Siegmund's narrative has shown that he is his family's enemy and Hunding has the duty to take vengeance on him. Here again the story of Paris and Helen in the *Oresteia* helped Wagner to dramatize his material.

The hearth is sacred in many cultures, including those of Northern Europe. But this close association with hospitality is specially emphasized only by the classical Greeks: the relationship between guest and host, called *xenia*, is basic to Greek society. Wagner encountered many clear examples of the procedures involved, when he read the *Odyssey*; and he used the pattern of actions of this Greek custom to order the sequence of *Die Walküre* Act 1. The relationship was initiated by taking refuge at the hearth—which Siegmund does in the first words of *Die Walküre*; and it was further advanced by eating a meal together, which is the first thing Hunding orders in scene ii.

*Xenia* was normally cemented by the exchange of gifts. But matters do not advance that far, in Hunding's hut. Just as the action of the *Oresteia* was set in motion by Paris' abduction of Helen so Siegmund now begins the main action of the *Ring* by abducting Sieglinde from Hunding's house. The parallel is exact:

> Such was Paris; he came
> to the house of the Atreidai
> and shamed the table of hospitality
> by the theft of a woman.
>
> (*Agamemnon* 367ff.)

By the conventions of Hunding's world, the hearth may be the centre of the house; Sieglinde—guided, as we shall learn in scene iii, by Wotan—now begins to indicate a new focal point. Hunding's hut, like that which the disguised Wotan built for his mortal family, is built around a central ash tree. And the ash that was burnt prefigures the ash that now stands. Both anticipate the cosmogony set out in the *Götterdämmerung* Prelude. There we will learn of the ash tree which is the centre of the world (in Teutonic myth, Yggdrasil). Wotan, who cut his spear from that tree, has pierced this tree with a sword. At this point Sieglinde's 'fixed, eloquent glance' is designed to direct Siegmund's eyes towards Notung.

When he is left alone, Siegmund's hope and apprehension mount until he gains the courage to cry out in a prayer to his father for the sword which he once promised; and the prayer is answered. But the firelight which reveals the hilt also blinds him, so that he cannot see clearly what it is. His perception is not yet great enough because, although their feeling of affinity has grown, it has not yet led Siegmund and Sieglinde to the fullness of love, in which they will recognize each other.

This affinity has, however, led Sieglinde to her decision to drug Hunding. The total congruence, when he is left alone, between Siegmund's mood, the blaze of the fire, and his memories of Sieglinde, prefigures the deeper congruence of his union with her, which will achieve full harmony with nature. The fire which blazes up for him and almost shows him the sword is the fire that binds his eyes to Sieglinde's, the fire of her gaze and of his response to it. And now Sieglinde returns; their love answers to their need.

This love is, nevertheless, hazardous. Drugging Hunding may be 'good deception'; but it remains deception. This may be an adultery of which we approve; it is still adultery, and will need to be defended against Sieglinde's husband. The shifty gleam in the eyes of the Volsung twins is matched by the gleam of the sword that Siegmund will need to use if their love is to survive.

As scene iii proceeds towards its conclusion, the feeling between the twins grows into love. It is a love so strong that nature bends to reflect it; winter storms yield before the springtime of their love, and in an extended love-scene Sieglinde and Siegmund gradually come to trace in each other's physical features (and lastly in their eyes) the deep affinity and resemblance between them. It is also a self-discovery, and a discovery of their father; and that enables Sieglinde to find the name that is right for Siegmund. 'Wehwalt' (Woeful) no longer, he is now styled Siegmund, 'the conqueror'.

To live up to that name, however, he must draw the sword from the tree. It is the sword of his *Not*. The German word conveys both need and distress; this is the sword which he must have to defend his life, and his newly acquired bride; but simply because it is an instrument of violence, it is also the sword of distress and misery. By punning on the two senses of *Not*, Wagner conveys all this in six lines, as Siegmund prepares to take the sword:

| | |
|---|---|
| Heiligster Minne | Holiest love's |
| höchste Not, | deepest distress, |
| sehnender Liebe | yearning desire's |
| sehrende Not | scorching need, |
| brennt mir hell in der Brust, | burn brightly in my breast, |
| drängt zu Tat und Tod. | drive me to deeds and death. |

(214–15)

And with these lines Ex.2 returns to the score of the *Ring*, clearly enunciated for the first time since the first scene of *Das Rheingold*. Wotan's agent Siegmund declaims the first four lines to the melody of Ex.2, fully exposed over a string tremolo. And so he becomes the first person to be placed in a situation fully parallel to Alberich's at the outset of the cycle. For Siegmund, like Alberich, has to accept power; he has a 'choice' which is no choice at all, since he has to face Hunding in the morning.

The paradoxes in the text are designed to alert us to the dangers; Siegmund's words invite ironic questions. Can a love be 'most holy' which causes 'the deepest distress'? Should it drive the male partner 'to deeds and to death'? Is a sword the most appropriate wedding gift for 'the fairest of women'? And the appearance of Ex.2, together with the name that Siegmund bestows on the sword, makes Wagner's meaning totally clear. This love can be preserved only by accepting the use of power; therefore, in Wagner's severe vision, it falls short of being a full, true love. That is why the Volsungs' congruence with nature is dissolved, in the opening music of Act 2, where the motifs of their love (Exx.13b and 17) are bitterly intertwined with Ex.1 in a passage of desperate strain whose musical symbolism is obvious. The love-music of Act 1 may be intense—but it is also tenuous, tragic and vulnerable. Death will be Siegmund's price for power, as lovelessness was Alberich's.

Sieglinde does not reveal herself to be Siegmund's sister until the last lines of the act. He then acknowledges and accepts this without hesitation: 'Bride and sister/are you to your brother' (239). Wagner has so far sought from the audience the fullest approval of Siegmund and Sieglinde; but now, with the open acknowledgement of incest, he foreshadows the threat that we may be obliged to change our perspective. In Act 2, we shall.

In the *Oresteia*, the brother and sister, Orestes and Elektra, do meet under oppressed conditions, by divine guidance and brought together by the father they have lost; but not until the second drama of the trilogy, and emphatically not to commit incest. Wagner elected to place incest at the centre of *Die Walküre* because it places the couple—and with them Wotan, who has created this whole situation—in an equivocal position, and so explains their downfall. They are Wotan's instruments, and he is the Klytaimestra of this drama; like her, he is going to find that his actions now will cost him his existence. Like Klytaimestra, whose daughter Agamemnon butchered at Aulis, he has the strongest of motivations; but also like Klytaimestra, he is going utterly against the social code of his society. Neither the breaking of the *xenia* code, nor even female adultery, held, in the second half of the nineteenth century, the intense power to shock which both possessed in fifth-century Athens. Wagner opens his trilogy, like Aeschylus, with an act designed to strike contemporary morality at its heart: the most sympathetic pair of lovers in the *Ring* break the one taboo which could be guaranteed to elicit the same horror in nineteenth-century Germany as the adulteries of Helen and her sister Klytaimestra in Aeschylus.

At the time when he wrote *Die Walküre*, Wagner held the view that nature—as opposed to society—has no objections to incest. He argued in *Opera and Drama* (AE 2.182–3) that since Oedipus and Jocasta had children, nature demonstrated that she was 'quite content' with their union. Indeed, Wagner did not even accept the view that inbreeding produces weaker offspring;

on the contrary, he followed his Icelandic source, the *Volsung Saga* (cc. 6–8), in which only the son of Signy by her brother Siegmund is strong enough to avenge her dishonour. In his 1848 sketch of the Nibelung myth, Wagner had made clear that in his version the union between brother and sister is essential 'to breed a true Volsung'; the Volsung blood *does* prosper from it, as Siegmund prophesies in the curtain line of *Die Walküre* Act 1. Siegfried is stronger, not weaker, than his parents.

Wagner does accept, however, that incest involves introversion. The text of the love-scene stresses the special nature of their affinity—to look at the other, they both say, is like gazing at their own likeness; the music here is also introspective, lying in stark contrast with the extrovert passion of Brünnhilde and Siegfried in the third act of *Siegfried*. And the Volsung twins are too close, not only to each other, but also to Wotan. The fire which they discern in each other's eyes is their inheritance from the old man who set the sword in the tree; the role of Ex.12 in the music of this act is designed to emphasize their position. Like the love of Paris and Helen, theirs is too tenuous and evanescent in its beauty to survive (*Agamemnon* 738ff.); and Siegmund, like Helen, is both a mortal and the chosen instrument of a god's will (cf. *Agamemnon* 747–9).

And so the spring after winter, the light out of darkness which their love achieves is premature, and will not last. Klytaimestra bends nature to her will, first with the relay of beacons and then with the two great speeches (958ff., 1372ff.) in which she almost blasphemously aligns the cycles of the seasons, nature and the gods with her own will and her determination to kill Agamemnon. Wotan is in a similar position. The storm that persecutes Siegmund, and the forced marriage that Wotan has left Sieglinde to endure until her saviour comes, are both Wotan's contrivances—just as much as the sword which he has left for Siegmund, and the spring night with which he signals approval of their union. In a thoroughly Aeschylean manner, the prospects for the Volsung twins point in two diametrically opposite directions by the end of Act 1: their love at once prospers under the influence of a god, and is also obviously hazardous, defensible only by violence.

## FRICKA

In Act 2 scene i, Fricka forces the ambiguity of Wotan's position out into the open; it is her role to bring home to him the first fruits of his own actions. The Norse gods and goddesses were believed to appear instantly to defend a hero, if he called on them for aid. Wagner employs this belief here, to provide Hunding, and the codes of society, with an advocate of formidable power. Fricka's case is presented unanswerably; and as her argument develops she finally undermines the conviction which Wagner successfully placed behind the power of the love of Siegmund and Sieglinde in Act 1. There we were invited at first to place our total approval behind them; the laws of kinship and the rights of a legal husband were presented unfavourably and embodied in the malevolent, sinister character of Hunding. By contrast, the forces of nature gathered behind Siegmund and Sieglinde, smiling upon their love and inviting us to give our full assent to it.

Wagner is as adept as Aeschylus in shifting our moral perspective as his tragedy unfolds. The rescue of Sieglinde by Siegmund is undermined now as decisively as the rightness of the Trojan expedition was undercut, as *Agamemnon* developed. In this scene Wotan attempts to counter Fricka's case by appealing to the power and beauty of love; as he does so the music echoes Siegmund's 'spring song', but nonetheless his attempt to justify the twins' sexual union in this way is simply bluster. They are too close to each other, and too close to Wotan, to prosper in the world of the *Ring*. For we are still too near to Alberich's original act, and Wotan's own theft of the ring. Love cannot yet proclaim its value unalloyed, and Wotan has only created a pair of true lovers at the price of endowing them with a bond of kinship too close for their liaison to survive.

So we are not yet dealing with 'right fighting against right' (*Choephoroi* 461). In both the *Oresteia* and the *Ring*, that situation will not be reached until the second drama of the main action. And there Orestes, and Siegfried, will achieve a deeper harmony with nature and its powers than could be achieved by their fathers. Here and now Wotan is as wrong as Aeschylus' Klytaimestra. Both attempt to go beyond society's limits. Klytaimestra commits adultery with Aigisthos, and then strikes further at the fabric of the Argive state by murdering Agamemnon, her husband and her king. Wotan, who founded the society which he leads by treaties—even if they include 'deceitfully binding' ones, in a revealing aside to Brünnhilde in scene ii—is now promoting incest and adultery.

Not that we fail to side with him. Like Klytaimestra, impelled to murder by the brutal sacrifice of her daughter, Wotan has been compelled to act as he has by a crisis of his own. The music is sublime and visionary, as he tells of his response:

> Hear this one thing!
> The crisis calls for a hero
> who, free from the gods' protection,
> can free himself from the gods' laws.      (315–16)

But this vision cannot yet be realized. Society, and Fricka, do not object to incest and adultery simply for convenience: these are real taboos, necessary to maintain moral stability and social order. Indeed, guilt at breaking them infects Sieglinde, in scene iii, even though she belonged to a man who obtained her without love. Only when society is being demolished, and the gods have accepted that they must pass away, can Fricka's claims be ignored. Wagner will not demand our approval for Gunther's claim to marry Brünnhilde. In *Die Walküre*, conventional morality must be obeyed—and Wotan is now forced to obey, right up to the final scene in which he has to punish Brünnhilde.

The confrontation with Fricka raises a further issue. Wotan's vision is indeed one for the future—for Fricka is absolutely right to argue that there is no new, separate hero 'free from divine protection' to be seen in Siegmund. Wotan gave him the sword—and his union with nature and with Sieglinde. And so in the remainder of the scene Fricka strips Wotan, with devastating power, of all the defences he has devised. First she makes him promise not to defend Siegmund, then she detects his evasiveness and forces him to prevent Brünnhilde from doing so either;

and finally, since she trusts neither of his promises, she exacts an oath from him.

The central issues here are responsibility and deception. In Act 1, Siegmund and Sieglinde introduced the first frankness and true sincerity into the *Ring*. But they have to use deception to escape from Hunding; and their protector uses sophistry, equivocation and deliberate omission in his attempt to save them. Fricka, as she strips Wotan of all his defences in this scene, forces him to act from now on with total honesty. In doing so she prevents all the gods and heroes in the *Ring* from using deception to gain their ends (after this drama, it is practised deliberately only by the Nibelungs); this paves the way for Siegfried, the hero who will fall because he is unable to deceive successfully.

The scene therefore stands in a complex relationship with Aeschylus. Like the world of Aeschylus' *Oresteia*, that of the *Ring* now becomes, by Fricka's triumph, a place in which responsibility is absolute and—*pace* Wotan's hopes at the close of *Das Rheingold*—one in which people will sooner or later receive their deserts.

The *Ring* is quicker to banish deception than the *Oresteia*. Deception is introduced into Aeschylus' trilogy by Klytaimestra herself in the first drama, and it reaches its height in the great scene where, after a totally hypocritical speech of welcome, she induces Agamemnon by specious arguments to invite the jealousy of the gods by walking into his palace over rich purple tapestries. Orestes then employs deception against her in *Choephoroi*, and is indeed commanded to do so by the god Apollo (*Choephoroi* 556ff.). It is only at the climax of the final drama, in the trial of Orestes, that we are finally invited to reject deception, and offered (in Athena and the Athenians) a model of how one can live and act without it.

The classical Greeks were notorious among foreigners for their use of deception—'trust nothing Greek', as Euripides' Iphigeneia tells King Thoas during a scene in which she is herself deceiving him (*Iphigeneia among the Taurians*, 1205). Goethe created his own play of this title to oppose Greek ethics on precisely this point: his Iphigeneia refuses to deceive Thoas, even to save her own life and her brother's.

In *Die Walküre*, Wagner shares Goethe's hostility to Greek pragmatism. The gods and heroes of the *Ring* must be made to transcend the use of deception as soon as possible. And so the music invests Fricka's closing words (339–42) with an intense nobility. Her demand that Wotan and Brünnhilde uphold her right is supported to the full both by Fricka's own formidable dignity and—as Ex.4c rises in the orchestra to accompany her— by the full power of the 'eternal feminine'.

After Fricka's intervention, Wotan must accept the constraints which his own actions—the building of Valhalla, and the creation of the Volsungs and the Valkyries—have caused. But he is not yet able to do so. He withdraws more and more into himself, and his misery and inner anger grow until, as the second scene begins, he bursts out:

> O divine shame!
> O shameful wrong!
> Distress for the gods!
> Distress for the gods!
> Endless rage!
> Eternal misery!
> I am the saddest of all beings.          (348–51)

The music is intensely expressive—but what it conveys is simply rhetorical emotion. Wotan bears the fullest responsibility for his deeds, and will suffer the consequences. He will be forced to recognize this, just as Klytaimestra will in her confrontation with the chorus of elders over the bodies of Agamemnon and Kassandra (*Agamemnon* 1399ff.).

## WOTAN BEQUEATHES THE WORLD TO HAGEN

The first part of the scene between Brünnhilde and Wotan is designed to draw out the full implications of his predicament. In a muted, fearful tone of voice Wotan reveals his position to her. Although he felt compelled to build up his power, he could not renounce love completely. He tells of the rise of Alberich, of Erda's warning, and his own quest for further wisdom; the creation of the Valkyries and their work of gathering warriors, to increase the strength of Valhalla and avert the fall of the gods.

And so to the present, and the position in which Fricka has left him. He cannot himself fight against Fafner, with whom he has made a treaty; but he has now been forced to admit that he has failed in his first attempt to find the hero who:

> a stranger to the god,
> free from his favours,
> unprompted,
> unwitting,
> with his own weapons
> might do the deed
> which I must avoid,
> which my counsel never urged on him,
> even though it is my only desire!                    (382–3)

His second outburst is as emotional as his first. The text may have developed: Wotan no longer simply rails at the shame which he is suffering, but expresses also a new self-disgust at the limitations of his power. The music, however, grows to an anguished, dissonant climax just as at first (388ff., cf. 348ff.); and Wotan's emotions burst out yet again. His expression 'changes from the most terrible suffering to despair': he now seeks nothing but 'the end' (406ff.).

These three outbursts exhaust Wotan's wrath. He now reflects more deeply on the events, and ends his monologue by consigning the world ironically, 'in bitter anger', to Hagen:

> So take my blessing,
> Nibelung's son!
> That which deeply revolts me,
> I bequeath to you—
> the empty glory of divinity:
> may your eager hate gnaw it away!          (418–21)

But now the music is different. As Wotan sings these words, Ex. 12 is bitterly split around Ex. 9, and broken into fragments. The symbolism is plain: Valhalla's strength is broken by the

Rhinegold, as Wotan accepts that the glory of his power is empty.

The central figures of Greek literature, from Homer's Achilleus to Sophocles' Oedipus at Colonus in the last surviving Greek tragedy, accept their death openly and directly, neither embracing the end in a melodramatic defiance of the reality of extinction, nor submitting passively to their fate. To take one central example: Aeschylus' Eteokles, in *Seven against Thebes*, at first rails against the curses laid upon the children of Oedipus when he discovers that he and his brother must encounter each other in single combat; but he gradually abandons his reckless urging on of fate, and departs to confront his death calmly, with complete equanimity—'when the gods give them, you cannot escape from evils' (719).

Wagner's portrait of Wotan here was profoundly influenced by this Greek stance. Wotan begins the scene in a torment of romantic anguish; but his wish for the end is not set to melodramatic music. Though the text of his final resignation expresses bitter anger, the music qualifies this mood. The security of Valhalla is now clearly illusory, and Wotan has conceded that his power, his fortress and its heroes were gained by disloyalty and deceit. There is a new kind of splendour to these broken fanfares. Wotan began by fighting against his fate; now he accepts it, in bitterness but also with nobility. And so he nears the classical stance. At the end of Act 3, he will attain it.

Fricka has forced from Wotan his promise that Siegmund will fall. That is indeed a 'Götternot', a crisis for the god. But why *should* the gods resign the world, either bitterly to Alberich's son or joyfully to Siegfried? Indeed, as Röckel pointedly asked Wagner on reading the poem in 1854: 'why, seeing that the gold is restored to the Rhine, is it necessary that the gods should perish?' (25/1/54). Wagner's own answer to this question then was evasive: he merely claimed that 'at a good performance, the most simple-minded spectator will be left in no doubt on that point'. While this is perhaps true, Wagner does not go on to explain *why* it is necessary (or even convincing) that his gods should perish at the end of the *Ring*.

Jakob Grimm argued that in Teutonic mythology, since all the gods came into the world after the creation, Wotan 'can do nothing against a higher constitution of the world, which exempts neither him nor victory-lending Zeus from a general destruction' (p. 856). The Norse sagas are obscure about the relative powers of fate and of the gods: Odin, like Zeus, is clearly neither omniscient nor omnipotent. But I know no passage in the poems or sagas that clearly shows Odin being overridden by the Fates or any other higher order. The fact that the Norse gods did come to an end at the Ragnarøk does not of course prove that they were doomed to do so.

Grimm's Greek parallel is unsound. In normal usage *moira* (the nearest Greek word to our 'fate') most frequently refers to a man's allotted portion in life—how long he is going to live. The main role of the *Moirai*—just like the Norns—was to determine a man's life-span; and in both Greek and Nordic myth, this allotted span was outside the control of the gods, in the sense that they did not normally intervene and attempt to control it. But in two famous passages of the *Iliad* Homer's Zeus contemplates doing just that. Observing that a hero particularly dear to him (Sarpedon in book 16, and Hektor in book 22) is about to be killed, Zeus asks the other gods whether he should not intervene to prevent their deaths. On each occasion a goddess objects (Hera in the first episode, Athena in the second) and they use the same words: 'do you really want to bring back from terrible death/a man who is mortal, long ago doomed to this fate?' Zeus is persuaded not to override the *moira* of his favourite. Yet both goddesses concede that Zeus could, if he wanted to, override *Moira* and postpone the mortal man's decreed time of death. All they (or presumably the Fates) could do is disapprove.

Wagner places Wotan in a parallel, but more disastrous position. He could save his favourite, Siegmund, from his destiny; but Fricka's arguments against this course of action are even more cogent than those of her Homeric counterpart Hera. And he is persuaded.

So Wagner's Wotan does not succumb to the power of destiny. It is indeed present here; Ex.4 rises darkly to punctuate Wotan's monologue, indicating the gentle, encircling presence of the female 'fate' represented by Erda. But that alone is not

enough to compel Wotan to resign the world, or even to assent to
the murder of Siegmund. There is another reason:

> I set hands on Alberich's ring,
> greedily I grasped the gold!
> The curse that I fled
> has fastened on me:
> I must forsake what I love,
> murder the man I cherish,
> deceive and betray
> the one who trusts me!            (398–403)

As Wotan speaks of the curse, Ex.17 is sounded, terribly distorted to convey his anguish; and so Wagner's meaning becomes
clear. It is precisely *because* he once possessed the ring, even for
a short time, that Wotan must fall. In the vision expressed here
by the music, Wotan's bitterness is so intense because he is
forced to accept that his power must come to an end, simply
because it has become tainted by the touch of corruption. The
distortion of Ex.17 expresses the blight which must fall (because
Wotan has touched the gold) on the first true love seen in the
trilogy—that of Siegmund and Sieglinde; this is why, when
Wotan proceeds to resign the world to Hagen, it is Ex.9 that cuts
through the fanfares of Valhalla. The taint of the Rhinegold is so
great that once forged it corrupts all who touch it. And that is
why the gods must perish.

Wagner claimed, in *Mein Leben*, that Wotan's voluntary
resignation of the world had an affinity with the philosophy of
Schopenhauer:

> It is from this perception of the nullity of the visible world
> . . . that all tragedy is derived, and such a perception must
> necessarily have dwelt in every great poet, and even in every
> great man. On looking afresh into my *Nibelungen* poem I
> recognized with surprise that the very things that now so
> embarrassed me theoretically had long been familiar to me in
> my own poetical conception. Now at last I could understand
> my Wotan, and I returned with chastened mind to the re-
> newed study of Schopenhauer's book. (p. 616)

But Schopenhauer's idea of renunciation is different from Wagner's. For the philosopher, saints can attain true renunciation by their own spiritual effort, after they have separated themselves, by their ascetic way of life, from the affairs of this world. All other mortals, even the most noble, can achieve resignation only when their suffering bestows that particular knowledge which acts as a 'quieter of the will'. This is 'the knowledge of its inner conflict and its essential vanity . . . True salvation, deliverance from life and sufferings, cannot even be imagined without complete denial of the will.' (1.397)

At the time when he was completing *Die Walküre*, Wagner paraphrased this doctrine in a letter to Röckel (ND: early 1855). According to Wagner, Schopenhauer's view is that 'redemption is to be found only in the deliberate negation of the will—that is, in realization of its corrupt nature'. The gloss is Wagner's own; the idea of corruption is not central to Schopenhauer's teaching at all.

The idea of corruption is, however, deeply Aeschylean. In the corresponding portions of the *Oresteia* the idea of tainted wealth is central to the chorus's meditations. To have a house 'teeming excessively with wealth', they argue in their second ode, is no protection to a man like Paris, who 'tramples on the grace of things inviolable' (371): he turns out, when tempted by the *daimōn* Persuasion, to have 'blackness fixed in him'—the inner corruption which cannot be hidden, but shines out, 'a direly clear light' (*Agamemnon* 389ff.). They pursue this analysis further in the third ode, just before the return of Agamemnon. For Aeschylus, wealth alone bears no hazards:

> . . . it is impiety which breeds
> a greater deed after it,
> like to its own race;
> for houses straight in their judgment
> have a fate of fair children for ever.
>
> But old violence is apt to breed
> among the dark deeds of men
> a younger violence sooner or later, when
> the appointed day comes round . . .

And Equity shines out in
   smoky homes,
   and pays respect to the moderate man;
she leaves mansions spangled with gold,
   where mens' hands are foul, with her eyes
turned away . . .
   paying no respect to the might of wealth
   that is stamped with false praise;
and she steers everything to its end.

                    (*Agamemnon* 758ff.)

Wagner's dramatic conception of Wotan in *Die Walküre* was
developed under the influence of these choruses. Wotan, like the
central characters of *Agamemnon*, finds that his success is
undermined simply by the violence which he has committed to
obtain it. And for Wagner as for Aeschylus, the corruption
which this violence has created is so powerful that the destruction which it causes is inevitable.

There is one marvellous dissent from Aeschylus' vision. Unlike Agamemnon or Klytaimestra, Wotan will finally—under
the pressure of a second loss, an exaction even harder than the
death of his son—come to accept his fate.

Brünnhilde causes that exaction, by rebelling against his decision. At the very start of this scene, Wotan was unwilling to
tell her why he is so unhappy: he fears that if he reveals his
dilemma even to her, the words will be released from the grip of
his will, and gain a power of their own. But she persuades him,
with her love.

It is also under the pressure of love that she rebels, when she
has heard that he must murder Siegmund:

        You love Siegmund;
        for love of you,
   I know, I must protect the Volsung.       (423)

This is why she rebels; but how *can* she?

## BRÜNNHILDE'S REBELLION

> You are speaking to Wotan's will,
> when you tell me what you intend;
> who am I,
> if not your will? (357–8)

These are the words with which Brünnhilde coaxes Wotan into revealing all his inmost thoughts to her. And Wotan accepts that talking to her is as good as leaving something unspoken: 'I am then just taking my own counsel/when I speak to you'. As she persuades him to speak, Ex. 17 sounds softly and caressingly in the horns; and it is her love that dispels his doubts. He 'gazes for a long time into her eyes, then strokes her hair with involuntary tenderness. At last he seems to emerge from deep thought, and begins very softly.' The music of his 'monologue' is hushed and whispered, as if she were *totally* part of him, and Wotan were truly speaking to himself alone. Slowly he abandons the muted, fearful tone in which he begins, and gains the confidence that he may safely speak out. But at the close, Brünnhilde rebels against his command that she must fight for Fricka.

Wagner goes out of his way to make the flowering of this rebellion psychologically credible. Brünnhilde's responses become steadily more agitated, as Wotan explains his situation and she comes to understand it for herself; when she defies him, this is the moment at which she begins to grow up. At the beginning of Act 2, she left Wotan to handle Fricka as best he could, taking an adolescent delight in her warrior skills and happily admitting that she is leaving him in the lurch. Now, however, we hear in the music the flowering of true feeling, as she sings:

> Him you have always
> taught me to love;
> his fine virtues
> are dear to your heart;
> against him I shall never be turned
> by your two-faced order! (425–6)

Although at this point her defiance may seem only like a girlish resolve that can be quelled by the sheer energy of Wotan's fury, our whole perspective is changed after he has departed. For the first time in her life, Brünnhilde's armour weighs heavily on her and she approaches her duty with reluctance. The music flowers into a full expressiveness, as she laments what she must do to her beloved Volsung: she has discovered the ability to feel pain, and the conflict between love and duty.

Is it possible for 'Wotan's will' to break completely away from him? In scene iv, when her new emotions receive a reciprocal echo in the anguished devotion of Siegmund to Sieglinde, Brünnhilde is deeply moved, and determines to defy Wotan in action, on the field of battle. For Bernard Shaw, Brünnhilde here 'is the inner thought and will of Godhead, the aspiration from the high life to the higher that is its divine element' (p. 38). But she is more than this. Schopenhauer wrote of the terrible miseries to be seen in great tragic drama as 'the antagonism of the will with itself, which is here most completely unfolded at the highest grade of its objectivity, and which comes into fearful prominence' (1.253) Wagner, even before reading Schopenhauer, shared his conception of the will as a power which extends not merely through the inner being of humanity, but throughout nature as well. Brünnhilde *is* the part of Wotan that aspires 'from the high life to the higher'; but that part is also independent, part of nature in her own right, and therefore able to rebel.

Brünnhilde was not deliberately created by Wotan: her creation, and that of her sisters, was the price that Erda exacted from him in return for greater knowledge. This suggests that the price of Wotan's knowledge is that it will turn against him if he misuses it.

Brünnhilde has the power to rebel. This is partly because, in her innocence of sex, she has not experienced the complexities, and in particular the fear, which sexual maturity and love bring together with their splendour and ecstasy. However, she is able to defy Wotan primarily because she is Erda's child, and above all because she is female. In the world of the *Ring*, her femininity gives her access to a level of insight which is deeper, and more direct, than that of men and gods. That is why she cannot accept Wotan's 'two-faced order'.

Wotan was looking for 'the other' in the wrong place. He sought to create a naturally rebellious male outsider who would be independent because he had been deliberately abandoned. Brünnhilde by contrast is female, and is so close to her father that she is not normally rebellious at all. She does not become independent until she forces Wotan to abandon her, by unexpectedly defying him.

Wotan has failed as a social innovator; Siegmund will fail as a defender of his bride. Brünnhilde's music, as her feelings mature throughout Acts 2 and 3, has a warmth and a strength (simply because she is innocent of deceit and violence) which are denied to Siegmund and his protector. Indeed, the deepest love attained by a male in Wagner's trilogy is that of Siegfried for Brünnhilde—and he must learn it from her. Brünnhilde, the god's virgin daughter, accomplishes that act of rebellion which, as Wotan ruefully admits in Act 3, he could not.

This is chiefly a criticism of nineteenth-century male attitudes and convictions (cf. Cooke 332–3); but here also Wagner begins that dissent from Aeschylus' vision of a world in which male power is fundamentally stronger than female, which will become a predominant concern of *Siegfried* and *Götterdämmerung*. Wagner felt a considerable distaste for the melodramatic plot of Sophocles' *Elektra* (D 1/11/77); nevertheless, he may well have noted and absorbed the way in which Sophocles and Euripides place the rebellious defiance of Agamemnon's virgin daughter Elektra at the centre of their plays about the deaths of Klytaimestra and Aigisthos. In the two *Elektra* plays, Orestes, even though he commits the actual matricide, is relatively unimportant—a drastic departure from Aeschylus' *Choephoroi*, in which Elektra plays a minor role, and does not appear at all in the second half of the drama. Where the ancients felt obliged to choose, and to place only one of Agamemnon's heirs at the centre of the play, Wagner characteristically takes the best of both worlds. In *Die Walküre* he takes Sophocles' path, and dramatizes the rebellion of the daughter, from within the household; in *Siegfried*, like Aeschylus, he deals with the return of the avenging son of the murdered father.

## THE KASSANDRA SCENE IN *AGAMEMNON*

One day in 1874, Cosima Wagner found:

> R. reading *Oedipus* in the evening, after his work, comparing the translation with the text. 'It is like a Persian carpet', he says, 'a torrent of beauty—now vanished forever; we are barbarians.' We then come to the *Oresteia*, the scene of Kassandra with the chorus, and R. declares it to be the most perfect thing mortal art has ever produced. (D 18/11/74)

This scene, for which Wagner expressed such high regard twenty years later, had played a significant part in influencing the dramatic development of scenes ii–v of the second act of *Die Walküre*.

It is an extraordinary scene, even by Aeschylus' standards of compression and richness. Agamemnon has gone into his palace, and the chorus of elders, although they welcome his return, cannot find any relief for their anxiety:

> a man's black blood once fallen
> on the ground in death, who then
> could call it back by singing any spell?
>
> (*Agamemnon* 1019ff.)

This new, dark thought, which will become a major motif of Aeschylus' trilogy, dominates the scene to follow. On one level, the audience might at this point expect Agamemnon's death-cry to ring out; but Kassandra remains standing, mute and quivering with terror, in the chariot which he has just left. Klytaimestra tries to lure her second victim within the house—and fails; frustrated and furious, she leaves Kassandra to the chorus and returns inside.

The Kassandra-scene itself now begins (*Agamemnon* 1072). Kassandra's terror and agony are those of a prophetess, a seer who possesses insight into the past, the future—and the hidden present. First in lyric outcries and later more calmly, in an extended dialogue with the chorus, she relates to Aeschylus' audience, for the first time, the past of the house of Atreus—the banquet of his own children's flesh which Atreus set before Thyestes and the Erinyes or Furies, the hideous *daimones* who have risen from the children's blood and now sit within this house, crying out for vengeance (1186ff.). Kassandra also gains insight into the hidden present: she speaks of Aigisthos, the surviving son of Thyestes, who is plotting to take vengeance on Atreus' son Agamemnon; of Aigisthos' adulterous relationship with Klytaimestra, and the monstrous preparations which she is making, under the guise of the rituals of welcome, for the murder of Agamemnon. At the end of the scene her vision extends beyond the present and immediate future into a vision of distant events to come which enables her to accept the imminence of her own death at Klytaimestra's hands.

Kassandra had accepted the gift of prophecy from the god Apollo—in return for the promise of her body. She later refused the price. The Greek gods could not retract their favours; for her refusal, Apollo added a penalty to her gift—what she said would never be believed. And so we watch the chorus of elders groping towards the truth. They cannot overcome the barrier imposed by Apollo's punishment, even when in desperation she tells them directly: 'I say that you shall see the death of Agamemnon' (1246). But at the end, they come as near as mortal men could to believing her despite the god. Her death confirms her insights, and they use the courage and vision which they have gained from her in their confrontation with Klytaimestra.

Kassandra, too, has a spiritual journey to make in the scene; but hers is far more terrible. Of all the human characters in Aeschylus, she alone has certain knowledge of her fate; her initial terror is that of one who knows, in this moment of vision, that Apollo has brought her to this place to meet her death. Her visions unfold, and through them she comes to realize the full extent of Apollo's punishment; finally, she comes to accept her destiny, and the closing mood is triumphant, as Kassandra gradually emerges from the possession of the god to full femininity, just before her death. Rejecting her role as Apollo's prophetess, she experiences a final vision, in which she sees far into the future and knows that neither Agamemnon nor she herself will die unavenged: the gods have sworn a mighty oath that Orestes will return from exile, 'a son to slay his mother, as his father's champion' (1281).

From this knowledge Kassandra gains the strength fully to accept her own death, rejecting both self-pity and delay. So many others, she observes, have been destroyed 'in the judgment of the gods'—both her own Trojans and their conquerors—that she draws a fierce consolation from realizing that she too is part of the pattern. 'It is enough; I go. I will endure my death.' (1290)

As she sets out, however, in her turn to cross the space between the chariot and the door, she hesitates. It is a *recueil pour mieux sauter*; she learns now to tolerate even the nearness of the stench of death. And with the certainty that even she—'a slave, an easy victim'—will be avenged in turn (when Aigisthos falls for Agamemnon, and Klytaimestra for Kassandra) she reaches in her last words a mood which is almost unique in Aeschylean tragedy. Poised just before the climactic moment of *Agamemnon*, the death of the king—with so much already related and so much of the future revealed to us—the poet and his character stand back, inviting us to seek a bitter, momentary comfort in the state of human affairs at large:

> Alas for the affairs of men; when they go well,
> they are but shadows, and if they go ill
> the touch of one wet sponge wipes out the picture.
> I pity both; ill-fortune even more.          (1327ff.)

The influence of the Kassandra-scene pervades every part of *Die Walküre* Act 2 except the first scene, and the qualities which Aeschylus embodied in his chorus and in Kassandra are widely distributed among the characters of *Die Walküre*.

There is no real parallel between the opening confrontation of Fricka and Wotan and the scene in which Klytaimestra persuades Agamemnon to enter his house over a rich array of tapestries. But the pressure which the two scenes exert on subsequent events is very similar. In both *Agamemnon* and *Die*

*Walküre*, the situation becomes so ominous that the characters who remain onstage are obliged to expand their perspective, to embrace the past and try to penetrate the future. Therefore, the first influence in *Die Walküre* of the Kassandra-scene is on scene ii; Wotan gropes, like the elders, in the riddles of the buried past, and the terrors of the future. But the influence of Kassandra on Wotan's thoughts goes further still: just like her, he gains the strength to face his extinction from the knowledge that all life is just a shadow and that his end is near.

Wotan is not alone in this, among the characters of *Die Walküre*. Sieglinde, too, will make a parallel journey, reaching in Act 3 a resignation and acceptance of her death, from which she is saved only when Brünnhilde tells her that she bears Siegfried in her womb. And it is of course Sieglinde whose development in Act 2 is most indebted to Aeschylus' Kassandra.

Sieglinde alone, among Wagner's characters in this drama, shares Kassandra's volatility, and both women are thrown into the agonies of prophecy by the realization that this is the place and time in which they are to suffer punishment. Like Kassandra, Sieglinde is first given insight into the hidden present: she sees the avenger preparing—Hunding in pursuit, with the hounds and kinsmen whom he has gathered together. From this she passes into the future, and her part in scene iii ends as she collapses under the pressure of a further vision: Siegmund dead, his sword shattered and the hounds devouring his flesh.

Aeschylus' Kassandra passes slowly from the trance of agonized vision to the calm lucidity of prophecy. Wagner reverses this process: the burden of Sieglinde's vision grows until she loses consciousness. Her limp, mute presence is essential to the scene that follows: the devotion of Siegmund to this fainting, helpless mortal woman is the factor which breaks down the barriers of Brünnhilde's reserve, and makes her decide to defy Wotan. Sieglinde is then left onstage for scene v, in which Wagner completes the parallel with Kassandra, by taking her, like Aeschylus' prophetess, back into her past. Already, at the close of Sieglinde's first vision, she has sung of Siegmund's death as the fall of an ash-tree (488): the ash is the centre of the house for the Volsungs, as the World-Ash is the centre of the

universe for their father (cf. Klytaimestra at *Agamemnon*
966ff.). At this point (after Siegmund has left her to fight
Hunding) Sieglinde, 'moving uneasily in her dreams', is trans-
ported back to the climactic moment of her childhood: the sack
and destruction of her house.

The fierce consolation which Kassandra drew from accepting
the sack of her city (*Agamemnon* 1287ff.) is denied to Sieglinde:
this vision ends with Sieglinde's terrible cry of 'Siegmund', with
which she suddenly returns to reality; her prophecy is fulfilled,
and her vision of the past is welded to the present.

Although Wagner gave Kassandra's powers to Sieglinde, she
moves into a mood of romantic self-sacrifice which is without
any parallel in Aeschylus. Sieglinde does resign herself to death,
but only in Act 3—where Ex. 2 sounds, slightly varied to express
her joyless resignation as she sings 'Do not suffer sorrow for
me;/all that I need is death!' (765). Sieglinde's final peace is
achieved, however, in realizing that her life will achieve its
purpose through her final sufferings, which will bring renewed
life. That is in the visionary assurance that Ex. 20 expresses,
when it is heard for the only time before the closing pages of
*Götterdämmerung* as she learns from Brünnhilde that she is

Ex. 20

with child (799ff.). In contrast, Kassandra achieves *her* true
greatness in the closing section of the scene, where she rises
gently to a total, welcoming acceptance of death. And that
Wagner took from Sieglinde, and bestowed on Siegmund.

Scene iv is of course the turning-point in the action of *Die
Walküre*. It is the first confrontation in the trilogy between a god
and a mortal. Wagner deliberately invests this scene with the
atmosphere of ritual, by the measured but inexorable pace of the
music, by the solemnity and restrained emotional strength of
the two principal themes (Exx. 21 and 22), and by the dramatic
technique. The scene is cast in the form of a sequence of matched

questions and answers, which is broken at the point where
Siegmund defies Brünnhilde's demand—'I will not follow you'
(516–17)—and so takes the leadership from her. It is Wagner's
re-creation of the stylized exchanges of *stichomythia* in the
*agōn*—the direct, formally structured contest between two
wills—which is a prominent feature of many of the surviving
Greek tragedies.

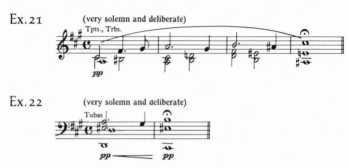

The subject of this *agōn* is Siegmund's defiance of the gods. It
is as though Kassandra could have confronted Apollo himself
with the courage and the acceptance of death, which she has
bequeathed to Wagner's Siegmund; for at the beginning of the
scene, Brünnhilde exhibits the glacial, distant calm which
Aeschylus' harsh Apollo seems to possess in *Agamemnon*. But
she is shaken by Siegmund's firm resolve. She promises him
that in Valhalla he will find *Wunschmädchen*—girls who will
fulfil all his desires; and in the orchestra, Ex.13 rises in its
pristine, undeveloped form, flowering into decorative arab-
esques as she describes them (504–9).

The figurations, however, are no more than decorative. To
Siegmund, the *Wunschmädchen* possess no allure. The music of
Act 1 has made us realize that, though it is doomed, the human
love of Siegmund and Sieglinde is deep and rich to an extent not
yet conceived of by any of the gods. Although Brünnhilde is
shocked, *our* deepest expectations are satisfied when Siegmund
rejects the 'frigid joys' of Valhalla and would rather live, or die,
with Sieglinde. Brünnhilde cannot understand why the woman
is everything to him, and his reply is piercing:

Siegmund (looking up bitterly at her)
    So young and fair
    you dazzle my eyes:
    but how cold and hard
    my heart knows you are!    (538–9)

At the end of scene ii, Brünnhilde showed that she has the potential to feel as deeply as human beings. Now Siegmund's distress and defiance reach her heart: when Siegmund shows that he would rather both he, and Sieglinde, were dead than that either should live on without the other, she resolves to fight for the Volsungs.

The ideal of Valhalla is finally undermined. Kassandra, by her power of prophecy, passes on to the elders of Argos the strength of insight which later enables them to defy and undermine Klytaimestra in her moment of triumph: in the same way Siegmund, by his power of devotion, passes to Brünnhilde the strength of insight which in Act 3 will enable her to defy Wotan and force him to accept his own destruction. The gods must now yield the world to heroes—for they have been shown to be the lesser race. Like Kassandra, who is a woman, a slave and a foreigner in Argos, the Volsungs are oppressed, persecuted and doomed to an early death in the world of the *Ring*. But Siegmund has the power in his last moments of life to influence the future decisively. We know already that Brünnhilde has the potential for deeper sympathy; and now, by the sheer intensity with which he faces the certainty that he is about to die, Siegmund, like Kassandra, communicates his feelings to his listener despite the barriers that prevent understanding. Kassandra overcomes the curse of Apollo; Siegmund breaks the Valkyrie's virginal reserve. The two characters 'live on': the pathos of their death is transcended by the effect which their influence now, in the moments before they die, will have on the world to come.

## WOTAN RENOUNCES BRÜNNHILDE

Act 3 begins with the assembly of the Valkyries. The main musical material here is of course Ex. 23, which was first heard at

Ex. 23

the start of Act 2, where it characterized the tomboyish vigour of
the obedient 'warrior maid' Brünnhilde. The sheer energy ex-
uded now by the other eight Valkyries prepares us for a powerful
contrast. Thanks to Siegmund, Brünnhilde has already begun to
develop towards a woman's full depth of feeling; she will continue that development until, at the end of this drama, she ceases
to be a Valkyrie at all. And so when Brünnhilde appears, riding
not in triumphant glory but with the intensity of one pursued,
carrying on her saddle not a dead warrior but the living woman
Sieglinde, the ensemble of the assembling Valkyries is disrupted; and the contrast between her and her sisters prefigures
the main issues of the act. Brünnhilde stands out sharply against
the other Valkyries: she is emotionally warm where they are
cold and conventional, and her fear of Wotan is human and real
where their reaction is shallow, adolescent timidity. She stands
out even more clearly when set against Wotan himself, who
arrives at the beginning of scene ii to exactly the same furious
music with which he began his pursuit of Brünnhilde at the end
of Act 2. To him, this is a simple matter of defiance and punishment.

   As the act develops, however, the situation's more complex
overtones intrude, and disrupt his expectation. The theme
(Ex. 24) which accompanies Wotan's pursuit of Brünnhilde was
first heard in his monologue in Act 2, when he accepts the
limitations of his position. Ex. 24 is related not only to the motif
associated with Wotan's power (Ex. 25) but also to the combina-
tion of Exx. 4c with 5. Indeed, it is the first stage in the evolution
of Ex. 25 towards the moment when it develops into Ex. 34 (see
p. 174) which is so closely related to Exx. 4c–5 that, in and after
*Siegfried* Act 3, it portrays Wotan's acceptance of his destiny.
His power is immense—but so also is the pressure on him of
forces beyond his control.

Ex. 24

(quite animated)

Ex. 25

Trbs.

Wotan's emotional position is now equivocal. While he is describing the extent of Brünnhilde's defiance, to justify punishing her, he is portrayed by the music as remaining detached; but when he lays down his sentence ('No more shall I send you out from Valhalla . . .' 847ff.), the feel of the music is altogether changed. The warmth of his affection for her sounds clearly, in both vocal line and orchestra, to belie the severity of the sentence. Before she has even begun to argue against him, this music holds out to us the hope that the sadness of punishment will somehow be mitigated: that what he imposes will in some way be 'right'.

In scene iii, when Wotan has dismissed the other Valkyries and Brünnhilde is left alone with him, she begins to argue her case from a position of total submission. She is lying prone on the ground at Wotan's feet, and even the eloquent woodwind meditations on the new melody, Ex. 26, which open the scene and prefigure some hope of peace, have died out into complete orchestral silence before she begins her defence. But we know, after what we have just heard, that her inner strengths will find a place in him to which they can appeal. As her plea develops, and she explains why she felt bound to help Siegmund, the music

Ex. 26    (a little bright)

Cl. solo

p dolce

surrounds her new maturity with an ever-increasing warmth
and beauty. Ex.26 plays a prominent role throughout this process, and it is this theme that flowers unrestrained at last, as she
completes her defence and invokes Wotan's own deeper self
against his present severity:

> He who instilled
> this love in my heart,
> the will, which
> allied me to the Volsung,
> I was faithful inwardly to him—
> though I broke your command.          (920–3)

Brünnhilde is 'inwardly' faithful to Wotan because she was
faithful to his ideals of love. The rich, warm textures here, and
the growth of Ex.26, portray the full strength of her love, which
begins to seem capable of overcoming even Wotan's rage.

*Agamemnon* ends with a fierce, bitter confrontation where
the only certainty for the future is the prospect of renewed
violence. But Brünnhilde's persuasive eloquence holds out the
possibility that in Wagner's trilogy love may be able to transcend violence even at this early stage. It creates the final dramatic issue of *Die Walküre*. Must Wotan look back, condemning
her to a pointless punishment out of bitterness because in Act 2
she was able to indulge her affection for Siegmund, while he
could not; or has he the strength to overcome his rancour and
look to the future, making creative use of the consequences of
what he has had to do?

When Apollo gave Kassandra the gift of prophecy, she then
refused to pay the price; the god, unable to take back his gift,
added instead a condition that destroyed its value (*Agamemnon*
1202ff.). To mark his dissent at this point from Aeschylus'
vision, Wagner places his Wotan in a parallel position: he is
unable to retract the punishment he has decreed (947ff.).
Brünnhilde now makes a proposal which precisely inverts the
Aeschylean situation. She begs Wotan to add to his punishment
a condition which converts it into a prize: a wall of fire which will
protect her:

so that only a fearless
completely free hero
will find me one day
here on the rock!                                    (956-7)

As she sings this, Ex.27 rings out in the orchestra; and the reference is clear. This theme has already been associated totally with Siegfried.

Ex.27    (pressing on)

In the last scene of *Agamemnon*, the chorus—armed with Kassandra's prophetic insights—threaten Aigisthos and Klytaimestra explicitly with their hope that Orestes will come back to slaughter them (1646ff.). This threat has no immediate effect. Klytaimestra is wearied by the conflict, and begs both sides for peace when Aigisthos and his bodyguard nearly come to blows with the elders. But she remains defiant to the end: she bids her new paramour:

Pay no regard to this empty wailing; I
and you are masters of this house, and will arrange all
    well.                                           (1672-3)

There is a central divergence from this sequence at the end of *Die Walküre*. Wagner makes Wotan accept extinction voluntarily. Wotan is being asked to resign his daughter—and with her his own fate—to the child of the race for which he has been forced to extinguish his love, and can now feel only hate.

Yet he comes to do just this. At the climax of the scene, all the tension between them is dissolved. Wotan raises Brünnhilde to her feet (so signifying that he accepts her plea), and begins an impassioned farewell. As he does this (968ff.) the full orchestra declaims three themes with the utmost clarity: first Ex.27, in token of the full acceptance of his own fate to which Wotan must now commit himself; then Ex.23, transformed for the first time to sound noble and truly serene as Brünnhilde, in her last moments as a Valkyrie, shows how much she has matured over the course of Acts 2 and 3; third, the new theme, Ex.6 (see p. 75), which was first heard explicitly when she made her last request—that she be surrounded with 'terrors that scare' (955ff.).

The process of evolution towards the open declaration of Ex.6 began much earlier, when Brünnhilde described her dilemma, and the anguish she suffered when she saw the extent, and the full depth, of Siegmund's love (905ff.). With its perfect poise and inner symmetry, Ex.6 expresses the new, fully altruistic love which Brünnhilde has learnt from Siegmund. It is the strength of this love which now inspires Wotan to embrace his loss.

When he entered in Act 3, Wotan was totally self-righteous— exactly like Klytaimestra at her appearance over the bodies of Agamemnon and Kassandra (*Agamemnon* 1372ff.). But the sequence after that point is precisely the reverse of Aeschylus'. The elders reduce Klytaimestra initially to the futile hope that she can make a personal pact with the *daimōn* of the house and gain exemption from its destructive powers (1567ff.); then to a final despairing plea—'the word of a woman, if anyone thinks it worthy of attention'—that Aigisthos and the elders do no more violence, but preserve the status quo, bitter though it is (1661ff.). She has already lost the total strength and confidence, uniting all the powers of the male and of the female, which she displayed while she prepared and executed the murder of Agamemnon.

Klytaimestra's hope, and her pleas, are futile because the forces which have been set in motion at the outset of both trilogies are too strong to be stopped simply by the wish of one character, however powerful, at the end of the first drama. Wagner extends to Wotan a contrasting possibility. He, too, begins the scene in righteous self-justification; but he proceeds, not to a pathetic hope of preserving the status quo, but to an active acceptance of all the implications of the change. This is caused by the influence of Brünnhilde's vision. The intelligence of 'this stupid girl' (as she ironically calls herself) has the power to transcend the constraints and fears which have oppressed

Wotan, and to make him turn from bitterness to acceptance. And so he begins, 'Leb wohl' (973).

The phrasing raises a precise echo: these are the exact words of the blessings which Goethe's Iphigeneia demands, at the end of *Iphigeneia among the Taurians*, from King Thoas. Refusing to be satisfied when he accepts only grudgingly that he must lose her, Goethe's Iphigeneia in her final speech begs Thoas to rise above his loss, and to mark their parting with the only words which can convey his full and open acceptance: Leb wohl—literally, live well. Goethe's Orestes has just spoken of the powers which his sister has shown in reconciling the Greeks and the Tauri:

> For force and cunning, proudest boasts of men,
> are put to shame by the truth
> of her great soul, and pure and childlike faith
> are her reward to every noble man. (2142ff.)

And so Wagner once again echoes Goethe's opposition to 'Greek' deception: as Ex. 26 evolves in this final scene towards its perfect culmination in Ex.6, we hear the growing power of Brünnhilde's depth and simplicity, the 'pure and childlike faith' which she, too, can now bestow. For Wagner's god Wotan as for Goethe's king Thoas, it is the noble, necessary act to cast off male violence and deceit, and to rise to full acceptance of a woman's depth of feeling.

There are three stages in Wotan's development after this point. First, he accepts Brünnhilde's last demand, and as he completes his promise to surround the rock with fire, the music slows and Ex.27 rings out in the horns, to show that as he accepts the loss of his daughter, he also fully accepts that he must lose his world:

> For one alone shall win the bride,
> one freer than I, the god! (988–91)

Now that Wotan has accepted this, and cast off his jealousy, the music can develop. Wotan embraces Brünnhilde for the last time; and the orchestra reaches an intense climax (994–7) as she gazes 'in solemn emotion' into his eyes. The woodwind and the strings echo each other, declaiming Ex.6 *fortissimo* in a perfect, symmetrical motion which expresses to the full the rightness of the decision which he has made.

The exaltation is succeeded by sorrow. As Wotan completes the words of his farewell, and prepares to bestow on Brünnhilde the kiss which will remove her immortality from her, Ex.2 sounds out, 'full of expression' in cor anglais and horn (1004). Here, at the end of this drama, Wotan accepts that he too must renounce love forever; Ex.2 is heard only now because, in explicitly bequeathing Brünnhilde to Siegfried, Wotan has at last accepted totally the exaction which he must face, in consequence of all that he has done. As Brünnhilde becomes a woman, she must leave Wotan's world forever. In Act 3 she has reached a plane of feeling beyond the reach of any god: Wotan can share it only briefly, in these last moments of temporary exaltation.

When Wotan has summoned Loge to surround the rock, he pronounces a final conjuration:

> He who fears the point
> of my spear,
> shall never pass through this fire!    (1032–41)

and from this point onwards a sequence of themes, always suspended under the ostinato of Loge's motifs, depicts the complex feelings with which Wotan departs from the rock. As he stretches out his spear 'as if casting a spell', Exx.27 and 6 are heard in perfect counterpoint, foreshadowing the glorious future union of Siegfried and Brünnhilde. Then, as he looks back sadly, an eloquent, plaintive theme (Ex.28) is heard in the cellos to convey Wotan's pain.

Ex.28

This theme was first heard in the moment of parting, as he kissed her farewell for ever (1049–55); but as it unfolds now, the musical emphasis passes elsewhere. In the upper instruments, Ex.6 proceeds steadily and expressively on its course. The future is indifferent to Wotan and his suffering. As he turns to go, Ex.6 is heard alone, now *dolce* as peace descends upon the scene. And when Wotan has finally left, the drama closes with the brass instruments solemnly sounding Ex.22, the gentle but severe harbinger of inevitable change.

The close, then, is a complex pattern of hopes and fears. There are two climaxes in Wotan's farewell, first the exultant glory of the embrace and then the resigned acceptance, at the moment where Wotan prepares to kiss Brünnhilde's eyes in final farewell, Ex.2 expressing all the pathos of his loss. Wotan attempted to remove from the world the effects of Alberich's seizure of the gold; but his own brief time as the possessor of the ring corrupted him too, before this drama even began; and so he finds himself compelled to lose not only his son, but his dearest daughter also. Hence the precise balance in the orchestral fabric, as Wotan slowly prepares to depart; Wotan's pain is overset by the certainty that Siegfried will come to free her—the repetitions of Ex.6 seem already to be beckoning Siegfried towards the rock, and undermining Wotan's attempt to foster his own backward-looking emotion; and then the implacable modulation of Ex.22 ensures that the resignation which Wotan has just made is final.

Wagner, thereby, completes his relationship with Aeschylus' finale. Just like the last third of *Agamemnon* (after Klytaimestra has appeared over the bodies of her victims and is confronted by the chorus) the last scene of *Die Walküre* is an *agōn*, a contest of wills which forces the murderers of Agamemnon and Siegmund to alter their perspective. Both Klytaimestra and Wotan must recognize the prospect that, in the next generation, an heir will return to avenge his father's murder.

As we have seen, they react in totally different ways. The reason for this is the fact that by the end of *Agamemnon*, the *daimōn* of the house of Atreus, the will of the gods, and the duty of Orestes to avenge his father when he comes of age are all working in harmony to fulfil the prophecies of Kassandra (1279ff.). There is no level of experience, whether 'material' or 'spiritual' in modern terms, on which Klytaimestra can evade the consequences of what she has done. It is, however, possible for Wotan to dissociate two such levels. Already, earlier in *Die Walküre*, other characters have willingly preferred to seek death rather than disgrace. Siegmund would rather murder Sieglinde, and commit suicide himself, than fight Hunding with the sword that will betray him; Sieglinde would rather die than live on after the death of Siegmund; and Brünnhilde herself begs that she might suffer death rather than be left on the rock, at the mercy of any man who comes to take her. For each of these characters, honour will transcend the material fact of death.

So, too, with Wotan, who completely dissociates his own material survival from his glory: he fulfils himself, creating his true glory, by rising above the concerns of this life, accepting his fate, and condemning himself to extinction. This conception of heroism, approached only by Kassandra in the *Oresteia*, is almost totally alien to Aeschylus' vision of the world.

There is none the less a deep parallel with Aeschylus' story-pattern in the contrast which is made between the first and the second principal agent of each trilogy. In the *Oresteia*, Aeschylus' Agamemnon sacrifices Iphigeneia under compulsion, while his successor Klytaimestra takes her revenge exultantly, glorying in her deed. Similarly, in the *Ring*: Wotan remakes Alberich's deed, sadly but voluntarily; to the music of Ex.2, he willingly accepts the sacrifice of love that tormented Alberich at the start of the trilogy. In *Das Rheingold* scene i, the dwarf could renounce love for gold only in fury and bitter distress. After all he has suffered in *Die Walküre*, Wotan has developed so far that he is now able to resign to another his dearest daughter—and with her his world; not, now, in anger to Hagen, but in full, calm acceptance to Siegfried.

# 5

# *Siegfried*

## SIEGFRIED AND ORESTES

With the second drama of both the *Oresteia* and the *Ring* a
young man becomes the central figure. In Aeschylus'
*Choephoroi*, the murder of Agamemnon and the usurpation of
his throne by Aigisthos are such serious wounds to the house of
Atreus that the outside world must recede from sight until the
third drama. The shed blood of Agamemnon confines the action
to this house simply because of the bonds of familial relationship:

> The cure for all this
> is lint applied inside the house
> and not by others from outside, but from its own,
> through savage, bloody strife.      (*Choephoroi* 471ff.)

In Greek belief, only children can save a man's glory, after he is
dead. A male heir must avenge his murdered father, or his
father's Furies will turn their wrath on him; and legitimate
power descends, with almost spiritually cogent force, from
father to son.

These basic social conditions are completely reflected in
Aeschylus' play. Only Agamemnon's heirs can lift the veil of
*miasma* under which this house now lies; only when
Agamemnon's son can take his father's throne will its greatness
be restored. The action has been locked into the house, and the
play begins in the atmosphere of darkness and repression set by

the first choral ode. *Choephoroi* then rises gradually to the point where Orestes has taken his revenge, and 'the light is here to see;/the great curb on this house has been lifted off' (961–2). But the rejoicing is premature: Orestes' victory is undermined, and in the last lines of the play his future lies poised between hope and total failure:

> Now he has come, the third, the saviour
> —or shall I call this death?
> Where, where will it end, where will it be sated,
> the pent-up force of destruction?            (1073ff.)

*Siegfried* is precisely parallel. Like Orestes, Siegfried succeeds where his father failed. Just as Orestes returns to the home that should be his and remakes his father's homecoming by killing the usurpers who in the first play welcomed Agamemnon so treacherously, so too Siegfried now embarks on a quest, the climax of which is the destruction of his father's murderer. And like Orestes, Siegfried is not simply remaking successfully the action which his father failed to accomplish in the first drama: he, too, achieves a success which was beyond the principal agent of the first drama. After killing the usurpers, Orestes for a few moments does attain the throne of Argos, which Aigisthos and Klytaimestra held precariously and without legitimacy; after defeating the Wanderer, Siegfried cleaves a path through the fire, and claims the bride whom his adversary left there. But in each case the attainment at the end of the second drama is undercut almost at once, and much must happen in the third drama before Orestes permanently resumes the throne of his fathers, and Siegfried attains, in death, eternal union with Brünnhilde.

*Choephoroi* is, so to speak, the dark night at the centre of the *Oresteia*: a narrow space into and through which the trilogy must move, in order to gain the greater, truer light and ever-increasing hope which come to it in the more open atmosphere of *Eumenides*. *Siegfried*, by contrast, is a drama of joy, which reflects the impetuous strength of its young hero and ends in the rich exultation of the closing duet (in the *Ring*, the counter-balancing darkness is reserved for *Götterdämmerung*, where the funeral music played before the final scene overwhelmingly emphasizes the tragic implications of Siegfried's death, before the final renewal); nonetheless, Wagner begins the second 'day' of the *Ring* in a very similar manner to Aeschylus. For both Aeschylus and Wagner, the second drama of the cycle must make a radical new beginning, and does so by starting in a distant place, returning only much later to the expected, ultimate scene—the palace of Atreus in *Choephoroi*, Brünnhilde's rock in *Siegfried*. The motif which unites the two beginnings is that of blight and corruption—a darkness into which the two heroes of the new generation bring a new hope.

Orestes approaches Argos from exile, and the world which is revealed to him, as Elektra and the chorus approach the tomb of Agamemnon bearing Klytaimestra's libations, is a dark and joyless one:

> O hearth of utter misery,
> o wreckage of the house;
> sunless, hateful
> mists of darkness shroud these halls
> whose true lords are dead.

> The glory that once irresistible, untameable, invincible
> passed deep into the ears and minds of men
> has now departed. All is fear . . .                    (49ff.)

Similarly in *Siegfried*: the prelude rises slowly from darkness, to depict Mime's sinister brooding, and the oppressive ambition for the ring which compels him to work endlessly at his anvil; and Mime himself dominates the action of Act 1. Orestes must return to a house dominated by his enemies; Siegfried, who like Orestes himself was the sole clear hope for the future at the close of the first drama, is trapped in his enemy's house.

In both cases this is fully expected. Orestes' coming was prophesied by Kassandra, at the climax of the most powerful scene in *Agamemnon*; and the oath which the gods had sworn was that 'the ghost of his dead father would bring him back' (*Agamemnon* 1285). The very opening of *Choephoroi*—Orestes' arrival before Agamemnon's grave—is itself the fulfilment of that prophecy. Towards the end of *Die Walküre*, Sieglinde fled to take refuge from Wotan's anger. The place which Brünnhilde chose for her is the dark forest which surrounds Fafner's cave—for Wotan, to avoid temptation, does not go there. But this ultimate advantage is accompanied by danger. Alberich and Mime are bound by no contracts to Fafner; and the ring draws them, weaker as they are, with a powerful lure. Orestes must return to the palace where Elektra is oppressed by the tyranny of Aigisthos and Klytaimestra; Siegfried is literally delivered into the hands of Mime. In both *Choephoroi* and *Siegfried* the new, young hero must attempt to break out of the constricting web in which the earlier events of the trilogy have placed him, and fulfil the duty which has been bequeathed to him.

Orestes and Siegfried have as yet performed no heroic deeds. They appear before us without the moral shadows which heroic achievement has already, before we first see them, cast over Agamemnon and Siegmund, and which, in *Agamemnon* and *Die Walküre*, rise up to cause their downfall. The two new heroes are both initially innocent, and therefore have the chance to succeed where their fathers failed; but, as if to compensate for this, they must begin by facing greater odds.

*Choephoroi* is a drama of sharp contrasts and rigorous divisions. Every person in the play is either a friend to Agamemnon and his cause or an enemy. In the Greek, these words do not denote affinities formed by personal preference: the 'friends' of Agamemnon are all those in Argos who retain their loyalty to its rightful lords, and the 'enemies' are Klytaimestra and Aigisthos. It was a truism in Aeschylus' world that allegiance is due to the rightful lord of a household; but the playwright accentuates it forcefully in the early scenes of *Choephoroi*, to prepare for the intense power of the play's tragic climax. Orestes is bound by every duty known to the Greeks to avenge his father; and his predicament is created, simply but profoundly, by the fact that in Aeschylus' version of the story he may do this only by killing his own mother. And so her Furies rise against him at the end of the play.

At first sight, Siegfried forms his allegiances electively. But this impression is misleading. As the work unfolds, Siegfried realizes his increasing capacity for an affinity and reciprocity with nature, an ability which enables his insight and understanding to grow until he has the power to defeat, not only Mime and Fafner, but the Wanderer as well. This ability is not an accident, but his inheritance as the child of Siegmund and—more especially—of Sieglinde.

At the end of *Siegfried*, Notung has been successfully remade and Siegfried unites in rapture with Brünnhilde. No *miasma* surrounds him, because he has not committed matricide. In Wagner's trilogy, the second drama does not end in tragedy.

This is closely bound up with the course taken by *Götterdämmerung*. Unlike the finale of *Eumenides*, the third act of *Götterdämmerung* does not provide a full and satisfactory outcome for all the surviving parties to the action of the *Ring*. Gunther lies dead, Gutrune heartbroken; Hagen and Alberich are not reconciled with Brünnhilde's dispensation of the world. Hagen makes a last bid of defiance, but is defeated as the Rhine-daughters reclaim their ring; even more importantly, Brünnhilde and Siegfried do attain eternal union—but only in their dying visions. At the end of the *Ring* there is a glory, and a hope for the future; but these are preceded by the intense tragedy of Siegfried's death, the fall of the Gibichungs and the defeat of the Nibelungs. Wagner has shifted the centre of tragic energy from the climax of the second drama to the climax of the third. The fundamental reason for this is Wagner's divergence in *Siegfried* from Aeschylus' view of a son's loyalties. As Apollo asks at the trial of Orestes, which is the 'true parent'—the father, or the mother? For Aeschylus' characters in *Choephoroi*, the answer is unequivocal: although Klytaimestra is presented with some sympathy, Orestes hesitates for only a moment when she appeals to him, and then implacably rebuts every argument that she makes in her defence. He does so with all the force of the first half of the play behind him: Orestes' words and actions at the grave of Agamemnon have brought him into a full and reciprocal relationship with his dead father and with the gods, both above and below the earth, who then support him in his enterprise. Our perspective is, of course, considerably developed in *Eumenides*; but in the central drama Orestes' position is placed beyond doubt as he begins his attempt at vengeance. It is his mother's power that he must destroy, his father with whom he must align himself.

The second drama of the *Ring* is designed to set out a diametrically opposed view of the world from that of Aeschylus. Nature is female for Wagner; indeed, Siegfried begins his path to insight by learning that he had a mother, and beginning to develop a warmth of feeling towards her. In Wagner's vision it is the father-figure who must be destroyed before the human male can attain true independence and be capable of adult love. Hence, in the first two acts, the meticulous care with which he studies the growth of Siegfried's harmony with nature, and with the spirit of his mother, as they gradually liberate him from Mime's false claim to be his father.

This theme is pursued to the climax of *Siegfried*. Siegfried should avenge his father's death on Hunding—as he did in Wagner's 1848 sketch. But in the actual text of *Siegfried*, Wagner made the hero confront Wotan himself at the foot of Brünnhilde's rock. The Wanderer seals his fate when he declares that the spear which he holds has broken Notung before—therefore, that he is responsible for the murder of Siegmund. Earlier in the scene he first rouses Siegfried's impatience when he asks for respect because he is old:

> That's rich!
> All my life
> an old man stood
> right in my way;
> and now I've swept him away.          (898–9)

In the course of *Siegfried*, the hero destroys all three of the older male figures who cross his path.

For Wagner as for many other Romantic writers the feminine is the sphere of instinctive or intuitive insight, as opposed to that of reasoning and intellectually acquired knowledge. This explains the fundamental difference between Orestes and Siegfried. Both stand in firm contrast with their predecessors, Agamemnon and Siegmund; but the contrasts lie in opposite directions. The 'young Siegfried' is distinguished from Sieg-mund (and indeed from Wotan) by his spontaneity and his lack of hindsight. The burden of the past does not weigh on him. It is precisely this 'naturalness' which gives him the ability to attain a greater affinity with nature than Siegmund, and therefore, at the end of the drama, to achieve a radiant, guiltfree union with Brünnhilde.

For the Greeks, however, increasing success was to be gained only by intelligence and prudence. Orestes is distinguished from Agamemnon and Klytaimestra by possessing a greater degree of insight than theirs. Throughout the drama, he is aware of his place in relation to the past, his understanding of the powers that surround him and of the deed that he must do. His stance from the outset is calm, thoughtful and reticent, in utter contrast with Klytaimestra's reckless assumption and execution of the will of the gods, and her grand hypocrisy. Orestes makes it clear that he is acting at the stringent command of Apollo (269ff.): his own personal motives, though real and emotionally compelling, are subordinate. At the moment of crisis, he weighs his victim's case, as if she were on trial. And he knows that what he does is itself wrong (930). In him there is nothing like Klytaimestra's growing thrill of anticipation before the deed, or her proud exultance after it has been done. Orestes mourns the sufferings of all his house, and does not glory in his victory.

Although this deed is committed with due reticence and moral awe, it is still an act of vengeance and matricide. And with the ability to think and use forethought comes the use of deception. Orestes is vulnerable, and is deservedly pursued by Klytaim-estra's Furies, because he must take on 'the manner of the snake' to overcome Aigisthos and Klytaimestra. As Klytaimestra says, at the moment when she realizes that she is trapped, 'we are being destroyed by treachery, just as we ourselves killed' (888). Treachery and deceit may be the method that Apollo ordained he should use, and the only means by which Orestes may succeed. Nonetheless, they remain undesirable qualities, and it is difficult to see them as virtues in a matricide when he denounces them in Klytaimestra. Nor does Aeschylus ask us to do this. Precisely *the* difference between Apollo and Athena is that in *Eumenides* she and her citizens will not countenance the kind of deception which Orestes employed in *Choephoroi*.

Again, Wagner presents a contrasting vision. Deception is utterly foreign to Siegfried's nature: in *Siegfried*, it is Mime's province. Just as Orestes' use of deception prefigures and explains his vulnerability in the world of *Eumenides*, where the Furies' charges against him carry ever-increasing weight, so too Siegfried's essential innocence remains with him, and will become *his* weakness when he descends from the mountain at the start of the main action of *Götterdämmerung*.

Aeschylus makes his audience perceive the relationship between Klytaimestra's deed and Orestes' by creating parallels between the structure of *Agamemnon* and *Choephoroi*. Just as in *Agamemnon*, the first half of *Choephoroi* shows the ever-increasing power of the avenger. In each drama a turning-point is reached with the arrival of the rightful lord before the palace of Atreus: in the first play, to be deceived; in the second, himself as the deceiver. In both, there are two victims, one of each sex; and the man is lured first into the house: the woman goes only when the audience has seen her face the certainty that she must die. This preparation ensures the impact of the central parallel. At the climax of both dramas the murderer emerges victorious, standing over the two corpses of his victims. But the glory of Orestes' triumph is then undermined, just as Klytaimestra's is: in the final scene, her Furies drive him from the stage.

The text of *Siegfried* is based, with a number of alterations of detail, on that which Wagner wrote early in 1851 for *The Young Siegfried*. It was, therefore, written before Wagner had decided to dramatize the whole of his Nibelung story by adding *Die Walküre* and *Das Rheingold*, and it was not altered in any essential way when it became the text for the second 'day' of the *Ring* trilogy. But Wagner wrote the text for *Die Walküre* in such a way that formal parallels between the two dramas could, in the manner of Aeschylus, highlight the similarities and the differences between Siegfried and both Siegmund and Wotan.

*Die Walküre* and *Siegfried* both begin indoors, with the hero

suffering persecution at the hands of a host not of his choosing—
a representative of the forces of darkness. And in both dramas
the closing part of Act 1 is an extended, self-contained lyric
sequence in which the hero realizes his identity and so gains the
power to break out from his bondage to a hard-won independence. This self-liberation is symbolized in the wielding of
Notung by each hero for the first time at the end of the act. (In
the first draft of *Die Walküre*, Wagner reinforced this parallelism even further, by making Wotan appear in person at the
centre of Act 1, just as he does in *Siegfried*: but Wotan's intervention in *Die Walküre* was distinctly artificial, and Wagner
later wisely abandoned this scene.) In both plays, the second and
third acts are set outdoors, and the second consists of a sequence of
intense confrontations, which lead in *Die Walküre* to Brünnhilde's defiance of Wotan and Siegmund's death, and in
*Siegfried* to Siegfried's conquest of Fafner.

Both dramas then conclude Act 3 with an extended duet on
Brünnhilde's rock. And Wagner, just like Aeschylus, uses the
strong and obvious parallel between the two closing scenes to
bring out to the full the difference between Wotan, who must
renounce and lose the daughter he loves, and Siegfried who has
finally won her.

Siegfried awakens a girl who has been laid to sleep; Orestes
assassinates a tyrant and commits matricide. Despite the immense contrast, the basic development of *Siegfried* remains close
to that of *Choephoroi*. The hero's gradually increasing harmony
with the powers of nature is as central to Aeschylus' second
drama, as to Wagner's. *Choephoroi* moves steadily from the
separate offerings and prayers made by Orestes and Elektra (at
the tomb of Agamemnon), via the extended lyric scene in which
they and the chorus seek to bind themselves totally into union
with the powers which surround and can support them, towards
the moment just before the climax, in which Klytaimestra
throws all the power of her motherhood into her appeal to
Orestes—but is defeated through the voice of Pylades, whose
three lines answer by placing all the force of the gods, their laws,
and of the natural order into the balance against her. At the close
of the play Orestes exhibits a calm faith in Apollo, who had both

commanded the deed and warned him that, if he did not do it, he would face the anger of his father's Furies. He can now reveal that Apollo has promised him deliverance from his pursuit by the Furies of Klytaimestra, if he goes to Apollo's own shrine at Delphi. This promise seems a just reward for the union with nature which Orestes has attempted to cultivate throughout the play. Orestes has striven successfully, and has overcome Klytaimestra, who as *Choephoroi* unfolds is increasingly presented as a monster, a perversion of the course of nature.

All this is mirrored in *Siegfried*. Mime has been corrupted, and reduced to a distortion of his original self, by the pursuit of the ring. And Siegfried, just like Orestes, begins to break free from his influence as soon as the drama begins. The famous entry accompanied by a bear is the first token that Siegfried has a greater affinity with nature than with his supposed father; as Act 1 develops and he gradually forces the truth out of Mime, Siegfried's first tremulous attempts to sense the nature of his mother prepare the ground for the meditations in Act 2. There, as he rests under the linden tree, he achieves a harmony with nature which, with a reciprocity which is truly Aeschylean, as it deepens gives him ever greater rewards. Siegfried then has the strength to overcome not only Mime but Fafner and the Wanderer as well; his road then lies open to Brünnhilde.

Here lies the most important difference between Aeschylus' vision and Wagner's. For Aeschylus, the hero's road to achievement is overcast by darkness; the whole play is beset by doubt whether any cure can be found for the wounds which have been inflicted on the house of Atreus in the first play of the trilogy. And Orestes' 'cure' is so drastic that, although he frees the house and the kingdom from the blight of the usurpers, he himself cannot yet take the throne of his fathers. All the harmony he has attained with Agamemnon and with the gods cannot save him from the legitimate wrath of his mother's Furies.

Siegfried has less insight than his predecessors—not more, like Orestes. He is simply unaware of the central dilemma of the *Ring*, because he is too immature to understand it. For this reason the 'renunciation of love' theme (Ex. 2) is not heard in *Siegfried*; there is no question of Siegfried having to renounce love for power in this drama, since he finds out what love is only in the final scene; and his innocence allows Wagner to examine the main preoccupations of the trilogy through two other characters. First, he explores in depth the Wanderer's movement towards his joyful resignation from the world: a victory over 'fate' of a kind that Aeschylus does not extend to any of his characters until the third play—and then only tentatively. Second, Siegfried's naivety demands that Wagner devote much of the final scene not to *his* growth of self-awareness after the act (as in Aeschylus) but to Brünnhilde. The closing scene of *Siegfried* is a penetrating and extended study of Brünnhilde's gradual development from an adolescent fear of sexual union to the glory of full womanhood. This study lays the essential foundations for the way in which, in *Götterdämmerung*, she is able to learn from and rise above her sufferings.

## THE YOUNG SIEGFRIED

'In Siegfried I have tried to portray the most highly developed and complete human being I can conceive of, and one whose highest attributes manifest themselves only in his immediate, current concerns' (R 26/1/54). In Act 1 of *Siegfried*, spontaneity and naturalness are the key elements in Siegfried's responses and actions; later in the drama, they will evolve into a deep sympathy (in the full Greek sense of fellow-feeling) with nature which has eluded all the other characters so far in the *Ring* except at brief, transitory moments—a deeper strength, and a greater capacity for love.

The essence of Siegfried's character is not merely boyish, impetuous vigour but the fundamentally direct response to experience which that behaviour expresses. It has rightly been noted that Act 1 of *Siegfried* contains more closed forms than any other part of the *Ring*: Wagner uses simple, symmetrical songs and song-like patterns to characterize the openness of the young Siegfried, and his basic honesty. And he also uses them to express Mime's caricature of a similar honesty, the feigned simplicity with which Mime tries to deceive Siegfried. The first question raised in *Siegfried* is simply how Siegfried can break out of the clutches of Mime.

When Wagner sketched the text for *The Young Siegfried*, he added a note to himself on the characteristics needed in the music of the prelude: 'mysteriously undefined sense of brooding on legend, making itself more and more rhythmically animated to accompany Mime's hammering'. This accurately describes the music which Wagner later wrote to introduce *Siegfried*: when the curtain rises it becomes clear that the brooding is associated with Mime—his theme, Ex.29, is heard as soon as Mime first breaks off from his work (19); and the matters on which he is brooding are indeed the fundamental, legendary concerns of the *Ring*. The way in which Ex.15 is used to impart the main rhythmic impetus to the earlier pages of the prelude is the most important feature here; Mime's calculations take us back to the world of Alberich's dreams in *Das Rheingold* scene iii. Once again, Ex.15 denotes an obsessive need to accumulate and acquire.

Ex.29     (moderate tempo)

Urged on relentlessly by the ostinato of Ex.8, the music builds to a dissonant climax (7–8), after which the ring motif (Ex.11) is heard in the woodwind. Even in the *Ring*, Wagner's orchestral music is rarely so programmatic. The world established by this prelude is that of Mime's obsessive desire for the ring; and the only music in the entire prelude which is not claustrophobic is the single appearance of the sword motif (Ex.1) on p. 11. Wagner extends this one ray of hope to us, set against the darkness of Mime's ambitions and his determination to bend Siegfried to his will. Just as Orestes' presence at the start (even before the coming of the libation-bearers begins the main action of *Choephoroi*) prefigures the prospect of a 'light out of darkness', so too does the promise, implicit in the clear sounding of Ex.1, that Notung will be reforged. Wagner, like Aeschylus, now devotes his main dramatic energies to portraying the way in which his hero gains the power to fulfil that promise and defeat the forces of darkness. *Siegfried* portrays Siegfried's development to full maturity.

Mime has kept Siegfried in ignorance, to make him his dupe. No less than Orestes, Siegfried has been deprived of his birthright. The drama begins as he starts to reclaim it, and escape from Mime's influence. Siegfried's entrance with the bear does not just establish his youthful exuberance. As soon as Siegfried recovers from the amusement which he has gained from the joke, the vigorous repetitions of Ex.30 vanish at once from the orchestra, giving way to more lyrical music as Siegfried explains why he brought the bear home with him: 'I wanted a better companion (*Gesell*)/than the one who sits in my home.' With a naturalness which defies translation into English, the word

Ex.30

*Gesell* embraces every one of the creatures with whom Siegfried achieves a relationship in *Siegfried*, from the bear at the start of the drama to Brünnhilde at its end. The bear is obviously only a temporary and inadequate substitute for Mime; but by sounding his horn in the forest, Siegfried has begun his quest in the right way—seeking better *Gesellen* by asking Nature for them. As the drama unfolds, Nature will respond reciprocally, sending him more and more appropriate *Gesellen* as his harmony with her processes becomes more deep.

This first stage of Siegfried's quest is immediately rewarded with new insight. Mime pretends to be upset when Siegfried rejects his food, treats him to an extended, sentimental recital of his own virtues and Siegfried's debts to him ('So that is love's/ bitter reward! . . .' 6off.), and concludes with a torrent of self-pity and sobbing. But Siegfried's response is new and wise. In the stage-direction: 'Siegfried has now turned round and is gazing quietly into Mime's eyes. Mime meets Siegfried's eyes and slyly tries to conceal his own.' (69). Once again, as in *Die Walküre*, eye contact is Wagner's token of honesty and lack of hypocrisy; Ex.31, which first entered the music to characterize

Siegfried's aggressive rejection of Mime, returns softly, so that the orchestral textures emphasize Siegfried's affinity with nature (70ff.). Siegfried, although he cannot express it yet, has

Ex. 31    (Very fast)

achieved the ability to see through Mime's hypocrisy. Because he finds all the animals, trees and birds dearer to him than Mime, Siegfried now has enough insight to refuse to accept Mime's explanation of why he keeps returning to the house.

During the following scene, Mime keeps trying to claim that he is Siegfried's parent, 'father and mother both'; and gradually Siegfried makes use of all that he has learnt in the forest and comes to realize that this is false. He has seen the birds and the deer mating, and felt their love for each other; he has looked in the stream also, seeing the reflections of all the trees and animals 'just as they are':

> And there I saw too
> my own image;
> I knew that I was
> quite different from you.    (98–9)

Here, in the horns, Ex. 27 sounds for the first time in *Siegfried.* As he starts to discover who he is, Siegfried begins to become that hero who, at the end of the previous drama, would alone be worthy of Brünnhilde. For Siegfried realizes that he is staying here only because Mime alone knows his true parentage. And he forces the story out of the reluctant dwarf.

This is another significant step forward. Watching the deer, the foxes and the wolves, with the male bringing food and the female suckling the young, Siegfried began to 'learn/what love is'—but the music at this point (93) though warm, is delicate, and lacks the richness of the themes that characterize human love in the *Ring*.

The account of Sieglinde's death brings adult human feeling for the first time to Siegfried. Even Mime is sufficiently moved by her fate to charge his narrative with emotion; and as Siegfried tries to absorb the fact that bearing him caused his mother's death (115), his music is muted and introspective for the first time in the drama. He stands 'lost in thought' as a solo clarinet portrays his emotions by playing Ex. 32, the principal theme of the compassion felt by Siegmund and Sieglinde in *Die Walküre*. A true, deep feeling has now been born in Siegfried, and his

Ex. 32

deeper meditation on his mother's fate, under the linden tree in Act 2, gains him the still closer contact with nature which (through the voice of the woodbird) will save his life from Mime and lead him to Brünnhilde.

First, however—because in Wagner's overall plan this relationship is less important—the other parent. As soon as he sees the fragments of Siegmund's sword, Siegfried senses that his mission in life is to wield it. He orders Mime to forge the sword and when Mime has failed, he does so himself. Act 1 is complete when, like Siegmund before him, he possesses the sword and hails it by the name of Notung.

Siegfried reduces the two halves of the sword completely to powder, and forges it anew. The symbolic meaning of this is clear. The sword which shattered in Siegmund's hand, because it was wielded to defend an incestuous liaison, is now purged (in Siegfried's final forging song) from all the *miasma* which it acquired in *Die Walküre*. The text of the Act 1 finale emphasizes the purity of all the equipment which Siegfried uses, the complete reduction of the sword, and the total rebirth which he then achieves for it. And the vigour and energy of the music fully support this vision.

Notung has not changed its name, and its motif (Ex. 1) rises in exactly the same form in the closing moments of Act 1 as it did when Sieglinde first directed Siegmund's gaze towards its place in the tree in *Die Walküre*, Act 1. Innocently wielded it may now be, in the hands of Siegfried; but Notung—and later the

Tarnhelm and the ring—remain themselves despite Siegfried's ignorance of their powers. Wagner's hero may be without the deception which is an integral part of Orestes' role in *Choephoroi*, but Siegfried begins in this act to acquire tokens of power which in Wagner's world are as dangerous to him as Orestes' questionable means are to him in Aeschylus'. Orestes must kill Klytaimestra, and his deception is the method commanded by the god Apollo (*Choephoroi* 557ff.); Siegfried must wield Notung to pass by the Wanderer and win Brünnhilde. The tragedy which they share is that for all their harmony with nature, both are ultimately undermined by the means which they have been obliged to employ.

## MIME AND 'LEARNING FEAR'

Mime is the exact reverse of Siegfried not simply in that he is weak and ugly where Siegfried is strong and fair, but also because he has knowledge but no power. He begins the act wasting his time trying to forge yet another ordinary sword, although he knows that it will be inadequate for Siegfried and that Notung must be forged for Siegfried to kill Fafner. At the start of the act, he is merely dejected; but after Siegfried has left, demanding that he forge Notung this very day, Mime cries out in bitter despair:

> This Nibelung's hate,
> pain and sweat
> will not rivet Notung for me,
> won't weld the sword into a whole!          (152–5)

As Mime concludes, the chords of Ex.33 enter on horns and Wagner tubas, smoothing away the turbulence evoked by Mime's anxiety and imposing a total calm. The source of this

Ex. 33     (moderate and rather solemn)

new mood is the Wanderer, who makes his entry at this point and advances slowly but inexorably towards Mime's hearth, where he takes his seat for the famous scene of questions and answers (Act 1 scene ii), at the end of which Mime's life is left forfeit to 'the one who knows no fear'.

The scene between Mime and the Wanderer is closely modelled on *Vafthrudnírsmal*, a poem of the Edda in which Odin resolves to test the strength of his own knowledge. He travels to the halls of the giant Vafthrudnír, and (disguised under the false name of Gagnrad) engages him in a contest of wits. At the giant's suggestion they stake their heads on the outcome when 'Gagnrad' has proved he is worthy of the contest; and Odin proceeds to ask Vafthrudnír an extended set of questions, first about the past of the world, then about the role of the warriors at Odin's court, and finally about the future and the downfall of the gods. Vafthrudnír succeeds in answering all the questions, and then he is asked: 'What did Odin whisper in the ears of his son/before Baldur was borne to the pyre?'

This is the climax of the poem; in the last stanza, the giant recognizes his adversary and knows he is doomed:

> You alone know that, what long ago
>     You said in the ears of your son.
> I doomed myself when I dared to tell
>     What fate will befall the gods,
> And staked my wit against the wit of Odin,
>     Ever the wisest of all.

Recognition is also a central element in Wagner's contest of knowledge. Though the audience knows that the Wanderer's broad hat and long dark cloak conceal Wotan, the characters whom he encounters in *Siegfried* do not. Of the four people whom he meets on his wanderings, only Alberich recognizes him at once (and that through a trick of the light); the others do not, even though two of them have known Wotan all too well in the past. In each of the three scenes with Mime, Erda and Siegfried, the moment at which he is recognized is deliberately delayed, and marks a turning-point in the action. When the Wanderer completes his steady, unperturbed advance despite

Mime's protests, and reaches the hearth at which his host can no longer refuse his supplication for hospitality, Ex.25 blares out with the utmost force from the trombones. We now know without doubt who the Wanderer is. But Mime, by convention, cannot hear the orchestra, and the Wanderer's identity remains hidden from him for a little longer. Like Vafthrudnír, he recognizes his guest only from the course taken by the contest of wits. For Mime's third and last question invites the Wanderer to discourse on the nature of the gods.

We learn much from his reply. Wotan styles himself 'Licht-Alberich', acknowledging for the first time the reciprocal relationship between himself and his principal adversary; then he tells us, also for the first time, the source of his power. Wotan's spear is carved from a sacred branch of the primeval ash tree.

To illuminate this moment (191–2), Ex.4b is introduced. By accepting that all his powers have their source in the 'eternal feminine', Wotan is moving towards that positive acceptance of equilibrium and harmony, against which he strove so vigorously in *Das Rheingold* and *Die Walküre*. A new theme, therefore, surges forward in the orchestra at this point: Ex.34, which in *Götterdämmerung* will become central to Wotan's ultimate attainment of peace (through the Prelude, the Waltraute-scene and, thirdly and finally, in Brünnhilde's immolation at the close), is heard now for the only time in *Siegfried* (pp. 193–4). In

Ex.34   (moderate tempo)                    Trbs.

this theme, Ex.25 is matched by a corresponding preliminary upward movement, to create a male pattern with the same symmetry and balance as that expressed elsewhere in the *Ring* by the pairing of Erda's themes, Exx.4c and 5. Its emergence here foreshadows the moment in Act 3 scene i where the Wanderer will become able actively to embrace his fate.

Having revealed himself so completely to us, Wotan reveals his identity to Mime. He 'strikes the ground with his spear as if by accident; a gentle thunderclap is heard, and Mime shrinks in terror'. From now on, Mime knows all too well the identity of his unwanted guest.

This changes the situation radically. The Wanderer's own questions lead inexorably towards the topic of forging Notung, and when Mime cannot answer his third and most crucial question, the Wanderer calmly observes that:

> you asked about
> meaningless, distant things;
> but what is really close to you,
> what you needed to know, didn't occur to you.
>
> (230–1)

Why didn't it?

Bernard Shaw is one of the few commentators to have asked this question, and he judged the dwarf severely:

> Here were Mimmy's [sic] opportunity, had he only the wit to ask what he wants to know, instead of pretending to know everything already. It is above all things needful to him at this moment to find out how that sword can be mended; and there has just dropped in on him in his need the one person who can tell him. In such circumstances a wise man would hasten to show to his visitor his three deepest ignorances, and ask him to dispel them. The dwarf, being a crafty fool, desiring only to detect ignorance in his guest, asks him for information on the three points on which he is proudest of being thoroughly well instructed himself. (p. 46)

But Mime's three questions are not hastily conceived. In the stage directions, he asks the first 'after cudgelling his brains', and the second while 'sunk in still deeper contemplation'. The music reflects this, coming almost to a complete halt in each case while Ex. 29 is enunciated twice, slowly in the bassoons. And by the time he reaches his third question, Mime 'is completely wrapped up in his dreams'.

Mime does not yet know who his visitor is. The calm authority of the Wanderer's entrance forces him out of the despair in which he was sunk when Siegfried ran out, and his first reactions are suspicion and terror. The formality of the contest of wits,

and the Wanderer's assurance and ease, lull his fear but not his
suspicions. Mime is so obsessed with the ring that the last thing
he wants to do is to share his thoughts with anyone else. Hence
the irony of the situation: precisely *because* he is so concerned
with trying to work out how to forge Notung, Mime deliberately
asks three questions designed to remove his guest's thoughts as
far as possible from his own plan to acquire power over the world
through Siegfried. But the Wanderer's expansive answers force
Mime back to the subject. He does not just name the inhabitants
of each sphere of the world, but goes on to speak of their three
lords and the way in which each acquired his power.

Then, in the second contest, Mime's own head is pawn in its
turn. Now Wotan chooses the questions. Mime is therefore
obliged to turn to the very subject which, before he knew who
the Wanderer was, he avoided at all costs—the destiny of the
Volsungs. And his reactions are fascinating. As he succeeds in
answering first one question, and then a second, about his closest
concern, Mime becomes 'more and more oblivious of his present
situation, and vividly stimulated by the topic'. But when he fails
to answer the third, Mime is thrown back into abject terror and
despair—just like his outburst at the end of scene i, and accompanied by the same music. Mime has learnt nothing and has
failed to develop.

Mime fails because he is constrained by fear. Wagner's
words to Röckel are central to the meaning of *Siegfried* Act 1:
'We must learn to die, and to die in the fullest sense of the word.
The fear of the end is the source of all lovelessness . . .'
(R 25/1/54). In Wagner's scenario (as in the *Edda*), Siegfried
gains Brünnhilde because he does not know fear; and Wagner
uses to the full the contrast between Siegfried's fearlessness and
Mime's uncontrollable timidity. At the beginning of the drama,
Mime's predicament is that he needs the ring which Fafner
possesses, but is too weak to obtain it himself. As Act 1 unfolds
we gradually see his fear and suspicion warp his judgment more
and more. His despair when the Wanderer strikes home with the
one question that he cannot answer is pitiable enough; it is then
followed by the extraordinary monologue which opens scene iii.
Mime, left alone, is deluded by the sunlight flickering through

the trees. His delirium mounts to a feverish level, and he seems at first to see flickering, roaring flames and then Fafner himself attacking him.

This is the second time that Mime loses touch with reality in Act 1. The third occurs at the end of the forging scene. Here Mime has 'solved' the problem of how to dispose of Siegfried after Fafner's death by brewing a poisonous drink for him. (He is apparently blind to the fact that Siegfried already rejects any food or drink that he offers.) And Mime's satisfaction reaches a ludicrous climax when he imagines himself as king, 'prince of the dwarfs, lord of the world!' This delusion is duly under-mined in the final tableau of the act, when Siegfried cleaves the anvil with his new sword and brings Mime down to earth, literally as well as metaphorically.

Mime's false expectations, and his delusions, are both symp-toms of his extreme fearfulness. Wagner uses a musical image which brings this out to the full, to portray Mime's rising hysteria after the Wanderer has departed: the predominant motifs here are Loge's shifting, chromatic figurations. Loge's fire has already been established at the end of *Die Walküre* as the supreme test of fearlessness. The same figurations return later in the scene, when Mime tries to describe fear to Siegfried.

The echo of *Die Walküre* rises to undermine Mime's expecta-tions. For as Mime warms to his subject and sings of *burning* fear, Ex.6 enters the textures and returns again and again, just as at the end of the previous drama (276ff.). And (as if he had heard, with us, the powerful allure of that music), Siegfried replies calmly, 'reflectively', that fear must be a very wonderful feeling; a solo oboe and horn quietly, gently play Ex.6 in quite another way, presenting the beckoning charm of the emotion which Mime has described to him. It terrifies Mime so much that he has hallucinations; but it inspires Siegfried to pleasurable anti-cipation. Mime's hope that Siegfried will learn fear from Fafner has been totally undermined in our eyes before they have even reached the dragon's lair.

Mime's inability to transcend his own fear leads him beyond attempting to deceive others, into deceiving himself: his need for the gold is so great that he is now rejoicing at the forging of

Notung; rejoicing, that is—in view of the Wanderer's last words—at the achievement which will seal his own fate.

Siegfried will not learn fear from Fafner. But that strength is also a weakness, for the appearance here of Ex.6 does not only undermine Mime's ambitions. Siegfried now is like the animals, knowing no fear. When his fearlessness has won him his bride, he must first learn fear from her, and then learn to transcend it. But he will never be able to transcend it totally; the awakening of his senses to love will itself be enough to cause his downfall, in *Götterdämmerung*.

## ALBERICH AND THE WANDERER

Act 2 is set in front of Neidhöle, the 'cave of hatred' in which Fafner holds passive custody of the treasure—and of the ring. It is a place of allure—but also of danger; and here the central issues of the trilogy, long buried by the failure of Wotan's first attempt to breed a hero who could gain the ring for the powers of light, reassert themselves powerfully. The music of the Act 2 prelude makes us aware of this. Rising slowly out of the depths, its dense and mysterious depiction of Fafner's brooding is rudely interrupted by a strident, aggressive re-formation (*sforzando* in woodwind and pizzicato strings) of the ring motif (Ex.11); after this new figure has intruded and retreated twice from the music, a motif appears which has not yet been heard in *Siegfried*. Ex.3 is heard twice, clearly enunciated on the trombones; and after the sinister, syncopated thirds in the woodwind, which introduced Alberich's curse in *Das Rheingold*, have also been introduced (completing the musical argument of the prelude by prefiguring his close involvement in the scenes to follow) Ex.3 rises in the brass for the third and final time—but now on solo bass trumpet in E flat with a yearning expressiveness and intensity. The prelude closes with a searing climax, after which Ex.5 cascades tumultuously downwards in the strings (pp. 457–9).

At this point in the trilogy, every part of the sequence has dramatic significance. One again (and for the first time since *Die*

*Walküre* Act 2) Alberich and his ring have come to the centre of the action. We will see him at once, when the curtain rises, keeping a vigil he cannot escape, bound to the quest for his ring as closely as any of the victims of his curse. Ex.3 is the most significant theme here. Thrice reiterated, and with such yearning at the third recurrence, it does not simply warn of the power which the curse on the ring will possess even over the 'innocent' Siegfried. In this music there is an intense desire for the end, a need for resolution, which is new to the *Ring*. Wotan, when he appears, has placed completely behind him the anguish he showed in *Die Walküre*, Act 2.

Both 'Licht-Alberich' and his shadow have reached a new stance; but in different ways. Like Mime, Alberich has less insight than the Wanderer, different expectations, and greater anxiety. Both Alberich and the Wanderer have come to the mouth of the cave to watch, and not to intervene; both have confidence in their own vision of the future. Nevertheless, Alberich's opening monologue is full of nervous uncertainty. He wrongly misreads the bluish light, which gleams out of the distant edge of the forest, at first as the approach of dawn, then as that of Fafner's assassin. The music, with its partial echoes of Exx.23 and 34, already gives us reason to suspect that he is wrong, even as he speaks; and when a sudden flash of moonlight reveals his adversary's face to him, Alberich is surprised as well as angry.

The Wanderer by contrast is utterly calm. The chords of Ex.33 now take on an even deeper meaning than in Act 1, as they support to the full his declaration that 'I came to observe/not to act' (pp. 477–8). Already in Act 1, when he spoke about himself to Mime, the Wanderer showed that he has a far deeper regard than in *Das Rheingold* or *Die Walküre* for the treaties which he has made; and throughout the contest, even when his own life was at stake, the Wanderer's music displayed serenity, a comfortable ease and acceptance of the nature of the world. By contrast Mime's preoccupation with the prospect of power made him highly emotional, and liable to over-react.

Alberich is a more worthy opponent; but he too remains corrupted by the lure of the ring, albeit more subtly than his brother. He tries to browbeat the Wanderer, first by reminding him of his contract with Fafner, and secondly by threatening him with his own curse on whoever comes to possess the ring. But his vision carries him away:

> . . . if I grasp it once
> again in my fist,
> I shall use the power of the ring
> very differently from foolish giants:
> so tremble, sacred
> guardian of heroes!
> I shall storm
> Valhall's heights with the hosts of Hell:
> then I will be ruler of the world!     (493–9)

As Alberich concludes his threat, the music rises to a ferocious, malevolent climax and concludes in a little dance of triumph. This sequence has been heard before: Alberich's mania for power deludes him here just as it did in *Das Rheingold* scene iii.

Then, of course, he possessed the ring, and Wotan had no response except to steal it from him by trickery; matters are now very different. His reply is quiet: 'I know your intentions well;/but they do not worry me'. Alberich then shifts the conversation to the subject of Siegfried, and the style of the music changes suddenly, as the Wanderer replies:

> The one I love,
> I leave to look after himself;
> he may stand or fall,
> he is his own master;
> only heroes can be of use to me.     (506)

At the third line, as soon as the Wanderer openly achieves the detachment which he sought in vain in *Die Walküre*, the music foreshadows the new, totally detached style which will be fully established in Act 3, when he begins his confrontation with Siegfried. Unlike Alberich, the Wanderer is now wholly a spectator of the events: he has freed himself completely from the need for power.

There is a further example of the Wanderer's impartiality.

After he has roused Fafner from sleep, and Alberich has failed to disturb the *Wurm*'s complacency, the Wanderer offers one final warning: 'All things go their appointed way,/and you can alter none of them.' As he does so, Ex.4b rises gently in the lower orchestra; the Wanderer is not simply detaching himself from personal involvement, but moving towards the deep harmony with nature which will culminate, in Act 3, in his final resignation.

When the Wanderer has departed, Alberich acknowledges ruefully that the Wanderer has left him with nothing but anxiety and humiliation. The orchestra accompanies his expression of pain with the plaintive melody (Ex.28) which conveyed Wotan's sadness as he left Brünnhilde, in the closing stages of *Die Walküre*. As Donington rightly remarks (p. 188), this music expresses more than simple grief: 'the nobility of the progression tells us that the grief is in some way accepted, and the nobility and the acceptance mingle with the grief in most moving fashion'. What the Wanderer suffered then, Alberich suffers now. The 'shadow' has not advanced as far towards detachment, and is, therefore, more emotional and involved. But Alberich has guessed one thing correctly, despite his more limited insight:

> Just laugh on
> you light-spirited,
> pleasure-seeking
> gang of gods!
> One day I will see you
> all pass away! (525–6)

Ex.3 returns here, rising three times in the orchestra to close the scene as it began it. The Wanderer may have detached himself from the events and harmonized himself with nature; but he has not yet cleansed the ring from Alberich's curse. The scene has brought the power of the ring, and the inevitability of destruction for all who touch it, back to the centre of the action; and Fafner's dying words to Siegfried will reassert this.

There are no close analogies to these events in the *Oresteia*. But Wagner's overall strategy at this point is very similar to

Aeschylus', at the parallel point in *Choephoroi*. *Siegfried* Act 2 scene i emphasizes the inevitability of the events, and the desire of the characters to hasten the outcome; an exactly similar mood pervades the corresponding scenes towards the centre of *Choephoroi*. From the *kommos* at Agamemnon's tomb onward, the chorus of *Choephoroi* feel a growing certainty that events are moving on a destined course, and they attempt to hasten that course even further forward. The two odes which they sing, while Orestes embarks on his attempt at vengeance (585ff. and 787ff.), are designed to demonstrate first the many ways in which Orestes' return and his attempt fulfil the laws of Fate, and then the reasons why Zeus, Apollo and Hermes should, without hesitation, embrace Orestes' cause. And as if these intense lyric arguments and appeals were not enough, the chorus proceed to intervene (in a manner without parallel in any other surviving Greek tragedy) to direct the action in favour of Orestes, by persuading the nurse to change her message (766ff.). Finally, they lure Aigisthos to his death by words of studied ambiguity (847ff.).

As each trilogy nears its midpoint, both Aeschylus and Wagner portray their characters hastening towards an event which, despite its horrific nature, is becoming not only more clearly inevitable, but also more necessary. Klytaimestra and Wotan increasingly submit—she out of weariness, he with ever greater joy—to the course of events which will shortly ensure their destruction. Both are now near to accepting the full consequences of their past actions.

## SIEGFRIED AND THE CREATURES OF THE FOREST

In Act 1 Siegfried shows the beginnings of a true affinity with nature, and an ability to learn from his observation of natural life, which give him the power to see through Mime's prevarications and begin the path to self-discovery. In Act 2, in the deepest part of the forest, his affinity with nature develops further, to the accompaniment of some of Wagner's most tender and delicate music. The forest seems almost to be reaching out to embrace Siegfried; at the very first moment when Mime offers to leave Siegfried alone, the 'forest murmurs' begin to steal into the orchestra (552ff.).

Like Orestes, Siegfried has no experience of the world in which he must now play such a prominent part. Orestes has never been prince; Siegfried has never learnt fear. They have been brought up in exile and as orphans. Their development is studied in depth at the focal point of the central drama of each trilogy precisely because these apparent weaknesses are, by paradox, the sources of the strength which will enable them to succeed where their fathers failed.

As soon as Mime has finally departed and Siegfried lies down comfortably under the linden tree, the murmurs re-enter the orchestra with renewed strength and greater persistence. They rise and fall, in pitch and intensity, together with the mood of Siegfried's musings: this is a process of mutual exploration. And as the scene proceeds, it becomes clear that it is also a process of reciprocal exchange: for each further stage of understanding that Siegfried attains, the forest extends a reward to him which in its turn stimulates further insight. First, his 'silent thoughts' lead Siegfried to speak of his father, and by understanding that Siegmund would have looked just like himself, he is able to complete the rejection of Mime towards which he was moving throughout Act 1. He then falls into 'deep silence'—and Ex.32 emerges on a solo clarinet, from forest murmurs of ever greater delicacy and subtlety (564). Siegfried is moved to fall into a deeper reverie. As he broods on his mother's beauty and (his voice becoming ever softer) on his own loss, he becomes for the first time capable of feeling compassion. His reverie ends thus:

> Oh, if only I, her son,
> could see my mother!
> My mother—
> she was some man's wife! (567ff.)

It is a moment of unutterable beauty and pathos; and it is one of the great turning-points of the *Ring*. As Siegfried ends his meditation, Ex.4b returns to the orchestra, with the original figurations which were heard supporting it in the prelude to *Das Rheingold*; and Ex. 13a rises from these textures on a solo violin, to become embraced by rich and beguiling harmonies—just as on the occasion when Loge stated that nobody is willing to exchange anything for 'woman's beauty and worth' (569ff. = *Das Rheingold* 273–4). Siegfried's affinity with and compassion for his mother makes him able to grasp all the meaning of the fact that 'she was some man's wife'. These simple words mark the moment at which Siegfried gains both full consciousness of himself, and desire for woman.

This desire is not the cynical lust of the gods, giants and dwarfs in *Das Rheingold*. The 'eternal feminine' manifested itself to Alberich in the form of the Rhine-daughters, whose whoreish teasing and circular, seductive but ultimately empty melodies were precisely appropriate temptations for his all too corruptible eyes. Siegfried's total innocence and powerful energy make him worthy of a deeper, more forward-looking insight—which he now receives. The woodbird calls to Siegfried, and the four related melodies of her song sound out in the orchestra. Each has a different effect on him. Ex. 35a is the motif by which the woodbird first engages Siegfried's attention, while Ex. 35b is the langourous, sensual coda which, when it follows Ex. 35a, completes the pattern and arouses Siegfried's curiosity.

Ex. 35c will be the motif to which the woodbird imparts knowledge, when Siegfried has gained the power to understand it; it therefore plays a central role when Mime returns, illustrating the way in which Siegfried's new understanding prevents Mime from concealing his murderous intentions. And Ex. 35d, a development of and coda to this melody, is the fully forward-looking theme which will conclude the act: the motif of wisdom attained and assimilated.

This sequence is prefigured now; all four aspects of Ex. 35 are displayed in order on clarinet and oboe (573–5). But the woodbird remains beyond Siegfried's comprehension, and so the full significance of her four separate motifs is withheld from us. He is not yet capable himself of fully looking forward (he still hopes that the bird will tell him something 'about his dear mother'). Then he tries to create a deeper relationship with the woodbird;

Ex. 35

he fails, because he tries to rival her on her own terms. He carves a pipe from a reed, and tries to play Ex. 35c himself (584–5). But Siegfried is not female, and he has not yet developed enough sensitivity, and affinity with the wisdom of female creatures, to succeed. She remains beyond his understanding. So he turns instead to his own instrument—the horn, the symbol of adolescent male strength.

He wrongly thinks that the woodbird is male. Ex. 30 has musical affinities with some of the themes of the female creatures in Wagner's universe (cf. especially Exx. 35c and 48); these affinities prefigure his ultimate, successful union with Brünnhilde. But for the moment, though he is now worthy of more than temporary playmates like the bear of Act 1, Siegfried is still not sensitive enough to femininity to gain insight into the world of women. And so—since in the *Ring*, as in the *Oresteia*, the characters receive their deserts—his aggressive second horn call (Ex. 27) brings out the right *Gesell* for his present stage of development: Fafner. For now, *als Wurm*, Fafner is also a creature of the forest, and Siegfried's encounter with him is an important stage in his development.

Fafner has become gentler and calmer. Donington rightly remarks (p. 186) that his new motif (Ex. 36), when contrasted with its original (Ex. 7), shows that: 'It is not only his destructive capacity but also his healing capacity which Fafner has increased by his voluntary transformation. He is potentially more

Ex. 36    (sluggish and dragging)

formidable than before, but also he is wiser, and as events will show he is even in some strange manner milder.'

Fafner is defeated because of his complacency, which is as much a part of his character as brash assertiveness is part of Siegfried's. (In their different ways they are counterparts, since neither recognizes the existence of danger and fear.) But Fafner attains wisdom and nobility in his last moments. He realizes that Siegfried did not devise the plan to kill him for himself; and he can guess who did:

> Look clearly around you,
> radiant child;
> he who prompted you, in your blindness, to this deed
> is now planning this radiant hero's death.        (620–1)

At this point Ex.3 rises in the orchestra. All this is the inevitable consequence of Alberich's curse; and Fafner, like Aeschylus' Kassandra, gains a foresight beyond his previous powers from the imminence of death: 'Take care how this will end!/Recall my fate!' (621–2).

Wagner's Siegfried is a 'radiant child'. His counterpart in the *Edda* conceals his identity from Fafnír to the end; but Wagner's Siegfried is frank, and wants to give what return he can for Fafner's wisdom. He discloses his name to the dying giant. He does this because he is now awakened, and capable of showing pity for Fafner in his dying moments, despite the ferocity with which the dragon had provoked him earlier.

By this gesture Siegfried shows that he can understand and learn wisdom from his experiences; and so Fafner's death becomes more than simply another failure by Siegfried to win a *Gesell*. In return for his understanding, Fafner yields to Siegfried the vital key to the new world which he must enter. Fafner's blood allows Siegfried, for the first time, access to the rest of nature. He can now understand the song of the woodbird, who tells him three vital things. The first is that he must take the Tarnhelm and the ring. Siegfried can do this without taint: as he emerges from the cave Ex.10 is played in its original form, as in the first scene of *Das Rheingold* (658ff.); and as he muses on his prize, the orchestration takes on the distinctive hues and luxuriant textures which will not be heard again until we encounter the Rhine-daughters once more, in *Götterdämmerung*, Act 3 scene i. In Siegfried's hands, it is as if the ring had not been forged, and were pure Rhinegold again. Siegfried's innocence has the power to weaken and delay the force of Alberich's curse.

Siegfried, although he has yet to become vulnerable to the curse, is already learning much. Hints at Ex.6, therefore, steal into the orchestral music as he places the ring on his finger and the Tarnhelm on his belt, declaring that he still has not managed to learn fear (663). This music makes us anticipate that he soon will; but there is one final obstacle. The woodbird's second piece of advice concerns Mime; as the next scene unfolds, Siegfried, with the aid of his new insight, sees completely through Mime's murderous intentions. When they become intolerable he kills Mime instinctively, in a sudden access of revulsion. He has now secured his freedom, and in his last meditation he rests for the second time in the drama (his third, and therefore final, rest will be in his union with Brünnhilde).

Siegfried's recent experiences have given him yet more insight and the ability to express his need: he is lonely, and still lacks a *Gesell*. His plea to the woodbird is his third attempt to find one; and by her third and final answer (which is itself delivered in three sections to emphasize its finality), the woodbird turns Siegfried from backward-looking meditation to forward-looking questing. In learning of the bride whom he alone can win, he also rightly realizes that she can teach him fear.

It is a moment of triumph, and the act ends in the tumultuous celebration of Siegfried's departure. Siegfried, naturally, feels only the joy of his desire, which is now fully awakened. But the woodbird has also sung of the sadness that accompanies her own joy, warning Siegfried that 'only lovers know what I mean'. The words could be an epigraph for *Götterdämmerung*.

Throughout Act 2 insight and reciprocity with the forces of nature are central to the gradual increase in Siegfried's strength, as he moves nearer to the challenge of confronting the Wanderer. This is parallel to the first half of Aeschylus' *Choephoroi*, and in particular to the impassioned lyric *kommos* sung by

Orestes, Elektra and the chorus at the grave of Agamemnon (306–487), where Orestes' increasing use of his insight and resolve bring in return the support of the powers which surround him—the gods of heaven above, and the darker powers of the earth below. In both Wagner and Aeschylus the process of attaining harmony with the gods occurs at the mid-point of the trilogy, so that the hero may gain the strength which he will need for the now imminent conflict with his human parent.

There is of course one central difference. For Aeschylus' Orestes, it is his father buried in the earth below who is supported by the forces of nature; and it is his mother against whom Orestes hardens himself. Klytaimestra, by killing Agamemnon, has placed herself outside the fabric of society; in Aeschylus' vision the gods themselves—first Apollo, and then at the climax of *Eumenides* Zeus himself—will support the social order.

In Act 2 of *Siegfried*, Wagner puts forward a contrasting vision. As in Aeschylus, all the support of the dead parent is needed to confront and defeat the parent of the other sex; but the supreme challenge that Wagner's hero must face is the confrontation with Wotan; he must achieve harmony with his mother, and with a nature which is female, in order to find the necessary strength. That is the purpose of the scenes under the linden tree in Act 2.

For Aeschylus, in the famous central ode of *Choephoroi* (585ff.), the monsters of the earth are female, and Klytaimestra is among the worst of them, in the eyes of Orestes and his allies. In Wagner both the monster whom Siegfried kills in Act 2, and the parent who must be destroyed, are male. This is the central divergence between Aeschylus' classical vision and the romantic perspective of the *Ring*. The 'bias' towards the female which is begun in *Siegfried* will continue into *Götterdämmerung*. For at the climax of the closing drama Wagner once again opposes an Aeschylean judgment in favour of the male.

## THE WANDERER RENOUNCES THE WORLD

The sheer energy of the prelude to Act 3 does not merely stem from Wagner's own exuberance as he returned to the *Ring* after an interval of twelve years. Nor is the mastery with which the themes are woven together, in a manner quite new to the score of the cycle, simply a celebration of the fact that Wagner could now apply the contrapuntal techniques which he had developed for *Die Meistersinger* to the musical themes of his beloved *Ring*. Both have a specific role to play in the dramatic structure. Indeed, it could be argued (though only, admittedly, with the benefit of hindsight) that if his increasing preoccupation with *Tristan und Isolde* had not led Wagner to break off the composition of the *Ring* after sketching Act 2 of *Siegfried*, he would have had to do so anyway, in order to develop a musical richness adequate to the challenges of Act 3 and of *Götterdämmerung*.

For the music of the prelude offers at once a new kind of hope. The opening theme is Ex. 4c, but each of its rising movements is made complex and effortful by the turbulent, staccato ostinato in the upper strings. This struggle is rapidly shown to be a productive one. The two themes which were totally opposed in *Die Walküre*, Act 2 scene i, since they were associated with Wotan's power and with Fricka's opposition to it, now appear together, fully integrated into the argument; and as the prelude begins to move towards its climax (764ff.), Exx. 4b and 5 are heard in sequence, with a perfect symmetry which prefigures the peace at the end of the entire cycle, supported and impelled forward by the Wanderer's chords (Ex. 33). Already, before the curtain goes up, the music has prefigured a reconciliation between the Wanderer's male power and the female fate which surrounds and earlier opposed him.

The reconciliation is, however, on extraordinary terms. When the curtain rises the Wanderer is seen conjuring Erda to appear from the depths of night, rousing her from the sleep of knowledge to acquire information:

> From your wisdom
> I would dearly like to know
> how to stop a rolling wheel.  (817–19)

As the scene proceeds, the Wanderer's continuously restless music gives the impression of one literally wrestling with fate. The confrontation between the Wanderer and Erda turns out in a way which surprises both of them. It is inspired by the Eddaic poem *Baldur's Dreams*, in which Odin assumes the name of 'Struggler's Son, Strider, Tamer of Ways' and conjures the spectre of a Wala from her tomb near the gates of Hel, to discover how his favourite son, Baldur, would die. The climax of the poem comes when the Wala suddenly recognizes her visitor from the direction of his insistent questions and his obvious personal concern, and it ends with mutual recriminations:

> Go home, Odin; air your triumph.
> No guest shall again my grave visit,
> Till wild Loki tear loose from his bonds,
> And the world-wasters on the warpath come.

Wagner's Wotan also comes to the Wala in disguise, refusing to name himself as anyone but 'the one who woke you'; and here, as in the *Edda*, he reveals his identity by the direction which his questions take. It is Erda, he sings, who once plunged 'the dagger of worry' into Wotan's heart, enchaining his spirit by fear of his own downfall. And what the Wanderer now wants to learn from 'the world's wisest woman' is how the god can conquer his anxiety. To which Erda replies:

> You are—not
> what you call yourself!                   (841)

And the Wanderer retorts:

> You are—not
> what you think yourself!                  (842–3)

There can be no accommodation between them; for if she is shocked when she realizes who her turbulent visitor is, he himself has already faced a greater surprise. When he summoned her from sleep, the Wanderer offered an extended paean to Erda's wisdom and insight. But Erda's response reveals that much has changed since she first appeared in *Das Rheingold*. She who was then the 'archetypal prophetess', warning Wotan of a crisis which threatened to cause his immediate shameful downfall, can now do no more than refer her conqueror to the Norns, despite their inability to change or reverse the course of events.

The strange sequence of events which has occurred since then has robbed Erda of the ability to give wise counsel—and even of factual knowledge: she learns of Brünnhilde's punishment for the first time, and is incredulous. The world is askew, the preacher of rebellion has punished rebellion:

> Does the defender of right,
> the guardian of oaths,
> shun what is right,
> rule by falsehood? (833–4)

In the music, a tremendous descent on the last word prefigures Ex.40, the dominant motif of Hagen's rising power in *Götterdämmerung*. The deeds of men, since the time when Wotan and Alberich first sired heroes to fight for the world, have dimmed her wisdom.

Their freedom, however, has given the Wanderer his strength. For now, when his passion and fear force Wotan to reveal his identity, the Wala's new weakness, and her inability to advise him how to conquer his anxiety, are all that he needs in order to conquer it himself. 'Your knowledge will vanish/before my will', he asserts, with commanding authority and a new confidence—which, as we shall see at the opening of *Götterdämmerung*, is fully justified. 'Do you know what Wotan wants?'

A long silence follows this question. And then the Wanderer answers his own question because the Wala—who will not be heard again—cannot. As he does so, themes 4c and 5 appear in sequence, in perfect symmetry and perfect peace (845–6). They play without the turbulence which drove them on in the prelude, and which has dominated the mood of the confrontation between the Wanderer and Erda up to this point. Wotan has fully absorbed and accepted the inevitability of the end of the gods— 'because now it is my desire'. And he proceeds to explain how he will carry out happily and gladly the plan which in *Die Walküre* he was forced to adopt in despair. As he does so, the music takes on a spacious, open mood which is quite different from anything yet heard in the *Ring*; and the new theme which now appears (Ex.37) eloquently portrays the Wanderer's joy in bequeathing the world to Siegfried; his active desire for, and joyful embracing

of, the end make his victory certain. It is precisely because he has thrown off his anxiety and fear that he has gained the ability to prophesy, while Erda, whom he now rightly terms 'the mother of primeval fear' has lost it. He can see forward, not only to the way in which Siegfried's noble character will exhaust Alberich's curse, but also as far as Brünnhilde's act of wisdom at the end of the cycle (the return of the ring to the Rhine-daughters) which will redeem the world.

In this scene the second major dissent of *Siegfried* from *Choephoroi* is brought out. Now, at the crisis, the victims who will fall to the avenging son have taken the stage; and the stances of Klytaimestra and the Wanderer are totally opposed. In *Choephoroi*, Klytaimestra appears diminished in stature, far removed from the triumphant murderess of *Agamemnon*. Receiving the disguised Orestes into her palace, she goes out of her way to follow the normal Greek custom, offering hospitality and insisting that if the visitors have any business to transact, then 'that is the work of men, and we will inform them' (673). The overall picture is of a passive character borne down by her fate, resigned to the disasters which have overtaken the house of Atreus; and the only point which she has in common with the Wanderer is the one electrifying moment immediately after the death of Aigisthos, when she calls for an axe and attempts to fight back, in a last surge of the 'manly' defiance which she exhibited in *Agamemnon* (*Choephoroi* 885ff.). But after that the contrast with the Wanderer is total. Although she is trapped, Klytaimestra resists her fate throughout her dialogue with Orestes until the moment at which she knows she is doomed. Weakened and vulnerable though she is, and certain of her own death once Aigisthos has been killed, Klytaimestra pleads for her life against a son who becomes ever more implacable as her pleas continue (907ff.). She remains actively opposed to Orestes even after her death: her ghost appears in *Eumenides* (94ff.) to stir on her avenging Furies, who have been drugged into sleep by Apollo and need her to arouse them to renewed pursuit.

Significantly, Wagner gave that scene not to Wotan but to Alberich (*Götterdämmerung*, Act 2 scene i). It is central to the meaning of the *Ring* that Wotan should not only 'reach the tragic height of willing his own destruction' but should ascend to an even greater height, mastering fate by *joyfully* willing his own destruction. In his earlier operas Wagner repeatedly extended to his central characters the prospect of obtaining glory through self-destruction; and this characteristic motif of his work now inflects the central climax of the *Ring*. Here, as again in *Götterdämmerung*, Act 3 scene i, Wagner's vision of transcendence is wholly opposed to the viewpoint of his Greek model; in the confrontation with Erda, Wagner gives Wotan a power which would have been beyond the comprehension of Aeschylus and his audience, since they recognized no perspective from which extinction could be glorious for either a god or a mortal. As the shade of Achilleus tells Odysseus, when he summons up the dead souls from Hades to speak with him in the *Odyssey*:

> I would rather follow the plough as serf to another, a man with no land allotted him and not much to live on, than be a king over all the perished dead.　　　　　　　(XI. 489ff.)

Scene ii corresponds with the climactic confrontation between Orestes and Klytaimestra in *Choephoroi*. In both dramas the son remakes his father's deed; just as Orestes successfully achieves the homecoming which his father failed, using deception in his turn against the deceiver of Agamemnon, so too Siegfried wields ths sword Notung which he has reforged against the spear of Wotan, on which it shattered in Siegmund's hands at the climax of *Die Walküre*, Act 2. Both scenes are cast in the form of a strange dialogue, fierce but detached; it is so full of emotional significance for Klytaimestra and for the Wanderer that their feelings are almost masked behind the ritual quality of the moves they make. Both scenes reach their climax in a moment of tragic recognition: Klytaimestra reads her dream and recognizes in Orestes the snake which suckled at her breast, while in

*Siegfried* it is Siegfried who makes the act of recognition, impelled to final courage against the Wanderer by coming to know that the spear in his hands is that which defeated Siegmund.

Of particular interest is the need, felt by both Aeschylus and Wagner, to have their protagonist make one last act of defiance. In the previous scene the Wanderer has proclaimed his joyous resignation; and as soon as Siegfried and the Wanderer come into close confrontation (883), the music adopts a new style, emotionally distanced in a way unlike any previous music in the *Ring*. (Wagner was alluding to the Wanderer's almost ironic detachment when he called this scene a 'buffo duet', D 13/7/69.)

This seems to herald a voluntary yielding by the Wanderer. Wagner, however, is far too good a psychologist to allow his most powerful character to 'go quietly'. And so the Wanderer bursts out into defiance like Klytaimestra—but against his will: he insists on barring the way to Brünnhilde even against the heir whom he loves and who, because he knows no fear, has the power to overcome whatever the Wanderer may do. Siegfried's patience is small, even before this man whom he senses he must for some unknown reason treat carefully, and he orders him out of the way. The Wanderer 'breaks out angrily and imperiously', and Loge's music erupts fiercely in the orchestra (914) as 'the lord of the ravens' forbids the path to Siegfried.

According to Wagner: 'the god has now become so completely human that, contrary to his high resolve, there is once more a stirring of his ancient pride, brought about by his jealousy for Brünnhilde . . .' (R 25/1/54). But the commentary is quite misleading. The Wanderer resists Siegfried at this last moment simply because 'the man who can win her/makes me powerless for ever' (918). By barring the way, he shows the sheer strength of the forces which Siegfried must oppose if he persists. For as these words are sung, Loge's music surges forward at full strength, and the Wanderer extends his spear in the direction of the flames.

When Orestes approaches her in *Choephoroi*, Klytaimestra pleads with him, pouring all the influence of her motherhood into three of the most powerful lines in Greek tragedy:

Stay, my son, and show awe, my child,
before this breast, at which you often drowsily
sucked with your gums the milk which gave you life.
(896ff.)

And she is answered, from a spectacularly unexpected direction.
Orestes' normally silent companion Pylades speaks, almost with
the authority of the gods themselves, and Orestes accepts his
advice. From this point onwards to the end, every argument that
Klytaimestra raises in her defence serves only to make Orestes
more determined, until she realizes that her pleas, like tears
upon a tomb, are in vain (926).

Her defences serve only to confirm Orestes' resolve, and even
the threat of pursuit by a mother's Furies, twice repeated, does
not sway her son. Likewise, the Wanderer's attempt to deter
Siegfried only increases his determination. The music which
invades the orchestral textures, as the Wanderer describes the
sea of flames engulfing the rock, is of fine ambiguity: full of the
terror which Brünnhilde begged him to surround her with, at
the end of *Die Walküre*—but also full of temptation. As the
Wanderer extends his spear, and the glare of the light from
above increases, the music and the spectacle both beckon to
Siegfried.

Klytaimestra acknowledges that she is doomed, and finally
accepts her fate, when she recognizes Orestes as the snake that
she suckled in her dream; and Orestes accepts her words:

> Klyt. Alas for me; I gave this serpent birth, and
> nurtured it.
> Or.  Indeed, the fear you suffered in your dream
> was no false prophet;
> You killed, and it was wrong; now suffer
> wrong.                                   (928–30)
> (*exeunt*)

The Wanderer, too, makes his destruction certain, when he
extends the spear against Siegfried, and tells his opponent that it
once shattered the sword which he wields. Siegfried recognizes

his father's enemy, and proceeds to remake his father's defeat as Orestes remade his father's murder.

In both Aeschylus and Wagner, this moment is marked by the attainment of symmetry, because it marks the climax of the central drama, the turning point in the action of the trilogy. All of Orestes' power and wisdom are explicit in the symmetry of the last line that he speaks (930) before leading Klytaimestra in to kill her. It communicates a feeling of balance and calm, even in this traumatic moment; and, therefore, extends a hope for the future.

So too in *Siegfried*. When the Wanderer's spear is shattered, themes 4c and 5 sound out mysteriously in tremolo strings (934), as he acknowledges his defeat. In the prelude to Act 3, they were yoked uneasily together, in turbulence and strife. Now they are calm again, as when he began to tell Erda that he now welcomes the downfall of the gods (845–6). The Wanderer's struggle is over and he vanishes instantly in the moment when he has been defeated and his role has ended.

## SIEGFRIED AND BRÜNNHILDE

Siegfried has remade his father's deed, and has taken the sword and the ring in such innocence that he does not yet incur the weight of Alberich's curse. And so at the end of scene ii he 'plunges into the sea of fire'. The music responds to this stage direction, engulfing his last words and absorbing the call of his horn into the textures of the fire music. Siegfried takes for his own and conquers, so to speak, both the music and the stage spectacle which the Wanderer had attempted to use against him. All memory of the past seems to vanish, cleansed by the bath of fire, as Siegfried reverses Wotan's departure from the rock at the end of *Die Walküre*, and Exx.6 and 27 combine in a powerful counterpoint to celebrate the fact that Siegfried has now won Brünnhilde.

This scene is in total contrast with the end of *Choephoroi*. There is, of course, no virgin bride, no sleeping princess waiting on her rock to greet the victorious Orestes and acclaim his matricide. On the contrary, the chorus, in their ode of rejoicing after Orestes has taken Klytaimestra in to die (935ff.), try to view what has happened simply as victory and the restoration of the rightful heir to the house of Atreus. This is reckless optimism. In the final scene, Orestes appears over the bodies of the usurpers and attempts to justify his deed. But madness comes: as she threatened, Klytaimestra's Furies invade his mind and drive him from the stage. Against that lies nothing but the promise extended by Apollo, god of healing, that he would succour Orestes if he can reach his shrine at Delphi.

Aeschylus' drama achieves a supreme power at this moment, chiefly because he concentrates on one single concern—Orestes' act and its inexorable consequences. As soon as he has expounded Orestes' position (precariously balanced between the terrors which afflict him now and his hopes for the future) Aeschylus concludes his second play and prepares to re-deploy the action in a new direction in the third.

Wagner's concerns obliged him to proceed quite differently. The closing scene of *Siegfried* is diffuse to a degree which marks it out from the rest of the *Ring*: Wagner studies at length not only the way in which Siegfried at last comes to learn fear from his first encounter with a woman, but also the gradual transformation of Brünnhilde. She begins the scene as a virgin Valkyrie who has not yet accepted that she is now a mortal girl, and passes through the adolescent fear of losing her own individuality in love to the radiant joy of a mature, adult surrender and acceptance.

This long (and uneven) scene has been much criticized, as if its length were due simply to a romantic need on Wagner's part to write an extended love scene for his hero and heroine—or even a personal celebration of the fact that Cosima von Bülow bore him a son as the composition sketch of *Siegfried* neared this closing part of the drama. There are, however, three sound dramatic reasons for Wagner's strategy. First, Brünnhilde and Siegfried are the second great pair of human lovers in the *Ring*: they remake on a newer, stronger plane the doomed love of Siegmund and Sieglinde in the previous opera. The music must express fully the differences between their rapturous union and the brief, tormented love of the persecuted Volsung twins. Second, they must remake not only the love of Siegmund and Sieglinde, but that of Wotan for his daughter. Siegfried has won his bride by defeating the Wanderer and passing unscathed through Loge's fires. They were set there by Wotan, when he broke the bonds of affection between himself and Brünnhilde for ever. The man who will replace him must show us that he is worthy to succeed Wotan—that he possesses a true affinity with Brünnhilde.

The third reason brings us to the fundamental point of divergence from Aeschylus. In Wagner's trilogy, the cycle is moving gradually upwards towards a love which is less trapped by the confines of the need for power than those which have gone before it. Brünnhilde and Siegfried exemplify for Wagner the final and most perfect type of love which can be achieved in our world. But that love is flawed: in *Götterdämmerung*, they are parted and their love is broken. There are no new characters in the final drama parallel to Athena and her citizens in *Eumenides*, whose approach to life is so radically different from that of the earlier characters that they can ultimately evade the tragic dilemma with which they are threatened. Brünnhilde herself, moulded by the intense sufferings which she undergoes in *Götterdämmerung*, must rise at the end to the heights which in Aeschylus are achieved with far less difficulty by the goddess Athena. And so the closing duet shows us not only the awakening and fulfilment of Brünnhilde in her love for Siegfried, but also the ominous aspects of their love.

In Aeschylus, the act of necessary violence which lies at the climax of the central drama is so intense, and so horrific in its implications, that its dispersal by the arrival of the Furies is as deeply expected as it is terrifying. In Wagner by contrast, the destruction of Wotan's power by Siegfried seems altogether desirable and by no means excessive. The result is that the 'catastrophe' of *Siegfried* is not a catastrophe at all. Wotan's disappearance is followed almost immediately by the exuberant, powerful celebration of his defeat in the orchestral interlude played while Siegfried ascends through the fire to Brünnhilde's rock.

As scene iii begins, it would seem that nothing can undermine the glory of Siegfried's achievement. But Brünnhilde, once she has been awakened, does not immediately fall into his arms. The final scene of *Siegfried* is long because Brünnhilde abandons her virginal, Valkyrie reserve only slowly and with difficulty. She rejects Siegfried's first, passionate embrace—not simply because she is suffering the terror of losing the security of girlhood, but because she is filled with apprehension about the future. Some remnants of her godly wisdom have not yet deserted her, and Brünnhilde's last true insight into the future is a fearful one: as her eyes grow (metaphorically) dim, Ex.3 rises in the woodwind (1084–6), and she senses pure horror about to overwhelm her.

Brünnhilde has accurately foreseen the course which events will take in *Götterdämmerung*, although her preoccupation with her own emotions now overcomes this vision. She casts off this mood—but not, as we might perhaps expect, simply by taking refuge in her love for Siegfried. On the contrary, her feelings of shame remain, and she attempts to retreat into a fantasy. The principal melody of Wagner's *Siegfried Idyll*—which in fact dates from Wagner's 'Starnberg days'—steals into the orchestra as she pictures herself worshipped from afar by Siegfried, left alone, pure and calm like the reflection in a clear stream of water.

It is an appropriate melody here precisely because it is both self-contained and alien to the musical world of the *Ring*. Siegfried must overcome both the undevelopable melody, and the metaphor of an unbroken water-surface, behind which Brünnhilde has attempted to hide. He has to break down her metaphor, because his parents sensed their own affinity by likening each other to their own images seen in streams, and now, at the end of *Siegfried*, we are moving towards an open love which is without the introversion of the twins' incestuous union. But his Volsung lineage also gives him power. A true child of his parents, Siegfried himself began to understand what kind of *Gesell* he needed by gazing at his own likeness in a stream. And so he can now break down the musical shell of Brünnhilde's self-contained melody as he triumphantly caps her metaphor. She is not simply a stream: she is a waterfall, a flood in which he would bathe. For the last time he demands: 'Awake!'

At last Brünnhilde moves towards the point of yielding. Her surrender is so powerful because we have now been made to realize just how much of herself and of her past she is abandoning for her love:

> Godly composure
> gives way to emotion;
> virginal light
> flares into frenzy;
> heavenly wisdom
> storms away from me;
> the joy of love
> chases it all away! (1127–9)

Siegfried has also abandoned his past. She challenges him for the last time, asking if he still fears the devouring surge of her womanhood and lust towards him; and she knows that he will not. The marvel is that, having learnt fear, he can now forget it again with the strength of maturity. There is a brief delay, and then suddenly Brünnhilde cries out, 'in the utmost joy of love':

> Laughing I shall love you,
> laughing I shall blind myself,
> laughing let us perish,
> laughing go down to death! (1144–6)

And the horns enter under the last words, followed immediately by Siegfried's voice, to begin the powerful *stretto* which drives the drama to its conclusion (Ex.38).

Ex.38     (Animated, but powerful and without haste)

In this last duet, Brünnhilde completely abandons all her cares. Valhalla may collapse, the Norns' rope break. The dusk of the gods can draw on, the night of annihilation cover them in mist. Siegfried is hers for ever: 'radiant love/laughter in death!' In the music, Siegfried's voice becomes finally united with hers only in these final words, as the orchestral music surges around them and Wagner forces the three main themes of the love scene together in violent counterpoint, driving the drama to its end in an unquenchable flow of triumphant melody.

The last few minutes of *Siegfried* have often attracted charges of crudity or banality. The closing music is certainly crude; and this is necessary. The apprehension which Brünnhilde felt, in the last moments before her divine wisdom deserted her forever, was totally justified. This is the reckless abandon of the young adult, giving herself totally to love for the first time. Every one of the possible concerns which Brünnhilde casts off in the closing duet does happen in *Götterdämmerung*. And by then she no longer possesses Siegfried's love.

The two early Norse sources for the awakening of Brünn-hilde—the *Volsung Saga* (chapter 20), and the *Poetic Edda*—both place much emphasis on Brünnhilde's prophetic powers, by having her give many runes of wise advice to Sigurd. Wagner has hinted that he will follow this pattern, by having the Wanderer prophesy to Erda that:

> when she awakes
> your child, in her wisdom,
> will redeem our world. (861–3)

The prophecy is misleading, however, since it is not fulfilled until the end of *Götterdämmerung*. In the last scene of *Siegfried* Wagner reverses the original version of the story. In his vision, her growing love progressively blinds Brünnhilde to the truth. As she comes nearer to union with Siegfried, Brünnhilde divests herself of her wisdom, and the lovers in their ever-increasing sexual rapture become almost as oblivious and defiant of reality as Tristan and Isolde in Act 2 of their drama.

At first sight this reckless, passionate finale has nothing in common with the controlled, objective stagecraft and precise moral balance which Aeschylus offers in the final scene of *Choephoroi*. Nevertheless, there remains a deeper affinity with Aeschylus. Orestes' defence of his deed, as he stands over the bodies of Klytaimestra and Aigisthos, may be more sober in its tone than his mother's was in *Agamemnon*; but whatever his justification, he remains, like her, a person attempting to be one-sided, in a world of ruthless symmetry. His father's Furies or his mother's; Orestes has made his choice, and as *Choephoroi* concludes the consequences of what he has done begin to overtake him.

Aeschylus' Orestes is undermined from within, by the law which has overshadowed the action of the trilogy since the murder of Agamemnon—'he who does, shall suffer'. Wagner proceeds in a comparable manner. He has not lost sight here of the main subject of his trilogy: the corruption which love suffers from the power needed to attain it. The sheer recklessness of their abandon shows that for Siegfried and Brünnhilde, the most promising lovers the *Ring* has yet seen, the seed of corruption is deeply embedded inside their love. They dismiss both the shadow of the past and any thought of its consequences in the future. 'Innocent' though he is, the ring still lies on Siegfried's finger; and the path to Brünnhilde was cleaved by the use of the sword Notung. As the curtain falls, the lovers may disregard Fafner's last warning—'Take care how this will end!'—but the radiant triumph with which *Siegfried* concludes turns out, in its own way, to be even more ominous than the new darkness which has been cast over Orestes at the end of *Choephoroi*. The length of time which is taken before Brünnhilde overcomes her resistance to love places the fullest emphasis on the way in which her premonitions become completely buried in the joy of sexual ecstasy. And Siegfried's position is no less ominous. Just before the final *stretto*, he sings of how he, 'the fool', has quite forgotten his fear in the joy of their first embrace. He means the description ironically; but in *Götterdämmerung* his newly awakened sensuality will indeed become the folly which leads to his downfall.

# 6

# *Götterdämmerung*

## *GÖTTERDÄMMERUNG* AND *EUMENIDES*

In both Aeschylus' trilogy and Wagner's, the action moves on to a new, more expansive plane at the start of the third drama. The constraints which bound the action and the characters into a confined, rigid space have begun to dissolve at the close of *Choephoroi* and of *Siegfried;* both dramatists now extend this process. The opening of the last work in the cycle is marked off as a decisive new beginning, by a radical change both in dramatic procedure and in style.

In both *Götterdämmerung* and *Eumenides,* the drama is begun by the appearance of seeresses, and in both cases the opening scene ends with their prophetic ability broken by the presence and rising strength of the powers of darkness. This casts a veil of uncertainty over the outcome of the action. And so we are to move not merely in a more expansive world—the unity of time, observed in *Choephoroi* and *Siegfried,* is now abandoned—but also in a plot with a looser framework. These are dramas into which an element of suspense and of melodramatic surprise has been injected, and this overlays the underlying pattern that has previously ordered both trilogies, by which expectations are first generated, and then fulfilled. Furthermore, there are now no obvious parallelisms between the new situations and those of the previous drama, such as guided our expectations by binding *Choephoroi* to *Agamemnon, Siegfried* to *Die Walküre.*

In the *Oresteia* the gods now take the stage for the first time; but their presence does not immediately elevate the tone either of the drama or of the poetry. On the contrary, *Eumenides* is a drama of clear, relatively simple poetry; it is filled with ethical and legal arguments, and is even prone to moments of sheer sophistry and rhetoric. Its climax is a trial scene of extreme suspense, the ancestor of all modern courtroom thrillers. Indeed, the looser forms of *Eumenides*, the spacious ease of the proceedings, the absence of 'tragic' violence, and a feeling that the poetry altogether lacks sublimity until the magnificent final scene, have led many critics to claim without hesitation that this drama is a weak conclusion to the *Oresteia*, an altogether lesser achievement than either *Agamemnon* or *Choephoroi*.

Wagner's strategy in *Götterdämmerung* has on occasion elicited an exactly parallel response—and for similar reasons. Bernard Shaw argued roundly that with *Götterdämmerung* the *Ring* descends to the level of 'a thorough grand opera' whose techniques are reminiscent more of Donizetti and Verdi than of Wagner's earlier aspirations to music-drama (pp. 54–5). This claim has more often simply been brushed aside—as by Ernest Newman, with his passionate insistence that *Götterdämmerung* exhibits a far higher level of musical invention than the three preceding Nibelungen dramas—than confronted squarely. Shaw's criticism, however, is an important one, which needs to be considered.

Until this drama the *Ring* has avoided ensemble almost completely, and Wagner has adapted all the forms which he takes over from earlier operatic styles completely to the distinctive needs of this drama-cycle. Wagner now reverses his technique. The 'lapse' into duet in the closing *stretto* of *Siegfried* is picked up, and compounded, by the extended interplay between the lovers' voices in the Prelude to *Götterdämmerung*; in the action to follow, there are unmistakable duets and trios, and even one extended scene (Act 2 scene iii) for the operatic chorus, where Hagen summons the vassals. This is the first use of a chorus in the whole of the *Ring*; the vassals then remain on stage, and are joined by their womenfolk, for the whole of Act 2 scene iv, which is the longest and most important scene in Act 2; here their comments punctuate the dialogue between the principals in a thoroughly traditional manner. Furthermore, the content of both the 'arias' and the 'ensembles' which stand out from the apparently seamless web of *Götterdämmerung* is no less traditional—the most prominent of them are of course a love-duet, an oath-taking duo, a vengeance-swearing trio and an extended death-aria for the *Heldentenor*. In this work even some of the scenic effects—as, for example, the sunrise at the start of Act 2 scene ii—seem to occur less because they play an integral role in the drama than as spectacle for its own sake. Wagner's reasons for this new procedure deserve examination.

Shaw makes a further charge against *Götterdämmerung*, which deserves no less attention, despite the provocative terms in which it is phrased:

> The musical fabric is enormously elaborate and gorgeous; but you cannot say, as you must in witnessing *The Rhine Gold*, *The Valkyrie*, and the first two acts of *Siegfried*, that you have never seen anything like it before, and that the inspiration is entirely original. Not only the action, but most of the poetry, might conceivably belong to an Elizabethan drama. The situation of Cleopatra and Antony is unconsciously reproduced without being bettered, or even equalled in point of majesty and musical expression. The loss of all simplicity and dignity, the impossibility of any credible scenic presentation of the incidents, and the extreme staginess of the conventions by which these impossibilities are got over, are no doubt covered from the popular eye by the overwhelming prestige of *Die Götterdämmerung* as part of so great a work as *The Ring*, and by the extraordinary storm of emotion and excitement which the music keeps up. But the very qualities that intoxicate the novice in music enlighten the adept . . .
> (p. 83)

*Götterdämmerung* raises clear echoes of Elizabethan and Jacobean tragedy at many points during the main action, as Hagen develops his intrigues in a manner reminiscent of Iago. In addition, there is the first part of the final scene, where vengeance is met with counter-vengeance, Gunther fights

Hagen and is killed, and Gutrune collapses on his body, crying out in anguish against both Hagen and Brünnhilde. Much of this ending is in the spirit of Middleton or Webster (or at best that of the final scenes of *Hamlet*) rather than of any surviving Greek tragedy.

Nor is it sufficient to argue that the text of *Siegfried's Death* was written some years before Wagner's design expanded to the point at which it had to become the basis for the culminating drama of an Aeschylean trilogy. Wagner was a consummate librettist, and by the time he came to compose *Götterdämmerung* he was fully capable of adapting any text to his will—or indeed of replacing it completely, if he had found it impossible to modify his earlier draft to his own satisfaction.

It is, therefore, clear that Wagner, like Aeschylus, deliberately chose in the plot of his final drama to avoid the kind of tragic pattern which is displayed in the earlier parts of his cycle. Why?

Other versions of the story of the house of Atreus place little stress on the events after Orestes' murder of Klytaimestra—his pursuit by, and eventual release from, her Furies. Aeschylus used and modified the Delphic legend that Orestes was purified by Apollo himself at his own shrine, and combined it with a story which is not attested before the *Oresteia*, and which may even be of his own invention. In *Eumenides*, Orestes is unable to gain full release from the rituals of Delphi; and in Aeschylus' version of the story, Orestes had to journey on to Athens as a suppliant, where his case became the reason for the founding of the Areopagos, the city's oldest most aristocratic court.

The main purpose of these innovations is clear: for Aeschylus, the act of matricide has consequences so serious, and so hard to resolve, that Orestes' fate and his just deserts demand far more exploration than could have been given at the end of *Choephoroi*. As a result, the last two dramas of the *Oresteia* study the whole of the relevant life of Orestes, from the moment when he comes of age and returns to Argos to claim the throne (which is his birthright) through to the moment when he is finally able to regain it.

Similarly, the *Ring* in its final form studies Siegfried's life from the moment when he first becomes conscious of who he is and what he must do, through his attainment and subsequent loss of Brünnhilde, to his death. In both trilogies this character development and analysis lies in a strong contrast with the portrayal of the earlier principals: Agamemnon and Klytaimestra, Alberich, Wotan and Siegmund. We do not see any of them for the first time until relatively late in their lives, near to their moment of tragic decision; and their influence fades gradually from the centre of the action after that moment. By exploring at length the fortunes of Orestes and Siegfried after their central deed, Aeschylus and Wagner are able to show first their relative 'innocence' and its rewards, and then (in the last drama) the extremes to which they are forced before their world can attain a final balance.

Each of them now plays a new, more passive role. Orestes in *Eumenides* is under the guidance of Apollo; his stance throughout the action is of passive confidence, in strong contrast with his resolution and vigour in *Choephoroi*. Similarly, when Siegfried first appears in *Götterdämmerung*, Brünnhilde gives him Grane as a symbol of the degree to which the strength for his adventures comes from her love; and he explicitly declares that his power now lies in the wisdom which she has bestowed on him. But Wagner goes further. When Orestes on his travels arrives in the developed community of Athens, he remains mindful throughout of the commands of Apollo. Siegfried by contrast succumbs instantly and totally, when he arrives at the court of the Gibichungs, to Hagen's potion and the charms of Gutrune.

The newly introduced setting, atmosphere and style of these final dramas are all designed to emphasize the fresh situation which the hero from the previous drama has now to confront. Aeschylus begins *Eumenides* at the centre of the Greek world, the *omphalos* or navel of the earth at Delphi; while Wagner's Norns (to emphasize at the outset his more pessimistic vision) have had to abandon their normal place at the centre of *their* world, the World-Ash—Wotan has had it cut down, to furnish the kindling for the fire that will destroy Valhalla. After this prologue, the two heroes journey down from the radiance of Apollo's temple and of Brünnhilde's farewell into the world of men, and again the contrast with Aeschylus is firm: Wagner sets the deceiving, treacherous world of Hagen's power over Gunther and Gutrune against the honesty and fairness of Athens and its tutelary goddess.

All this is in preparation for the complete contrast which Wagner draws as the climax of his drama. Aeschylus' Orestes passes from the thick veil of *miasma* under which he lay at the close of *Choephoroi*, through a gradual process of purification to his eventual complete release by the Athenian jury. Wagner precisely inverts this sequence. Siegfried closed the previous drama in naive joy, echoing Brünnhilde's words in the duet as she blissfully consigned to oblivion all that she ever cared about in the past. But in the world of Alberich's curse, even innocence, although it carries with it *some* immunity, is ultimately destructive to the possessor of the ring. The very fearlessness and heroic ardour which made his deeds possible in his own drama bring Siegfried to his death in the web of deception and intrigue which he encounters in *Götterdämmerung*. This is immediately apparent when he sets foot in the palace of the Gibichungs. Under Hagen's influence, Siegfried is easily corrupted and projects on to Gutrune all the sexual desire which he had first bestowed on Brünnhilde. After that he rapidly becomes the willing instrument of Hagen's schemes. He wrests the ring back from Brünnhilde, gives her to Gunther to be his bride, defies the Rhine-daughters in an act of reckless stupidity—and as a result ends the cycle not released but dead. Wagner uses the funeral music to place the fullest emotional weight behind the pathos of Siegfried's fate; but although Siegfried transcends his death in his last vision of Brünnhilde, he is not absolved by any recognition of his own misdeeds. Absolution is conferred on Siegfried only at the end of the drama, by Brünnhilde's self-sacrifice.

Siegfried's funeral music is the climax of *Götterdämmerung*, as Orestes' release is the climax of *Eumenides*. But both cycles have raised larger issues than the fate of the two young heroes; and to resolve them, both Wagner and Aeschylus now add to this first climax a still greater one to conclude the entire sequence. In the two final scenes, Athena and Brünnhilde come forward, to take for the first time a wholly commanding position; the remaining problems of each trilogy are resolved by the power of their wisdom. Here Wagner makes his final and most striking dissent from Aeschylus, countering the closing vision in *Eumenides*, of peace through perpetual mutual renewal, with his own vision of peace coming only through the total destruction of the gods and heroes, and the return of the gold, now 'purified', to the waters of the Rhine.

Neither *Götterdämmerung* nor *Eumenides* was intended by its author to make the same kind of impact on its spectators as *Die Walküre* or *Agamemnon*. They are the closing dramas of their respective cycles, and both are designed to show how the issues which led earlier to stark, unredeemed disaster can be resolved when their settlement finally devolves out of the hands of heroes into those of a wise goddess-woman.

This quest for final resolution is necessarily an anxious one. As *Eumenides* unfolds, Apollo's cause gains ever-greater strength, until it seems that Orestes deserves to go free; yet at the same time we come increasingly to realize the power and the value of the Furies. So too in *Götterdämmerung*: while Brünnhilde's sufferings lead her ever on, from her refusal to return the ring (Act 1 scene iii) to the final scene in which she achieves an even greater wisdom than that which she possessed as a Valkyrie in *Die Walküre* Act 3, Hagen at the same time gains continuously both in stature and in power.

This means that neither third drama can follow the pattern set by their respective predecessors. *Agamemnon* and *Choephoroi*, *Die Walküre* and *Siegfried* are single-minded works, in which, as the plot unfolds, everything comes more and more to point our expectations towards one outcome—the outcome which does in fact occur at the climax of each drama. These four dramas are, so to speak, Iliadic works, in which the tragic outcome is as deeply expected by the time at which it occurs as the moment in *Iliad* XXII when Achilleus, killing Hektor in implacable revenge for the loss of Patroklos, embraces the certainty of his own imminent, inglorious death.

In the *Odyssey*, however, Homer also provided an alternative possible exemplar for subsequent western fiction. During the battle with the suitors of Penelope in Odysseus' halls on Ithaka, there is so much power deployed against the hero that his fate remains uncertain, for the audience, almost to the last—even though the poet has made clear from the outset that his gods give men their deserts, that Zeus and Athena are now behind Odysseus, and that his victory is the only outcome which will satisfy our expectations. Aeschylus elected to follow this pattern in *Eumenides*; and Wagner followed him in *Götterdämmerung*.

Klytaimestra's death at the hand of her own son is an outrage so great that Aeschylus' gods and goddesses must take the stage in *Eumenides* to resolve the consequences; and the shattering of Wotan's spear by Siegfried has implications that are no less severe. The first is that Alberich's curse has the power to rise, in the Prelude to *Götterdämmerung*, and break the rope of fate. Events will no longer take a predictable course. And so the final drama in both trilogies is an *agōn*, a contest between the powers of light and darkness, through which each dramatist offers us his vision of how we may gain release from our toils. And though the outcome in both cases works in the theatre, it is not deeply expected in the manner of the earlier climaxes of both cycles.

This is the reason for the clarity, directness and overt 'theatrical' power which have so often, and so wrongly, been criticized in *Eumenides*: it also explains why Wagner could retain most of the text of *Siegfried's Death*, which differs in a similar way from those for *Siegfried* and *Die Walküre*, as the basis for *Götterdämmerung*. But Wagner was faced with a further problem which did not impede Aeschylus; and the exceptionally rich musical resources of *Götterdämmerung*, to which Newman rightly called attention, were needed to solve it.

By his radical decision to place the gods and the Furies on stage in person, Aeschylus both ensured that he had the range necessary to explore Orestes' predicament in depth, and provided himself with the characters necessary to achieve an elevated and satisfying conclusion to his entire trilogy. It is, however, basic to the meaning of the *Ring* that the gods have increasingly faded from the scene, as they are supplanted by human beings (indeed, Wotan has now adopted a totally passive position, in anticipation of his own imminent destruction). As a consequence, the new level on which the main action of *Götterdämmerung* takes place is not more elevated than the scene of the previous dramas, but less: the hall of the Gibichungs is both literally and morally lower than any other place to which the *Ring* has taken us since the first act of *Die Walküre*. Some counterbalance was essential.

Wagner first addressed himself to this problem by changing the title of the drama to reflect the cosmic implications of its action, and by reinflecting the actual text. The Norns' scene was expanded, and 'Hagen's watch' added to the close of Act 1 scene ii. Wagner then replaced the original, almost redundant scene in *Siegfried's Death* where the other eight Valkyries visited Brünnhilde on her rock, by the new scene between Waltraute and Brünnhilde, which goes straight to the heart of the meaning of the trilogy. He also made important adjustments to the words of Alberich's dream-appearance to Hagen (Act 2 scene i) and of Brünnhilde's final monologue.

These alterations and additional scenes alone were not enough, however, to give *Götterdämmerung* a power and signi-ficance comparable to that which makes *Eumenides* a more than worthy conclusion for the *Oresteia*. The main action of Wag-ner's final drama is necessarily centred on the palace of the Gibichungs, where three of the main characters—Siegfried, Gunther and Gutrune—are wholly ignorant of the cosmic im-plications of what they are doing, and the other two have good reasons for not discussing them with anyone: Hagen because he is plotting to regain the ring, and Brünnhilde because first her love, and later her betrayal by Siegfried, ensure that she does not regain the wisdom she possessed as a goddess until the final scene of the drama. Therefore, music has to play an entirely new role in *Götterdämmerung*, in comparison with the earlier dramas of the *Ring*; and the exultant contrapuntal mastery and advanced harmonic procedures, which Wagner brought to *Sieg-fried* Act 3 from his work on *Die Meistersinger* and *Tristan und Isolde*, have now to be put to a new and different use.

The music of *Götterdämmerung* is an intricate mosaic in which the principal themes and motifs of the *Ring* are used, far more often than before, to make specific musical allusion to previous dramatic events. A dense tissue of cross- and back-references surrounds the human drama onstage, providing a depth of commentary and insight which is needed to make sense of the action, and which cannot be expressed in the text because the characters themselves lack adequate understanding. This technique is not confined to reminiscences of the powers from the previous dramas which overshadow the action of *Götter-dämmerung*: there are hidden forces behind the action in the present also, as in the climactic scene of Act 1, where 'Gunther' overpowers Brünnhilde and repeated, ever more strident outbursts of Hagen's motif (Ex.40, extended to a fall of an octave) drive the act to its conclusion to emphasize how much Siegfried's blind action is impelled by his ever-rising power.

The score is also far more homogeneous than its predecessors. The consistency and even fabric of the orchestral music in *Götterdämmerung* is so cogent that its 'arias' and 'ensembles' blend naturally into, and grow out of, the textures of the whole. In *Eumenides*, the central role which the chorus takes in the action prefigures and prepares for the closing harmony. Similarly, the all-enveloping role of Wagner's orchestra in *Götter-dämmerung* implies that at this late stage in the action of the *Ring* (in the last moments before the fall of the gods) the men and women of Wagner's world are bound together more than they ever imagine: their thoughts and reactions are closely connected even at moments of apparent confrontation. And so the ensembles and other operatic devices of *Götterdämmerung* fulfil a deeper role than their participants suspect—just as Apollo (for all his prescience) and the Furies, as they argue their rhetorical cases for and against Orestes, pave the way for an accommodation between Athens and the Eumenides which is far beyond the dreams of either side. With the profound music of his richest score, Wagner places the fullest emotional depth behind the death of Siegfried and the sufferings of Brünnhilde. In Act 3 his hero and heroine attain a transcendent glory which rises, as in Aeschylus' final scene, far above the deception and intrigue that dominate the plot in the earlier stages of *Götter-dämmerung*.

## THE END OF PROPHECY

Both Aeschylus and Wagner establish the new plane on which the final drama will take place, by introducing it in an expansive and relatively leisurely sequence of scenes. In these, the opposing forces which will dominate the action are brought before us, first separately and then together. *Eumenides* opens with the Pythia's prayer, and after she has gone we see in sequence first Orestes' champion, Apollo, giving support to his protégé and sending him on to Athens; then the ghost of Klytaimestra, attempting to rouse *her* champions, the Furies; and then the Furies themselves. When they have shown us that their resolve to pursue Orestes is as strong as Apollo's determination to defend him (178), Apollo re-enters, and the Delphic section of the play ends with an initial inconclusive confrontation between him and the Furies.

Wagner follows this succession almost exactly. After *his* prophetesses have left the scene, here too the forces of light first appear; Siegfried is given encouragement and sent on his way by Brünnhilde in just the same way as Orestes by Apollo. If Aeschylus' sequences were followed precisely, the next character to enter should be the apparition of Alberich—but Wagner delays his appearance to the beginning of Act 2, for reasons which will become apparent. This apart, the strategy remains the same as Aeschylus' as Act 1 begins: in scene i we see Hagen and the Gibichungs alone, beginning their plot against Siegfried and Brünnhilde. Then in scene ii, Siegfried arrives, and the tremendous outburst of Ex.3 in the trombones, over a timpani pedal, which marks this moment (262-3), leaves no doubt that now, as Siegfried meets Hagen for the first time, the contest between light and dark is joined in earnest. But here as well the outcome is inconclusive. As scene ii proceeds, all goes as Hagen would wish; and in the famous vignette known as 'Hagen's watch' he anticipates his eventual success with as much confidence as do the Furies at the end of their confrontation with Apollo. The preceding scene, however, remains a preliminary skirmish just as much as its counterpart in *Eumenides*. The new dramatic issues cannot be fully joined, in Aeschylus' vision, until they can be crystallized around a new place, and the new character of Athena; likewise, the confrontation begun in *Götterdämmerung* Act 1 scene ii cannot be fully developed until Brünnhilde has been brought back into the drama.

Both *Götterdämmerung* and *Eumenides* will ultimately turn out to be concerned with far more important issues than would appear from these opening scenes. Apollo's vehement loathing for the Furies, as he expels them from his temple (179ff.), will later be shown to be an inadequate perspective—and so will their calm confidence that, for all he has said, their pursuit of Orestes will never cease until they have succeeded (225ff.). The progression in the *Ring* is similar. Hagen's confidence, in Act 1, that his pawns Gunther and Siegfried will deliver the ring into *his* hands, is as misplaced as the Furies'; while Brünnhilde's rapturous certainty, as she bids Siegfried farewell, that:

> Parted, who can separate us?
> Separated, who can divide us? (134–7)

is as emotionally excessive, in view of the realities of the situation, as Apollo's abuse of the Furies. Both the light and the dark are limited in their vision and overconfident at this stage, in the two trilogies; but Hagen in his watch shares with the Furies a calm stance, which promises that his power, like theirs, will continue to grow in the next stages of the drama.

So the positions of *both* parties in the last drama will be undercut almost as soon as they have made their opening moves. The main function of the two prologues—the monologue for the Pythia, the prophetess of Apollo, in Aeschylus and the dialogue between the Norns in Wagner—is to supply us with a new perspective from which we can realize this in advance; both prologues open up the real issues of the final drama, and hint at the ultimate way in which the trilogy may end—over the heads, so to speak, of the characters who appear in the next few scenes.

There is, however, a difference between the Pythia's role in *Eumenides* and the Norns' in *Götterdämmerung*, which is the focal point of Wagner's dissent from Aeschylus' vision of the world. We first see the Pythia as she offers up her morning

prayer before going in to take her accustomed place for prophecy, seated on the sacred tripod. Her prayer is a thinly disguised
paean to Apollo: by selecting the most favourable versions of the
sequence of events by which the ancient oracle at Delphi came to
be his, the prophetess creates the impression that Apollo is the
source of every civilizing influence in Greece; and she emphasizes that Apollo's prophetic power comes from his father, Zeus
(1–19). After offering prayers to the principal Olympian gods,
she goes into the temple of Apollo.

The Pythia returns only a few moments later, reduced to
crawling on all fours, powerless in the face of what she has seen.
Orestes is seated as a suppliant at the *omphalos*—and his com-
panions:

> They are not women—are not even Gorgons;
> once I saw some creatures in a picture, those
> who stole the meal from Phineus. But these have no wings
> and they are black, and utterly abominable.
> They are snoring, and their breath is insupportable.
> Then, from their eyes there pours a stream of filth;
> their dress is such as no one should see fit
> to wear approaching either images of gods, or even any
>        human home. (48ff.)

As the scene ends, her calm returns. Apollo is the lord of this
temple, and he is able to cope with the situation:

> Loxias is very strong;
> he heals by divination, reads portentous signs,
> and he can purify the halls of other men and gods. (61ff.)

She then departs—not into the temple which she has just left in
terror, but to return to her residence. There will be no prophecies made this day at Delphi.

The Pythia's opening calm and reassurance, the way in
which she places at the centre of this drama the power and
continuity of the Delphic tradition, and her full and reverent
prayer to the other chief Olympians, establish at the outset a
picture of an ordered and stable universe. Although this picture
is undermined almost at once by the intrusion of the Furies at

the very centre of the Earth, it is the picture which will ultimately prevail. Apollo *can* deliver his temple from the pollution which has afflicted it; and the priestess' emphasis on his role as the prophet of Zeus (19) is not misplaced. Zeus' backing will turn out at the trial to be the ultimate factor behind Orestes which resolves his predicament and gains him his freedom.

Matters are very different at the opening of *Götterdämmerung*. The orchestra makes an attempt to restate the glorious chords to which Siegfried awakened Brünnhilde; but the textures are more veiled, and each of the weary attempts by Ex. 46 to rise through the suspended chords (as did Ex. 13a in glory at that moment) is undercut by the mysterious figurations which will punctuate the colloquy of the Norns. After this sequence has led at the second attempt back to a fortissimo restatement of the opening chord (4), the enterprise is abandoned.

As the Norns begin to sing, the reasons for this weariness and justified pessimism emerge. Unlike the Pythia, the Norns have been obliged to abandon their central place of prophecy: *Eumenides* begins at the *omphalos* in Delphi, but in *Götterdämmerung* the World-Ash has been destroyed. Just as in *Eumenides*, we hear, for the first time in the trilogy, about the origins of divine wisdom. But there is no suggestion of over-confidence; and when the Norns, like the Pythia, have confronted the rise of the powers of darkness, *they* leave us in no doubt of the implications. At the end of the first scene of *Götterdämmerung*, prophecy is suspended not for one day but for ever.

As the narrative unfolds, taking us from the time when Wotan paid his eye as forfeit and received wisdom in return, through to the prophecy of the third Norn that when the logs cut from the World-Ash take fire:

> the eternal gods' end
> will then dawn (*Dämmert*) for eternity          (38–9)

both text and music move ever more animatedly with a desire for the end. Earlier in the third Norn's narrative, the new symmetrical theme (Ex. 34) appears in a form which foreshadows the moment at the end of the work when Brünnhilde herself will prepare to set that fire; and when she comes to sing these words, Ex.5 descends in tremolo violins (38). As *Götterdämmerung* develops, this theme will become the symbol for the nearing of the end.

The Pythia emphasized the continuity and stability of Zeus and the Olympians, which will become central to the settlement achieved in the closing stages of *Eumenides*. Wagner's gods, by contrast—led by Wotan—have now resigned themselves passively to their fate; and the whole action of *Götterdämmerung* is overshadowed by the gathering twilight as the extinction of the gods comes ever closer.

In consequence, darker forces have now been released; and so the Norns are interrupted in the ritual of question and answer, turning and binding of the rope of fate through which they have till now been able to see into the future. Ex.11 enters the textures, and the first Norn's vision becomes dimmed; Alberich's curse rises into their minds, and the rope falls into danger. But Siegfried's horn call (Ex.30) breaks out almost hysterically in the horns (61); the crisis has been created not by Alberich, but by Siegfried himself—first by breaking Wotan's spear, and then by the attempt that he and Brünnhilde will make, in the very next scene, to convert Alberich's ring into a token of their love. And so, as the rope of fate is broken, Ex.3 sounds out 'with extreme strength' in the bass trumpet (62). The Norns' 'eternal knowledge' is at an end; and the world is now freed from predictability. The road is, therefore, clear for the curse to take on new powers, and assist Hagen in his attempt to regain the ring. Just as in Aeschylus, the new urgency of the issues in the last drama is established at once—with the news that the Furies (invisible even in the climactic last scene of the previous drama) are physically present and surround Orestes even as he seeks to purify himself in the temple at Delphi—in Wagner, the breaking of the rope of fate is the mark of the new urgency which Alberich's curse has gained.

Alberich's curse disrupts the world of the Norns even more decisively than the appearance of the Furies did that of the Pythia. But as the Norns rescue the pieces of the broken rope, Ex.5 flows calmly down in the woodwind:

Our eternal knowledge is ended!
We will tell the world
our counsel no more.                                  (62–3)

While they sing these words, Ex. 3 is heard once more; this time
muted, tamed by their placid acceptance. In Aeschylus, the
world of the Olympians is seriously disrupted when the Furies
are roused by the murder of Klytaimestra to appear in physical
form on this earth; equilibrium is restored to the world of the
*Oresteia* only after the protracted, severe struggles which occupy
the remainder of *Eumenides*. Wagner sets out a far more pessimistic vision. The World-Ash is already dead; and so, as soon as
the curse rises, his fates accept without resistance that their role
is now completely ended. The first part of the *Götterdäm-*
*merung* Prelude holds out no hope that *any* closing equilibrium
may be reached. Our only consolation is, apparently, to be found
in the calmness with which the fates accept this.


## THE LIGHT AND THE DARKNESS

*Eumenides* is dominated by one question: whether Orestes
deserves to be saved or to be destroyed. Apollo, Orestes' defender, represents the forces that make his deed seem justified; the
Furies incarnate the opposition to this point of view—the claims
of the dead Klytaimestra. Athena embodies true wisdom, and
the spirit of fairness and tolerance which Aeschylus sees as
central to her city's virtues. The tension between these powers,
as Apollo and the Furies fight out the issues, enables Aeschylus
to explore Orestes' deserts in depth. As the play unfolds and the
fortunes of Orestes and of his pursuers fluctuate, the contest
between them in the theatre reflects the way in which our vision
of the strengths and weaknesses of their opening cases develops.

Aeschylus positively invites his spectators to take a moral
stance, and to respond to the changes in the two parties' relative
strength; the meaning of the drama is embodied in this process
of moral flux. The opening image is a simple one: Apollo, the
radiant young Olympian, male god of light, is pitted against the

hideous, old and female daughters of the Night, the loathsome Furies from the underworld. It is not difficult for the Athenian audience to take sides at the outset, and favour the defenders of Orestes. Nor are their expectations cheated: Apollo's side gains ever greater successes, until it appears that Orestes deserves to go free. Ultimately, appearances are not deceptive—but the Furies' case also gains cogency.

For Apollo, despite the Pythia, is not simply the great god of prophecy, long and legally established on his throne at Delphi. In *Agamemnon*, he drove the girl who broke her pledge to him to a hideous death; in *Choephoroi* he is ruthless once again, commanding matricide, warning of terrible penalties should Orestes try to evade it, and ordaining that Orestes must sink to treachery in order to achieve that end. Nor was his oracle, in real life, always above the charge of deviousness and trickery.

*Eumenides* seizes on these facts. By trickery, Apollo breaks the deadlock in which the play opens, and he argues with the Furies in a way that carries more vehemence than conviction. Then, at the trial, he cloaks the clinching arguments of Orestes' defence in sophistry and rhetoric. The 'right' case—or at least the one which comes to prevail—is increasingly undercut, and his disappearance as soon as the verdict is given (753)—a silent, unremarked exit which is without parallel in the extant Greek plays—seems appropriate for the advocate of a cause which has come to seem more hollow even as it nears its victory.

As Apollo's stance increasingly fails to carry conviction, simple pictures of the Furies also lose their force. The Pythia cannot find words to describe their appearance, and to Apollo they are 'born only to inflict harm', 'hated by men and by the Olympian gods' (71–3). In later antiquity, the impact of their first appearance was legendary: children were said to have fainted and pregnant women to have gone into labour as Aeschylus' chorus entered the orchestra. The intense, terrifying poetry of their first ode, as they awake under the lash of the plangent lament by Klytaimestra's ghost, and of the 'binding song' which they dance around their victim Orestes (when they have finally run him to ground at Athens (307ff.)), fixes firmly in our minds a picture of the Furies as evil.

In the remainder of the play, however, this conception of the Furies is equally firmly undermined. At Delphi they reply with courtesy to Apollo, even under a torrent of abuse and threats, and claim no more than their rights. In the 'binding song' itself, though there is savagery in the ritual refrains, the Furies emphasize the solemnity and importance of their duties. Then, in the fourth choral ode (490ff.), they develop this argument and begin to make the audience realize that they are essential to society: not despite, but because of, their fearful appearance and powers:

> There are places where the terrible is good,
> and it must stay there, firmly seated
> as the guardian of the heart.
> There is advantage
> in learning moderation from torment.
> Can the man, or can the city
> that nurtures no fear within the heart
> yet pay reverence to Equity?

> You should praise neither the life of anarchy
> nor that of subjection to one man. A god
> has granted victory in everything to the middle
> way . . .                                              (517ff.)

Athena echoes these words, as she founds the court of the Areopagos (681ff.). One of the Olympians may execrate the Furies; but another shares their ideals, and wants them in her city.

When the two sides come to trial, their cases have equal force. The Furies' wrath may justly be unleashed against the Athenians, if they are deprived of their victim. The majority of the human jurors vote in their favour, and Orestes is acquitted only because Athena, frankly acknowledging her personal bias towards the male cause, casts her own vote for Orestes—and so produces a tied ballot, which gives him his liberty, but no vindication. Then, in the final scene, Athena reaches an accommodation with the Furies; now their female sex, their sinister dwelling-place beneath the earth, and their power to inflict terror are all viewed in a new perspective. In the finale we become able to see that all those aspects of their being are positive benefits, and fill needs which any city neglects at its peril.

Athens will not neglect them. Under Athena's guidance, the city gives a place to the Furies, receiving them as honoured guests for all time; the trilogy draws to its close as the men and women of Athens escort the Eumenides to their new dwelling-place, placing around their black and loathsome bodies the scarlet robes which were worn in Athens by permanent foreign residents. The darkness and the light are one.

*Eumenides* is one of the shortest surviving Greek tragedies. Its sequence of events, which passes with total conviction from an apparently impenetrable opposition between the Olympians and the powers of darkness to the final, eternal reconciliation, is one of Aeschylus' finest achievements as a dramatist. Wagner offers no such reconciliation at the close of *Götterdämmerung;* and this divergence from Aeschylus at the final climax of his trilogy raises the gravest problems in the entire *Ring*. To understand the course which Wagner took, we must look closely at one aspect of the plot of *Götterdämmerung*.

In his final drama Wagner follows Aeschylus' basic strategy exactly: *Götterdämmerung*, like *Eumenides*, is a contest between the forces of darkness and the forces of light, which ends with Siegfried's two 'trials' in Act 3 scene i and scene ii, and is followed by the finale to the entire work, in which the music patently offers the audience a feeling of peaceful, complete renewal.

Like Aeschylus, Wagner gradually withdraws the simple 'black and white' image of the opening as the work proceeds. Siegfried's new theme in *Götterdämmerung* (Ex. 39) is a portrait of a greater man, more heroic now that he has become an adult by consummating his union with Brünnhilde. But when he arrives in human society Siegfried will not live up to the radiant image which Brünnhilde paints of him; he turns out to be completely vulnerable to Hagen's intrigues and the appeal of Gutrune's sexuality. Wagner's intention, in his characterization of the *Götterdämmerung* Siegfried, was to reverse the idealized, 'Hellenic' spirit of optimism in which he had first conceived the character during his revolutionary period.

Ex. 39    (very calm, without dragging)

In *Gotterdammerung*, as in *Eumenides*, we see a corresponding, steady increase in the power of the representatives of darkness. When we first encounter the Gibichungs, as the main action of *Götterdämmerung* begins, Hagen is an unequivocally sinister figure, openly committed to treachery, deceit and the manipulation of others. By the end of the second scene of Act 1 his success has already been formidable. Here Wagner inserted the short scena known as 'Hagen's watch', a powerfully evocative piece of music which spins a dense web of thematic allusions, drawing on the full resources of Wagner's mature style. It establishes completely the credibility of Hagen's aspirations. The underlay of the rich thematic tapestry is the motif that expressed Alberich's own bitter ambitions in the earlier dramas of the *Ring*. But its syncopations are now mellowed by rephrasing and by the instrumentation, so that it is imbued with a new spirit of confidence. With this as a basis, Hagen's own theme (Ex. 40) is heard invoking broken fragments of Ex. 30, in perfect symbolism of the power which he has begun to wield over Siegfried; and Wagner himself drew attention (in his essay of 1879, *On the Application of Music to Drama*, AE 6.188) to the use throughout the scena of Ex. 10, in a remarkable transformation (Ex. 41) which brings out to the full the increasing

Ex. 40    (very moderate tempo, slightly hesitant)

Ex. 41

(very moderate tempo, slightly hesitant)

power of the Rhinegold, as Hagen's plan nears its first fulfilment.

The most illuminating allusion of the music here is at the
close, where Hagen sings:

> Though you despise him,
> you will all serve
> the Nibelung's son. (363–5)

Ex. 12 is fractured around Ex. 9, just as in Wotan's 'monologue'
in *Die Walküre*, Act 2. The power that the god saw rising to
defeat the glory of his heroes—the lure of the ring, embodied
then as now in the creation and existence of Hagen—has now
come to fulfilment. Hagen's confidence is shown to be justified at
the end of Act 1, when tremendous outbursts of his music in the
orchestra leave no doubt of the extent to which his influence lies
behind the conquest of Brünnhilde; and this confidence continues in Act 2, where Hagen is able to offer firm and soothing
assurances to the anxious dream-apparition of Alberich—in
marked contrast to the drowsy murmurings which are all that
Alberich's Aeschylean counterpart, the apparition of Klytaimestra, is able to elicit from the sleeping Furies (*Eumenides* 94ff.).
Indeed, Hagen's plans to regain the ring for the Nibelungs
proceed with ever-increasing power, right up to the last scene of
the drama. And he becomes an ever more formidable figure,
rising in strength throughout *Götterdämmerung* to the
tremendous moment in Act 3 scene iii when he comes forward,
acknowledges that he killed Siegfried, and claims the ring.

Hagen does not simply grow in power. The audience also lose
some of their initial hostility towards him. Just as the Furies are
marked off from the other gods, forbidden to share in the
company of the Olympians because their work is so hideous
(*Eumenides* 349–86), so too Hagen, in Act 1, is seen isolated
from the other heroes by his illegitimacy, his premature ageing,
and the cold, stagnant blood which runs in his veins. These
characteristics are brought out further in Act 2 scene i. There
is a real pathos to be heard in the music as he rebukes his
father:

> If my mother gave me strength,
> I owe her no thanks,
> that she succumbed to your trickery:
> old in my youth, sallow and pale,
>     I hate happy people,
>     I am never glad!                    (559–63)

But Wagner is unable to develop this aspect of the drama any further. Siegfried must die for his treachery to Brünnhilde, and—given the characters used in Wagner's dramatization of the myth—Hagen must clearly be the murderer. We must ultimately, however, view Siegfried with sympathy, so that Brünnhilde may attain true glory by joining him in death. In Wagner's version, therefore, Siegfried made love to Brünnhilde only when he first came to her rock, long before he met Gunther and swore blood-brotherhood with him. In *Götterdämmerung*, Hagen's charge of perjury against Siegfried is simply false, and by murdering him Hagen becomes, in the final perspective of the drama, unequivocally villainous—'accursed Hagen' as Gutrune calls him in her last outburst. And so, although he—unlike the Furies—has achieved ever-increasing power throughout the action of the drama, in its final scene Hagen is denied both sympathy and victory.

In this there is an important difference from *Eumenides*. Aeschylus also asks his audience to take sides, to engage in moral debate about the actions of his characters. But his understanding of their motivation goes so deep that, ultimately, the *Oresteia* is objective and morally neutral. Klytaimestra's enemies are, naturally, vehement in their condemnation of her; the playwright himself makes no such judgment. She has to die, because of the wound which Agamemnon's murder has inflicted on the order shared by the gods and by human society; yet the *Oresteia* also contains moments of genuine sympathy for her motherhood, her loss of Iphigeneia, and her own suffering after the murder of Agamemnon. In the final perspective of *Eumenides*, though Agamemnon's case has Zeus' sympathy and Orestes is eventually released from the Furies' pursuit, the values of femininity, which were blighted and made sterile in Klytaimestra, are restored to full strength in the city of Athens by the creative harmony between Athena and the Furies.

The *Ring*, however, cannot develop in a similar direction. Siegfried's character is such that, eventually, the curse on the ring is bound to bring him down. Wagner explores the ways in which this came about, and also the fate of Brünnhilde who, after failing in Act 1 to escape Alberich's curse on the ring, finds a way, after Siegfried's death, finally to cleanse it.

This strategy leads to drastic consequences in the finale. If Brünnhilde is to take the ring and return it to the Rhine-daughters, then Hagen must not take it. But there is literally no earthly reason why he should not do so, after he has removed the final obstacle by killing Gunther; Wagner was obliged to provide a supernatural one. In an arbitrary and highly melodramatic gesture, the hand of Siegfried's corpse rises to defend the ring. Hagen accepts this portent, with a superstitiousness which is wholly out of character, and makes no further attempt to regain the ring until it is too late. After 'watching Brünnhilde's behaviour with ever-growing anxiety', he attempts to retrieve the ring only when the Rhine has flooded over her pyre and its daughters come to reclaim their gold. The curse is broken at this point (in the orchestra, Ex.3 is graphically snapped in mid-utterance, 1333), and two of the Rhine-daughters drag Hagen down while the third recovers the ring.

This is not an implausible outcome for the plot of the *Ring*; but it falls unavoidably short of our best expectations. In Aeschylus, the Olympians and the Furies came into conflict only at the moment (more than half-way through the trilogy) when Orestes murdered his mother. Even so, the reconciliation at the end of *Eumenides* is deeply satisfying. In the *Ring* on the other hand, the gods and the Nibelungs have been in open hostility since the third scene of *Das Rheingold*, and our need for a profound resolution to their conflict is correspondingly greater. But for Wagner the power of the Nibelungs is ultimately disruptive to society. Despite all the moments at which sympathy is extended to the dwarfs during the course of the trilogy, Hagen must fall at the end of the cycle. For all its power, his music is ultimately sterile, and lies in profound contrast to the

thematic richness which is bestowed upon Siegfried and Brünnhilde.

There is no room in the *Ring* for a conclusion parallel to the
almost miraculous revelation, in Aeschylus, that there lies within the terrifying power of the Furies an essential power which
mankind needs for its own good. In the final reckoning, Hagen
must be seen as evil so that Brünnhilde's glorification of Siegfried and of love-in-death can make any kind of sense. Wagner's
vision of life forced him to abandon, at the end of the *Ring*, the
classical objectivity towards which he struggled in *Lohengrin*,
and which he had sustained throughout the earlier parts of the
cycle; and *if* his strategy in *Götterdämmerung* feels right to us
today, that is the measure of the extent to which our hopes have
been diminished, and our fears increased, in contrast to the
world of Aeschylus.

## BRÜNNHILDE'S REVENGE

In the *Oresteia*, the fourth and final predicament of the trilogy
devolves upon an entirely new set of characters. Athena and her
citizens are faced with the impossible choice between abandoning Orestes, who has taken refuge in their city as a pure suppliant (the rights of suppliants were guarded, in Greek belief, by
Zeus himself), and dismissing the claims of the Furies, who—as
Athena rightly predicts—will seek to exact compensation by
unleashing their powers against Athens if it wrongs them.
Wagner has already experimented with the possibility of a
double exaction from one character—Wotan suffers the fate of
Agamemnon in *Das Rheingold*, and of Klytaimestra in *Die
Walküre*; and now he does so again, to crown the final drama.
Where Aeschylus' Orestes rises gradually during the course of
*Eumenides*, from the madness into which the Furies had thrown
him at the close of *Choephoroi* to the point where he gains
release from their pursuit at Athens, Siegfried by contrast is in
decline throughout the action of *Götterdämmerung*. Dwarfs,
giants and gods have all proved themselves in turn to be inadequate to overcome the lure of the ring; now Siegfried's

'innocence' leads to his downfall at the hands of Hagen, when even he, the finest hero whom the world of the *Ring* has seen, has proved his inadequacy by rejecting the plea of the Rhine-daughters (Act 3 scene i). 'Siegfried does not know what he is guilty of; as a man, committed entirely to deeds, he knows nothing, he must fall in order that Brünnhilde may rise to the heights of perception.' (D 6/9/71) Brünnhilde becomes the final agent in Wagner's cycle: it is she who gains the power to give back the ring to the Rhine-daughters, and so purge the world from the influence of Alberich's curse. She develops gradually through the course of the drama, to achieve that degree of response and understanding which Athena, in Aeschylus' trilogy, achieves effortlessly, simply because she is a goddess.

Here Wagner's strategy brings nothing but gain. Aeschylus achieves the resolution of his cycle by introducing a new character who is wise by definition; and she is joined by a group of jurors who, being citizens of Athens, may be assumed to be so by a deft flattery of the poet's audience. In the *Ring*, by contrast, the final resolution is achieved, after suffering and conflict, by a character with whose emotional development we have already become intensely involved. Brünnhilde has played a major role in the first two dramas of the main action; now, in *Götterdämmerung*, she comes to the centre.

In the second part of the Prelude, Wagner portrays Siegfried and Brünnhilde in terms which make plain that their love incarnates his supreme ideal, the total giving of one's self which leads to true interdependence, and a union of personality between man and woman:

Siegfried     . . . I am no longer Siegfried,
                  I am just Brünnhilde's arm.
Brünnhilde   If only Brünnhilde might be your soul!
Siegfried     My courage is kindled by her.
Brünnhilde   Then you are both Siegfried and Brünnhilde?
Siegfried     Where I am, both are sheltered.
Brünnhilde   Then my cave will be empty?
Siegfried     We are one; it will contain us both!    (124–9)

Written—and set to ecstatic music—by the composer of *Tristan und Isolde*, these are not simply metaphysical conceits. The tragedy of *Götterdämmerung* lies in the fact that this, the most complete love to be seen in the *Ring*, is now broken; the redemption at the end of the drama is possible only because after Siegfried has betrayed her and died for it, Brünnhilde, 'woman, suffering and willing to sacrifice herself, becomes at last the real, conscious redeemer' (R 25/1/54). How and why does Brünnhilde become able to rise to that height?

At the end of *Siegfried*, Brünnhilde abandoned herself recklessly to her love, happily consigning the gods to oblivion. But when Waltraute comes to her now (Act 1 scene iii), we learn that the gods' situation is even worse than it appeared to be from the Norns' narrative. Wotan has willed his own destruction, has allowed his spear of power to oppose and be broken by Siegfried, and has prepared the gods and heroes in Valhalla to await their end. Nevertheless, he cannot bring about his own destruction. Wotan refuses to taste Holda's apples; but—perhaps in deliberate contradiction of the mythology of *Das Rheingold* (cf. Chapter 3, pp. 96–7)—that alone is not now sufficient to bring death to the god. He is trapped in a kind of limbo, and can only gain his release from the outcome of the deeds of human beings:

> 'If she would give the ring back
> to the Rhine-daughters far below,
>   from the weight of the curse
> both god and world would be redeemed'.   (440–2)

As Waltraute reports the last words of Wotan's wish, Ex. 12 is sounded in a new, developed form: the first truly beautiful shape which this melody has taken. Only in the total destruction of Valhalla will Wotan, and the world, be purged from the consequences of its creation.

Brünnhilde, however, is not yet capable of fulfilling the Wanderer's prophecy (*Siegfried* Act 3 scene i) that when she awakes she will be wise enough to perform the deed which will redeem the world. She rebuffs Waltraute's plea brutally. As she herself ironically says, she is a *Törin*, separated in her 'folly' from the world, and the wisdom of the gods. That 'folly' is her love. For Wagner, the deepest love that two people can achieve for each other must also be the most oblivious to external reality. 'From the moment that Siegfried had awakened her, she has no other knowledge than the knowledge of love. Now the symbol of this—after Siegfried's departure—is the ring . . . She knows also that one thing alone is god-like, and that is love; therefore let the splendour of Valhalla fall in ruins, she will not give up the ring (her love).' (R 25/1/54) This ring is 'Siegfried's pledge of love'; one glance at it means more to Brünnhilde than all the gods and their fate.

At the same time it is also Alberich's ring, and Brünnhilde's new innocence and mortality render her vulnerable to its power. So once more, as in *Die Walküre*, even human love is corrupted. Just as Siegmund moved from rapturous praise of Sieglinde to the drawing of Notung from the tree to defend his love for her, so too Brünnhilde first exults in Siegfried's love, and then concludes:

> About my ring
> you tell them this;
> I shall never give up love,
> they won't take love from me,
>     even if Valhall's radiant pride
> collapses into ruins! (469–72)

The third and fourth lines of this text are set to Ex. 2, enunciated with chilling power and total clarity in Brünnhilde's vocal line. Once again—just as with Alberich and Wotan—the Rhinegold has corrupted its possessor's sense and vision; and once again, as with Siegmund and Notung at the end of *Die Walküre*, Act 1, the peculiar horror for the audience of Brünnhilde's reaction lies in the delusion that a true, deep love can be defended by the use of power and remain intact.

At this point—partly because Brünnhilde's love is so intense that it has taken her completely away from any understanding of Wotan, and partly because at this stage in the trilogy, after Wotan's total resignation, the power of the Nibelungs has grown so great—Brünnhilde is the most cruelly and the most immediately punished of the victims of the ring. Almost as soon as Waltraute has left her, she hears the call of Siegfried's horn, and runs to the edge of the cliff to greet and fall into 'the arms of my god'.

This is *hubris*, in the full neo-classical sense of dangerous, arrogant pride; and it is immediately given its reward. Just as Alberich, in *Das Rheingold* scene iv, was forced to re-enact at Wotan's command the ascent to Valhalla which he dreamed of making in glorious conquest, Brünnhilde is now forced to undergo a hideous re-enactment of the closing scene of *Siegfried* as Siegfried, totally under the control of Hagen, impersonates Gunther and makes her—again like Alberich—suffer the removal of the ring by force:

> Everything totters around Brünnhilde, everything is out of joint; in a terrible conflict she is overcome, she is 'forsaken of God'. And moreover it is Siegfried in reality who orders her to share his bed; Siegfried whom she (unconsciously and thus with greater bewilderment) almost recognizes, by his gleaming eye, in spite of his disguise. (R 25/1/54)

Once again in the *Ring*, as in *Die Walküre*, Acts 1 and 2, the eyes cannot fully deceive—even though now all the powers of the Tarnhelm are aiding the deception.

This partial recognition is transformed into certain recognition during Act 2 scene iv. In the palace of the Gibichungs, Brünnhilde abandons her simple astonishment at the presence of Siegfried, engaged to Gutrune, and begins to realize the truth when her attention lights on the ring, which still lies on Siegfried's finger.

The fact that it does is central to Wagner's meaning: it shows that Siegfried, like every previous possessor of the ring, is brought down simply by its allure. For the influence of the ring has worked on Siegfried—albeit without his realizing it, and in a scene which is not shown to us onstage. In order to ensure that Brünnhilde was truly deceived, and so won for his blood-brother, Siegfried should naturally (were this any other ring than Alberich's) have passed it over to Gunther when he relinquished his disguise and placed Brünnhilde in his hands.

But he did not. Brünnhilde realizes the full extent to which she has been betrayed. She addresses the gods:

> Have you taught suffering to me
> such as no one ever suffered?
> Have you planned disgrace for me
> such as no one ever bore?
> Then plan for me a vengeance
> such as no one ever stopped!
> Kindle in me a rage,
> such as no one ever tamed!                    (765–9)

The symmetry of these lines makes them the pivot in the development of the drama. The suffering which has been inflicted on Brünnhilde, since she rejected Waltraute's appeal, teaches her her revenge; and the grief which she inflicts on herself, as she now revenges herself on Siegfried, will teach her the understanding which enables her, at the end of the trilogy, to achieve that deed which will redeem the world and which neither god nor hero could accomplish.

One of these two motifs is Aeschylean. There is a constant emphasis throughout the *Oresteia* on the idea of revenge. 'He who does, shall suffer' is almost a leitmotif of the first two dramas, while the law of retribution (the idea that every action has its inexorable due consequences) is of course a fundamental theme of the trilogy right up until the close of *Eumenides*. And the symmetry of Brünnhilde's resolve that as she has suffered, so she will be revenged, is no less true to the spirit of Aeschylus.

The idea of learning through suffering, which comes forward to dominate the closing stages of *Götterdämmerung*, is, however, foreign to the thought of the *Oresteia*. It is traditional to impose this overtone on Aeschylus' text; in the elders' famous 'hymn to Zeus' (*Agamemnon* 16off.) men are (in most versions) encouraged to worship Zeus because it is he who:

> set men on the road to
>     thinking, he who laid down
>   'learn by suffering' to be a law . . .        (176ff.)

But nobody learns by suffering in the *Oresteia*. In Aeschylus' vision, only time can heal. In *Eumenides*, Orestes gradually gains release from his pollution simply through the length of his journeys and the time which they take; and at the very end of the trilogy, the chorus hymn the Athenians who are, as it were, seated under the wings of Pallas, the goddess of wisdom herself, and so will 'learn wisdom in the course of time' (*Eumenides* 1000).

The Greek word *pathos* can mean suffering; but it can also, simply and neutrally, mean experience. Lexicographers have insisted that the correct translation of *Agamemnon* 178 is 'learn from experience'. Their voice has been drowned by generations of moralizing commentary; but they are right.

Wagner was misled on this point: partly by Droysen ('Zeus . . . uns in Leid/lernen lässt'), but far more by his own inclinations; for from this point on, the *Ring* moves ever more openly towards the theme of *Erlösung*—redemption. The word and its overtones are Christian, and in *Götterdämmerung* both Wotan's need for release, and Brünnhilde's gaining of wisdom through her sufferings, raise echoes of Wagner's earlier opera *Tannhäuser*, and of the preoccupations which were to dominate his last years and to lead to the composition of the work which he had long hoped to create, *Parsifal*. It is true that Christian ideas are only implicit in Brünnhilde's predicament, while they are explicit in *Parsifal* (here a loving woman may redeem the world when she regains her wisdom, but there only a chaste, male 'pure fool' may do so; here, suffering alone is enough to bring redemption, while there Amfortas cannot redeem precisely because he is suffering, and the knights of the Grail can achieve their deliverance only at the hands of one who has gained wisdom *durch Mitleid*, through compassion and sympathy with the suffering of others). The affinities are, nevertheless, still there.

Through his portrait of Brünnhilde in *Götterdämmerung*, Wagner set out a vision of the sources of true moral strength which achieves a total contrast with that offered by Aeschylus in *Eumenides*. First, Orestes' predicament is resolved by a silent court of Athenian elders—male, calm, and guided by the chaste virgin goddess of wisdom in person—while, in the finale, Athena herself achieves the power to transcend the last dilemma of the *Oresteia*, not by any display of emotion (let alone such an emotion as Brünnhilde's intense fury and its consequent suffering), but through the powers of patience, reason, and persuasion. Second, that dilemma is transcended not through any act of redemption or atonement for the past but—as we shall see—by facing up to the past and building on it for the future.

## HUMAN SOCIETY: HONOUR AND TREACHERY

Brünnhilde's sufferings and Siegfried's fall take place, like the resolution of Orestes' predicament, in the context of an open society. Just as the claustrophobic atmosphere of the house of Atreus gives place, in the final drama, to the civic focus of the proceedings at Athens, so too in Wagner the action which has so far in the *Ring* taken place in the wild, untamed surroundings of nature moves, in Act 1 of *Götterdämmerung*, to the civilized milieu of the hall of the Gibichungs.

In the Greek world, the need to maintain and increase his inherited honour or status in society was fundamental for every man of noble birth. The ends of acquiring *timē* (the inclusive word by which the Greeks denoted both the status itself and the material possessions which proved its existence), and of avoiding the shame of being accorded less *timē* than is your due, were never questioned; and anguished moral scrutiny of the means employed to achieve them was rare. Aeschylus closed *Eumenides* with a vision of a harmonious and stable social organization; and because the triumph of Athenian society is his theme, it is, I think, no accident that the settlement between the Athenians and the Furies is made to devolve entirely round the concept of *timē*, simply because it was so fundamental to Greek values. The Furies claim that the Athenians' verdict has thrown their *timē* into contempt, and propose to unleash their full destructive powers upon the city in retaliation. Athena persuades them not to do this. First she invites them to look at the outcome of the trial from a different point of view: Orestes was not vindicated, but released simply by being granted the benefit of the fact that she and her fellow-jurors were evenly divided in their votes; the Furies were not dishonoured (794ff. and 824ff.).

And then, if any slight remains, she proceeds to show them how her citizens can in the future more than recompense them for it, by offering them a role and honoured place in their society. The Furies will live in Athens, and their terrible powers will provide a check on the citizens, and a guarantee that they will fight not against each other but against their common foes; while in return for the *timē* that the Athenians will pay them, they will bless and give increase to the fertility both of the city's crops and of its people.

There is no suggestion in Aeschylus' finale that the audience is to frown either on the materialism of the negotiations, or on the Furies' feeling that their honour and prestige have been damaged and that they are entitled to react in a way which we might simply call vindictive. On the contrary, the strength of the final scene spreads out from the wealth of specific honours and functions with which the Athenians and the Eumenides are able to endow each other. Aeschylus is inviting his audience to feel relief on returning to the solidity of basic Greek values after the dubious metaphysics, *ad hoc* and *ad hominem* arguments, and blatant threats and bribes to the jury which resulted (in the trial of Orestes) from Apollo's attempt to hold a debate about moral issues. In Aeschylus, high talk of morality led to a lower, less honest level of debate than that which is subsequently achieved in the finale by attention to the real status, power, and deserts of the characters. And so Aeschylus' trilogy can reach its resolution in the playwright's triumphant celebration of the strength and the potential of the developed *polis*, the city-state of contemporary Athens.

In *Götterdämmerung*, Wagner reverses the Aeschylean position. Political society does not enter this trilogy as mankind's crowning achievement: on the contrary, the kingdom over which Gunther presides embodies Wagner's vision of nineteenth-century society in all its shallowness and hypocrisy.

Few of the principal motifs in the *Ring* are as empty and rhetorical as the theme (Ex.42) to whose accompaniment Gunther introduces us to both himself and his preoccupation with his *Ruhm*—his fame and his prestige. Gunther's needs, in themselves, are respectable by any standards, Aeschylean or

Romantic: marriage for himself, and for his sister. But his motives are suspect almost from the start. He asks Hagen:

> Whom do you suggest I marry,
> to give profit to our prestige? (209–10)

Wagner hardly expects us to view this favourably. And while Gutrune may be a slightly more attractive character than her brother, her theme (Ex.43)—for all its beauty—is not the music of a profound person.

Ex.42 (at a comfortable speed)

Ex.43 (very moderate tempo)

The moral shallowness of both Gibichungs is confirmed at the end of the first scene. When Hagen has unfolded his plot, both Gunther and Gutrune are immediately enthusiastic. They do not balk once either at the plan or its execution (though Gunther later shows some qualms about murdering his sworn blood-brother), and Gutrune's outbursts against Hagen, in Act 3 scene iii, when she finally realizes that Brünnhilde was the woman whom her drugged drink made Siegfried forget, sound more like the complaints of self-interest foiled, rather than any genuine moral protest.

Wagner's dissent from Aeschylus here is more than simply the reaction of a Romantic against the confidence in their material possessions which the aristocrats of classical Greece shared (albeit less hypocritically) with their nineteenth-century counterparts. The fundamental difference between Wagner and Aeschylus in the closing dramas of the two cycles is crystallized around the role played in each by treachery and deceit.

It is central to the design of the *Oresteia* that, where

Klytaimestra put on the mask of hypocrisy as the only means by which she could overcome Agamemnon, the god Apollo should ordain that her son must also use treachery as part of the fierce symmetry by which Orestes' deed must match and answer his mother's. The use of deception in *Choephoroi* was itself the most cogent indication that Orestes' murder of his mother can in no sense be the final, releasing act which he and his champion would like it to be: for Aeschylus, the position of Orestes and Apollo is undermined in *Eumenides* precisely because they have to stoop to treachery to maintain it. Apollo's drugging of the Furies at Delphi matches his unjustified contempt for them and for their duties; and it is then no surprise that, in the trial, he presents Orestes' case with ever-increasing speciousness and rhetoric.

Athena's conduct lies in total contrast with Apollo's. Though taken aback by the Furies' appearance, she refuses to judge them by it, saying that this would be unfair (413–14). She rapidly convinces them that she would be a fair arbiter for their cause. When they have lost, the Furies naturally take a less generous view of Athens and its goddess; but in the finale she embarks on the task of showing them that they are wrong to do so; and in this process persuasion, which has until her appearance always been used in the *Oresteia* to malicious and deceptive effect, at last ceases to be the means of deception. Now, it takes its place as the means by which two parties can become convinced of each other's fundamental honesty—and through that attain peace. In the third play, as Athena comes to the forefront and eclipses Apollo, deception is banished, gradually but completely, from the world of Aeschylus' trilogy.

In *Götterdämmerung*, deception is Hagen's chief weapon in his attempt to regain the ring; and it thrives on a scale unmatched even in *Das Rheingold*. When Hagen first indicates to Gunther that he could use Siegfried to bring him Brünnhilde (228–9), the Tarnhelm's motif returns to the score of the *Ring* in a spacious, leisurely form; and as he then describes the powers possessed by the love-potion which he obtained for Gutrune, it flowers into a new theme (Ex.44), which expands it both in length and in power (234). This theme then becomes, through-

Ex. 44

out *Götterdämmerung*, the token of the enhanced powers which deception has now gained. These powers are represented on stage both by the potion itself and by the increased capabilities of the Tarnhelm: it is now not simply capable of disguising its wearer and of making him invisible, but can also be used—as it is by Siegfried, at the start of Act 2—to transport him instantly from one place to another.

The role of deception in *Götterdämmerung* is not confined to the employment of magic devices. In the hall of the Gibichungs treachery is seen to undermine the whole fabric of society, which is symbolized here in the ideas of fidelity and the pledging of oaths. Each of the three great ensemble sections of *Götterdämmerung* is concerned with the taking of an oath; and ensemble is the appropriate musical procedure for these scenes because the characters involved have achieved a brief (and illusory) affinity with each other at the moment when they make their bond. In their duet Siegfried presents Alberich's ring to Brünnhilde 'as the sacred pledge of my fidelity'; in Act 1 scene ii he cements his assent to Hagen's plan in a duo with Gunther, where each swears that should he betray his friend his blood shall flow in streams to make amends. The tables are then turned on Siegfried in his own terms when Brünnhilde and Gunther unite with Hagen, at the end of Act 2, in an intensely powerful trio, to secure their vengeance for Siegfried's apparent breach of the oaths which he has sworn to each of them. Oaths suffer in the action of *Götterdämmerung*; so too, of course, does the ideal of marriage. Immediately after this ensemble, in the last tableau of the act, Gunther and Brünnhilde (striding separately towards the palace) find themselves confronted by the bridal procession of Siegfried and Gutrune. As the curtain falls, Hagen propels Brünnhilde against her will into taking up her place beside Gunther, to form the second couple.

With these actions, the *Ring* begins to move apart from the

*Oresteia* on the central issue of the dramatists' vision of society. Aeschylus' trilogy nears its resolution as Athena and her citizens successfully impose on Apollo and the Furies a correct use of social rituals—respect for the rights of suppliants, for custom, and for the powers of the newly created court of the Areopagos. But in the *Ring,* the twilight of the gods draws closer (after their withdrawal from the world) as two rituals which lie at the foundation of any society—that of sworn pledges, and that of marriage—are perverted.

In Wagner, therefore, treachery and dishonesty do not fade as the end nears, but gather a new strength. In Aeschylus, the *miasma* of his deed gradually fades from Orestes—as he himself says, 'time heals all things . . .' (*Eumenides* 286). This is not true in Wagner's world. The personal power of Alberich himself has indeed weakened: when he appears as a dream-figure to Hagen (Act 2 scene i), he is as diminished and wraith-like as Klytaimestra herself in the scene which Wagner is echoing here (*Eumenides* 94ff.). But this is not because the power of the curse is diminishing in any way. On the contrary, the fact that it has risen to split the rope of fate is itself the first indication that Alberich's curse has taken on new strength. Klytaimestra's case has to be carried on now by supernatural beings, because— unlike her husband—she has no mortal, living relative on whom the duty to avenge her death can devolve. Her intervention is not superfluous because her agents have failed her, and need her presence in their dreams to rouse them back to their duties. By contrast, Alberich's appearance to Hagen *is* superfluous: his son is a substantial being of flesh and blood, strong and intensely motivated in himself towards the goal which Alberich urges upon him. And, unlike the Furies, Hagen is fully in command of the situation when the dream comes to him, and is rightly confident that the action is proceeding as he has planned.

As always, the ring corrupts each of its possessors according to their nature, striking at and making a vice out of his or her highest ability. Fafner's giant strength becomes the sluggish-ness of a *Wurm*; Brünnhilde's profound love becomes an obses-sive refusal to release its token. When he arrives in the hall of the Gibichungs, the spontaneity and naturalness which gave

Siegfried all his power in the previous drama now cause his downfall. In the world of society, the child of nature is as vulnerable as was Alberich in the domain of the Rhine-daughters. He succumbs completely to the charms of the first sophisticated woman that he encounters, and with no less impetuosity pledges himself to her brother and hastens to help him win Brünnhilde.

Nor can Brünnhilde, when she is brought in her turn to Gunther's hall, turn for support to the ordinary people, his vassals and their women. In total contrast with the Athenian elders (whom Athena brings to join her in judging Orestes) and the men and women of Athens who lead the Eumenides into their city as the *Oresteia* closes, the chorus of *Götterdämmerung* are as gullible and manipulable in Hagen's hands as are their leaders, Gunther, Siegfried and Gutrune. Although their music is more vigorous than that of their mediaeval counterparts in *Lohengrin*, it is no more profound.

In the *Ring*, society offers no solution to the world's dilemmas. Brünnhilde is truly alone in Acts 2 and 3, both before and after the death of Siegfried.


## SIEGFRIED'S DEATH

At the end of Act 2, when Hagen and Brünnhilde are united against Siegfried, both appeal to their fathers: Brünnhilde commanding Wotan to look down and help, Hagen telling Alberich to summon up the Nibelungs from the darkness. But Alberich and Wotan do nothing in Act 3; Siegfried's destruction, like Orestes' liberation, is almost entirely effected by human beings.

Nor does Zeus intervene and impose his will on the Athenians. The highest arbiters of the world are absent as the hero's fate is decided in both cycles; but there are, nonetheless, some divine powers present at this moment. Athena herself shares with her citizens in the task of judging Orestes; and in *Götterdämmerung* Act 3, Siegfried suffers the first of his two 'trials', at the hands of the Rhine-daughters.

As the act begins, Ex.4 sounds out calmly and fully, almost

immediately after the opening flourishes; here and now thère is
at last a real chance that Alberich's original action will finally be
remade. The Rhine-daughters appear; and the contrast between their original melody (quoted on p. 249 as Ex.48) and the
two new inventions for this scene (Ex.45a and b) tells us that the
loss of the gold has taken away their former playful energy; but
during its absence they have gained in wisdom.

Ex.45

Siegfried, by contrast, has come to the end of his good fortune. This time the bear which he has hunted (he calls it a *Gesell*,
showing us that he has regressed once more to the 'innocence' of
*Siegfried*, Act 1) has led him astray: in reality, the ring has
brought him to the banks of the Rhine so that the Rhine-
daughters can now subject him to the test which he has so far
evaded, by his ignorance of the ring's powers. The question
which could not be asked at the end of his own drama is asked
now: can Siegfried surrender the ring freely to the Rhine-
daughters, and so finally release the world of the blight which
has been placed upon it ever since Alberich's choice in the first
scene of *Das Rheingold*? Like Orestes, Siegfried comes to trial;
and like Orestes, he proves that although adequate to the heroic
deeds of the central drama of the trilogy he is ultimately limited—unable to move forward and gain the new powers which
will be needed to bring the cycle to its close.

When we last saw Siegfried, he led the joyful, pastoral wedding procession which concludes Act 2; he was completely be-
sotted with Gutrune (as the procession passes behind the three
conspirators, the full orchestra works its way through more and
more inane versions of Ex.43). His total ignorance of womens'
moods and powers is to be demonstrated once more in this
encounter with the Rhine-daughters.

Siegfried, however, does not die for his sexual naivety alone.
He refuses to give the ring voluntarily to the nymphs because it
is his prize for having slain Fafner; and they then warn him
solemnly about the power of the ring:

> He who cunningly forged it
> and lost it to his shame,
> laid upon it this curse
> that into the depths of time
> it would bring to death
> the one who bears it.
> Just as you felled the dragon
> so you too will fall,
> and right this day
> —this is what we tell you—
> if you don't give us the ring. . .      (1013–17)

But Siegfried becomes even more reckless as the Rhine-
daughters begin to free him from his ignorance. Their threats do
not terrify him. If the rope of Fate has curses woven into it, one
cut from Notung will deal with that; he has already been warned
about this curse by Fafner, but he has no fear of it. He then tells
the Rhine-daughters that he would have given it to them in
return for their favours (this is surely false), but since they have
tried to get it by threatening his life, they could not have it now
even if it were worthless:

> For my limbs and my life,
>     look—this
> is how I throw them from me!          (1033–5)

To illustrate these words he picks up a clod of earth and throws it
contemptuously behind him.

How are we to interpret this? Bernard Shaw suggested that
the scene is to be read in the light of Wagner's famous comment
on the trilogy (R 25/1/54) that 'the fear of the end is the source
of all lovelessness'; for Shaw, Siegfried 'discloses to them as
unconsciously as Julius Caesar disclosed it long ago, that secret
of heroism, never to let your life be shaped by fear of the end'
(p. 81). In the original prose sketch of 1848, Wagner envisaged

Siegfried telling the Rhine-daughters that 'what my courage bids me is the law of my being' (AE 7.308).

Siegfried's genial, relaxed demeanour in the scene as a whole supports this view: he banters gently with the Rhine-daughters when he first meets them, calls them back cheerfully when they go away after his refusal, and even reflects contentedly, after they have finally left, that if he was not so devoted to Gutrune he would have enjoyed the delights of sexual sport with one of them.

The music at this particular point offers a different perspective. As Siegfried becomes more vehement in his rejection of what he calls their threat, the music rises with his emotions to a tremendous climax which unmistakably recalls the megalomaniacal ambition of Alberich in *Das Rheingold* scene ii and *Siegfried* Act 2 scene i. Siegfried has been corrupted by the ring as surely and as completely as its first possessor. Is his defiance heroic—or is Siegfried the blinded idiot that the Rhine-daughters now say he is?

Aeschylus and his audience would unequivocally have read the scene from the second of these two perspectives. From a Greek point of view, Siegfried's action is all too comprehensible: when he shows that he is prepared to give up the ring in return for the Rhine-daughters' sexual favours (but not in response to their solemn warning that if he does not, his *moira* will fall that very day) Siegfried is exhibiting the influence of the curse on the ring, and through it that blindness which the Greeks called *atē*. Aeschylus states that *atē* was working on Paris, when he chooses Helen's love at the price of his own and his city's destruction (*Agamemnon* 386ff.); and the solemnity of the music for the Rhine-daughters' appeal, the musical echo of Alberich's behaviour as Siegfried rejects it, and the closing commentary in which the Rhine-daughters draw out the implications for the future, all elevate this scene into a paradigm of warning and inevitable refusal—a cogent demonstration of how blindness can be inflicted on men, and forces them to the fate which gives them their deserts. It is very close in spirit to the final exchange between Eteokles and the chorus of Theban women in Aeschylus' *Seven against Thebes* (653–719), where the hero accepts the power of the curse on his race, and goes forth defiantly to meet his death.

From another point of view there is nothing Greek at all about Siegfried's defiance. No Greek warrior would have defied a prophet's warning that his *moira* was imminent if he persisted with a certain course of action, simply in order to avoid being seen to give in to threats. Appearances were very important to the Greeks; but life itself was far more so (consider for example Menelaos' predicament, and his decision, at *Iliad* 17.89ff.). The implication here of Wagner's text, that there is something admirable about Siegfried's refusal to heed the words of the Rhine-daughters, is quite alien to the Greek world.

Wagner is uncomfortably divided between his Romantic needs and his Aeschylean aspirations. On the one hand we have an Aeschylean Siegfried, who dies because he has been corrupted by the power of the ring, is prone because of that to self-delusion and gullibility, and, therefore, deserves his death. On the other hand we have a defiant Siegfried, heroic in the Romantic sense of the word, who creates his glory out of his nonchalance, and his ability to transcend the fear of death. This antithesis is never resolved in *Götterdämmerung*.

Siegfried's narrative in scene ii is a classical *anagnorisis*, or recognition-scene: a narrative organized in three parts which exhibits such total recall of the thematic materials and textures of *Siegfried* that the final vision of the awakening of Brünnhilde, and Hagen's revenge, are totally expected by the audience. It is then appropriate that, as Siegfried falls, the crashing chords, which will become the punctuating refrain of the funeral music, enter at once (1146).

Theatrically speaking however, the next few minutes come from another kind of drama—a nineteenth-century permutation of Jacobean revenge tragedy, in which the triumphant exit of the successful conspirator is followed by a final monologue for the wounded hero, in which his death is transcended as he recalls in ecstasy the only true love of his life. This is the high point of Wagner's vision, the moment at which the composer confronts at its strongest the classical momentum of the *Ring*, the urge to give each character his or her just deserts—and opposes it with

Siegfried's radiant vision of a hero and heroine who are united for ever (just like Tristan and Isolde) beyond the grave:

> Death is sweet,
> its terrors enchanting—
> Brünnhilde—welcomes me!    (1162–4)

The transcendent vision vanishes, and the classical spirit returns at once when Siegfried has died. 'I have composed a Greek chorus' (Wagner told his wife) 'but a chorus which will be sung, so to speak, by the orchestra; after Siegfried's death, while the scene is being changed, the Siegmund theme will be played, as if the chorus were saying: "This was his father"; then the sword motif; and finally his theme . . .' (D 29/9/71).

This commentary omits one central aspect of the funeral music. It is indeed a threnody, a summation and review of Siegfried's ancestry and of his life. It is punctuated and thrust forward by the traumatic, staccato chords of the refrain; and the rhythmic pattern of these chords is so close to Hunding's theme (Ex. 19) that with each irruption it seems more and more as if Siegfried, Brünnhilde and Hagen have re-enacted the destructive triangle of Siegmund, Sieglinde and Hunding.

As the threnody unfolds, the melodies which the orchestra reviews do indeed include those associated with Siegmund the Volsung (Ex. 46) and with the sword (Ex. 1). But greater prominence is given, both at the start and at the finish of the scenic

Ex. 46

transformation, to the music of women. Sieglinde's themes 32, 16 and 17 appear, in that order, to surround and set in context the full statement of Ex. 46; and when the threnody has reached its final climax with the paean to Siegfried's own achievement

(Ex.27 leading to Ex.39 *fortissimo*, 1178ff.), the music draws to its close with a plangent statement of the theme (Ex.47) which has been associated throughout *Götterdämmerung* with Brünnhilde's love for him. Siegfried and his deeds are, so to speak, surrounded on each side by his mother and his wife.

Ex. 47

The trial-scene in *Eumenides* is the climax of the struggle between male and female values, which has been a central thread throughout the action of the *Oresteia*. Orestes is saved from death by the Athenian jurors; but their verdict does not vindicate his actions, or Apollo's arguments in favour of the supremacy of the male. Ultimately, honour must be paid to both parents. The verdict of the Athenians recognizes this; and so does Wagner's funeral music.

Within the balance which both dramatists must offer in their final perspective on Siegfried and on Orestes, certain preferences remain. By the vote of Athena, Aeschylus conveys his own bias towards the male side; and here Wagner once again places to the fore his firm dissent from the Greek vision, by creating in his orchestral obituary a portrait of Siegfried's life and of his parents in which, though equality is maintained, primacy is given gently but firmly to the female.

## THE TWILIGHT OF THE GODS

Onstage violence was almost invariably avoided in Greek tragedy; the few moments in which the threat to commit an act of violence was translated into stage action, as when Ajax commits suicide in Sophocles' play, drew their intense dramatic impact simply from the rarity of what was being done. But the threat of onstage violence could still be made, even where the dramatist had no intention of letting it be implemented. The situation would then create a pressure on the other characters, which would force them to find another course of action, and so avoid violence. By freeing Orestes, the Athenians incur the threat of terrible vengeance from the Furies. As the final scene begins, Athena embarks on an attempt to persuade them out of their anger.

For the first time in the *Oresteia*, we have a strong hope and expectation that the character who is facing a crisis will succeed in avoiding disaster. Aeschylus has been careful to stress, from the mid-point of the drama onwards, the features which Athena and her city have in common with the Furies. In the speech (681ff.) where she proclaims the court which will try Orestes to be the Areopagos (the ancient aristocratic court which still played an active, and controversial, role in the political life of Athens in Aeschylus' own time), Athena was careful to stress that she recognizes the importance of an element of fear in any city or individual who aspires to inner harmony. And this, too, has been the Furies' main contention, when they argued for the importance of their own role in human affairs (526ff.). Before the votes are cast there is a hope that, even if the Athenians decide for Orestes, they may still have the power to come to an accommodation with the Furies. Athena herself is a virgin goddess, sprung from Zeus' head, and for that reason gives her own vote (which turns out to be decisive) to Orestes. But in far more ways she matches the Furies. She is female, courteous, fair, and above the use of deception. When she embarks upon her persuasion, there is no deceit; her gentle persistence answers the deepest expectations of the audience, and so both the avoidance of violence, and the lyric splendours of the final moments are felt as a compelling, true resolution to the last conflict in Aeschylus' cycle. Male intellect has, in the outcome, scored only a token victory in the case of Orestes; now balance can be restored, and the values of femininity achieve the full intellectual and emotional strength which has been their due ever since Aeschylus' cogent portraits of the sufferings of Klytaimestra, Kassandra and Elektra. The Furies, being goddesses of the earth, are powers of fecundity: they can bestow increase in place of blight. Therefore, in their concord with the Athenians a true harmony with nature is reached, and the images of creation and generation, so often perverted into metaphors of violence in *Agamemnon* and *Choephoroi*, at last regain their literal force. In Aeschylus' vision of the future, the gods, nature and human beings are at one; their mutual agreement will bring endless blessings to the city of Athens.

Wagner's closing disposition is very different. Violence does break out in the hall of the Gibichungs, as Hagen steps forward to acknowledge that he killed Siegfried, claims the ring as his legacy, and disposes rapidly of Gunther. Once again we are in a Jacobean rather than a classical theatre. The lurid, melodramatic coup de théâtre that deprives Hagen of the ring comes straight from nineteenth-century melodrama.

Wagner then seeks to regain a more classical balance. As Brünnhilde enters, and imposes order on the scene by her new authority (1226–7), the calm with which themes 4 and 5 interplay takes the drama on to a wholly new level. But for the brief outburst of Gutrune, and the equally brief words in which Brünnhilde disposes of her, the remainder of *Götterdämmerung* proceeds on a far more elevated plane. As she comes to understand all that has been done to her, Brünnhilde becomes able to accept her betrayal by Siegfried, and the sufferings which Wotan knew she would have to endure; through this she regains, on a far deeper level, the equilibrium that she achieved in her first ecstatic love at the end of *Siegfried*. This bestows on her the power which no one in the trilogy has possessed before—to take Alberich's ring and return it to the Rhine-daughters.

Brünnhilde is able to do this because her love is now so great that it has no need for power, and she is therefore not tempted by the ring. Siegfried seemed to be immune to the curse because in his naive strength he disdained to use it; but he has now been undermined by the ring as decisively as any previous agent in the trilogy, and we are, therefore, still in search of a person who may finally resolve the situation created by Alberich's theft of the gold—by actually being what Siegfried only seemed to be.

As in Aeschylus, that person is female and possessed of divine wisdom; but Wagner reverses (here as elsewhere) the sexual emphasis of Aeschylus' trilogy. Athena gains the strength to resolve the *Oresteia* from the fact that, as a virgin goddess, she lacks the full powers of female sexuality, and can therefore feel an affinity with, and be fair to, both Orestes and the Furies. Wagner's Brünnhilde by contrast achieves the transfiguring power to resolve this trilogy precisely because she possesses a total capacity for all the love of which a woman is capable.

Aeschylus concludes the *Oresteia* with a widespread harmony; old and new, male and female, the powers of the Earth below and the Olympians above all unite to bless the Athenians, and to celebrate the peace which they have achieved both with Orestes and his city of Argos, and with the Eumenides. In place of this, Wagner's stage action offers only division and destruction. Hagen and Alberich are not reconciled with Brünnhilde and Wotan, but are overcome by the Rhine-daughters. The last and greatest of heroes, Siegfried, is already dead; and he is joined now by Brünnhilde, by the dwarfs, and by the gods. The past action of the *Ring* offers no prospect for the future to the human beings who survive the action of *Götterdämmerung*. They must make their own world, unaided by gods or heroes.

At the end, therefore, Wagner opposes the heart of Aeschylus' vision. Where Orestes triumphed and resumed the throne of his father, Siegfried falls, and the first major orchestral climax of *Götterdämmerung* Act 3 is his threnody. And where Aeschylus' Athena closes the trilogy by reconciling the Furies with the people of her city, Brünnhilde withdraws, reaching in death a plane of feeling which is, by implication, beyond achievement in this life. Aeschylus' Zeus gains glory from the outcome and remains upon his throne; Wagner's Wotan achieves his full glory only in the moments when he finally receives his own extinction from another's hand.

As Orestes leaves Athens, he promises the Athenians a perpetual alliance with his kingdom of Argos. Then Athena begins her attempt to persuade the Furies by telling them that they have not really been wronged; but she rapidly moves forward from this argument to offer future benefits, which she and her city can give to them for all time. At the end of his trilogy, Aeschylus draws his audience forward from the mythical past in which the *Oresteia* is set towards the present and the splendour of Athens' own contemporary achievement.

Wagner looks back, both in the funeral music and here in the final scene. Two principal musical motifs dominate Brünnhilde's final monologue: and they, too, anchor what we are to see firmly in its relationship with the past. First Ex.34 returns to the score for the third and final time as Brünnhilde orders the pyre to be built. It speaks, as it already has in the Norns' scene and in Waltraute's plea to Brünnhilde, of Wotan's reconciliation with fate, and his intense desire for death. Then, at the moment when Brünnhilde prepares to ignite the pyre, proclaiming that 'the end of the gods/is now dawning' (1297–8) Ex.5 descends powerfully in the orchestra, to convey the almost desperate need for that end which has now been built up.

Where Aeschylus turns to the future and to the *polis*, Wagner turns to the past and to the individual. Brünnhilde gains the strength to return the ring to the Rhine-daughters from her own isolation, by meditating on Siegfried's deeds, realizing that he was a pure hero and that he had to wrong her unknowingly so that she herself would gain the wisdom needed to redeem the world and the gods. And the promise of happiness and renewal for the future is achieved in Wagner not by advancing to a mature organization of society as in Aeschylus, but by re-turning to the state of nature in which the trilogy began, with the gold restored to the Rhine-daughters. At the exact moment when Brünnhilde declares that she has the strength to return the ring to them (1282ff.), their original melody from *Das Rhein-gold* scene i (Ex.48) enters the score of Act 3, for the first time despite the fact that the Rhine-daughters themselves were the principal characters of scene i. It returns even more beautifully in the orchestral coda to the *Ring*, as we watch the triumph of the Rhine-daughters and the destruction of Valhalla. Here also Ex.12 at last attains full nobility—as Valhalla blazes. For Ex.48

Wagner, nature and society are totally opposed, and the world of the *Ring* can attain its final peace only when all social order is removed.

The closing catharsis of the *Ring* lies in total dissent from that of the *Oresteia*. In Wagner, simply because of the taint of power, symbolized in the curse on the ring, everyone in the *Ring* is denied that eventual peace within this life which time and patience grant to some of the characters of Aeschylus' cycle. The *Ring* has led us to the point where Brünnhilde's deep love can overcome the power of the curse; but only because her husband is dead, and she is on the verge of immolating herself to join him. It has led to a world which, as the curtain falls, is purified; but only because the men and women who survive the cataclysm, watching 'in the utmost consternation', are left without any gods or heroes to guide their path.

If we attend only to its *verbal* contents, Wagner's conclusion would appear to deny even that minimal degree of hope which the Greek tragedians extended to the audience in all but the very darkest of their dramas. This finale seems to bring the *Ring* close to Schopenhauer's conception of tragedy. For the philosopher:

> the purpose of this highest poetical achievement is the description of the terrible side of life. The unspeakable pain, the wretchedness and misery of mankind, the triumph of wickedness, the scornful mastery of chance, and the irretrievable fall of the just and innocent are all here presented to us . . . we see in tragedy the noblest men, after a long conflict and suffering, finally renounce for ever all the pleasures of life and the aims till then pursued so keenly, or cheerfully and willingly give up life itself . . .                    (1.252–3)

Wagner's last scene, however, is not wholly pessimistic. Set beside the close of *Eumenides*, the stage action is clearly 'negative'; but it is also profound. Aeschylus closes with a paradox: that from the terrible powers of the Eumenides can come almost infinite blessings. Wagner counters with an even sharper paradox; for through the *music*, he extends a contrasting promise filled with a strange and marvellous hope. In Wagner's vision, both sexual and political achievement attain true beauty and splendour only in their final extinction. As the end nears, Ex.20 enters the orchestra, to preside serenely—enunciated with piercing sweetness by all the violins in unison—over the catastrophic destruction which is proceeding on stage. Before the closing section of Brünnhilde's monologue, this theme had not been heard since its first appearance in *Die Walküre*, Act 3; it becomes the final motif to be heard in the *Ring*, because Wotan and Brünnhilde have at last reached that glory which Sieglinde attained in the one brief, visionary moment when she learnt that she bore Siegfried in her womb. It is the special glory which can be granted by knowing that your life will achieve its purpose, and so become complete, in its final sufferings and through their consequences. That is the reason why Brünnhilde gives orders where Athena offered persuasion; why Brünnhilde comes not to honour and be reconciled with the Nibelungs but to defeat them; and why her monologue turns increasingly inward, ever moving towards the goal of total contemplation of Siegfried and the past, where Athena turned outward and to the future. Throughout the scene, her music becomes increasingly invaded by a longing for the end; and the finale, in the sheer power of the orchestral portrait of the 'twilight of the gods', holds in itself the glory which for Aeschylus extended far into the future. Wagner's greatest achievement was to oppose that vision so completely, and to carry almost equal conviction as he did so.

The qualification is unavoidable. Wagner's ending turns to the past; but it does not truly build upon it. Aeschylus' ending, though forward-looking, has stressed its deep continuity with the past. The Furies become the Eumenides not by abandoning their old powers, but by turning them from the pursuit of Orestes to the service of Athens:

> In their terrifying faces
> I see great good for these our citizens.
> For while with good will you hold them ever in honour,
> their will shall be good, and you,
> guiding our land and our city
> on the straight path of equity,
> will be pre-eminent in every way.                    (990ff.)

It is precisely because they have such power to terrify that the Furies can bring great benefits to Athena's city.

In Wagner, the power of darkness is not reconciled but defeated. When Hagen is denied the ring, our needs are fulfilled; but here, for the first time in the *Ring*, a character does not receive his deserts. The defeat of the Nibelungs, though it may satisfy us, marks a decisive departure from Aeschylus' objective understanding. The delicate tissue of hopes and fears in the *Oresteia* is founded on the playwright's serene assurance that, terrible though this world is, its suffering ultimately makes sense. The undeserved defeat of Hagen heralds Wagner's departure from the world of the Greeks, and his return in his last drama to the Christian vision of transcendence, a redemption which human beings desire because it extends the hope that we can rise above the consequences of our sinful past.

At Athens each tragic playwright offered, after his group of three tragedies, a 'satyr-play'—a short, farcical postlude with a chorus of satyrs (creatures half man, half beast)—in which characters and situations drawn from a legend used in the preceding tragedies were burlesqued. After his estrangement from Wagner, Nietzsche enraged the Bayreuth faithful by suggesting (in *Nietzsche contra Wagner*) that:

> *Parsifal* was meant as a piece of idle gaiety, as the closing act and satyric drama, with which Wagner the tragedian wished to take leave of us, of himself, and above all *of tragedy*, in a way which befitted him and his dignity, that is to say, with an extravagant, lofty and most malicious parody of tragedy itself, of all the past and terrible earnestness and sorrow of this world . . . Is Wagner's *Parsifal* his secret laugh of superiority at himself, the triumph of his last and most exalted state of artistic freedom, of artistic transcendence—is it Wagner able to *laugh* at himself?

Since the publication of Cosima's *Diaries*, Nietzsche's reading of *Parsifal* has become increasingly plausible. Many of the comments recorded in Volume 2 bear testimony to Wagner's deep weariness as he composed this work—a distaste for his self-imposed labour which he never expressed when writing the

*Ring,* and which cannot be explained simply by his declining physical health. Other entries exhibit a cynicism, and a refusal to take the characters and situations seriously, which are equally unprecedented, and are quite remarkable even if we allow for the frequent coarseness of Wagner's Saxon sense of humour. On two occasions, as he wrote *Parsifal,* this most self-confident of composers confessed that 'I sometimes have doubts about the whole thing, whether it is not a nonsense, a complete failure' (D 8/8/78 cf. 9/8/81).

*Parsifal* transmutes the symbols, the images and even the characters of the *Ring,* very much as if it were a satyr-play to the trilogy. Wagner himself regarded Titurel as a reincarnation of Wotan (though Wotan has even more in common with Amfortas), and Parsifal as a development of Siegfried (D 19/2/78 and 29/4/79). Indeed, Kundry's evocation of Herzeleide in Act 2 reads (and sounds) like a malevolent parody of Siegfried's developing affinity with the memory of Sieglinde.

There are other, more sinister mutations. In *Parsifal* the heroic amoral hosts of Valhalla have become the Knights of the Grail, fervently committed to an unattainable ideal of chastity and to racial purity. The forest, which flourished in *Siegfried,* Act 2, simply because it is part of nature, has become the domain of the Grail; it suffers a constant blight and can gain renewed strength only when a redeemer comes. In the stunted landscape of this drama, the *Wunschmädchen* who in *Die Walküre* were the gift of a god, and the real temptation by whose rejection Siegmund proves his greatness, have become the decadent, artificial enchantments created by the literally sterile Klingsor. The music of *Parsifal* is filled with a serene beauty—especially in the outer acts—and a delicacy of texture which is new in Wagner's music. It also exhibits a deep understanding of suffering and of spiritual ecstasy. There is however—perhaps inevitably—one major difference from the *Ring.*

In his last drama, Wagner approached the themes of the *Ring* with the ironic, questioning glance of his last years, and so the moral balance of the *Ring,* and its fine understanding of the forces that compel men and women to inflict suffering on each other, have been lost. Kundry's music is enigmatic, Klingsor's empty. Once again we are in the world of *Tannhäuser*: sensuality and sexuality are set in combat with the values of spirituality—a combat which they are predestined to lose in the drama, to compensate for the fact that they always won in the composer's life.

Parsifal's innocence gives him, not the tragic fate that Siegfried deservedly suffers for *his* naivety, but the strength to resist sexual temptation, to overcome evil, and to redeem Amfortas' sin. He does this in the closing scene of Act 3, having learnt wisdom not, like Brünnhilde, from his sufferings but *durch Mitleid*—through compassion. These are Christian values. Wagner's vision of the world in *Parisfal* is bereft of that kinship with Greek tragedy which had led to the creation of the *Ring*, and his last drama has nothing in common with Aeschylus except the economy of its stagecraft.

Many critics would claim that he had never possessed any such kinship. To Hans Gal, for example, Wagner's whole endeavour was misguided. The world of the Greeks is irrevocably lost to us, it 'cannot be reconstructed, and its sociological, artistic and religious precepts cannot be transferred to a completely differently organized civilization. Wagner's entire edifice is an illusion.' (p. 159)

The challenge of the Greek vision is indeed intense. The *Oresteia* confronts the depths of human suffering with utter objectivity. Bereft of the consolation of any rewards in an afterlife, the poet and his characters confront the most acute miseries of existence directly, drawing no comfort from faith in any form of transcendence. Aeschylus celebrates, simply but profoundly, the fierce consolation which can be drawn from the knowledge that there is a pattern in human life; that every human action has its consequence, and that with patience and goodwill we may in time unravel their secrets and come to understand our fate.

At Athens, that strength of vision was broken during the Peloponnesian war. The West has never wholly regained it, and not even Wagner could match the unique achievement of Aeschylean drama. But he did create the *Ring*; and it remains a work of such compelling power that it speaks to our tormented century as directly, and offers us as much hope and consolation, as the *Oresteia* offered fifty years later to the men and women of a fractured Athens in the bitter years of war and defeat. Wagner's cycle stands beside the *Oresteia*, distinguished by the sustained strength and depth of its vision from every other modern attempt to imitate, echo or re-create the form and manner of the Aeschylean trilogy.

Wagner and Aeschylus address their trilogies to the same group of subjects: corruption and power, violence and its consequences, love and sexuality, hope and fear, and the choice which we must make between society and anarchy. Nietszche wrote in 1876, in the fourth section of *Richard Wagner at Bayreuth*, that:

There are such similarities and affinities between Kant and the Eleatics, between Schopenhauer and Empedocles, and between Aeschylus and Richard Wagner as to be an almost intangible reminder of the relative nature of all concepts of time; it almost seems as though some things belong together, and time is only a mist that makes it hard for our eyes to see that they do.

The differences between the *Ring* and the *Oresteia* are obvious. The profound affinity remains.

# Appendix

Pearl Wilson, in her 1919 Columbia dissertation, recognized the importance of the *Oresteia* to Wagner, and attempted to trace parallels between the two cycles. Her discussion was relatively short, and it failed to carry much conviction—chiefly because she took *Das Rheingold* to be parallel to the whole of *Agamemnon*, *Die Walküre* to *Choephoroi*, and was therefore forced to omit *Siegfried* completely from her considerations. She has been followed only by Curt von Westernhagen, who touches briefly on the affinities between the *Oresteia* and the *Ring* in each of his two biographies of Wagner. Everyone else who has written about Wagner and the Greeks has claimed that *Prometheus Bound* was the Aeschylean drama that most influenced Wagner.

*Prometheus Bound* is the only extant play about Prometheus; it was almost certainly the central drama of a trilogy which began with the theft of fire from the gods. Prometheus, a Titan, was the most intelligent member of the previous dynasty of gods that ruled the world before the coming of the Olympians. He defected to the side of Zeus, and helped him to gain his throne; but when Zeus resolved to exterminate mankind, he stole fire from the gods, and gave it to men, so that humanity could survive and begin to develop the rudiments of culture and civilization. The surviving play portrays the punishment which Zeus inflicted on Prometheus for this; though chained and impaled upon an isolated crag, the Titan, who is immortal, holds out against his tormentor. Prometheus knows a secret which he is confident will secure Zeus' downfall: it is fated that the sea-nymph Thetis will bear a son who is mightier than his father. As the play proceeds, Hera's persecution of the virgin Io (simply because her beauty attracted Zeus' lust) turns Prometheus' determination into open defiance. Zeus then sends Hermes, the messenger of the gods, to demand that Prometheus reveal his secret; when he refuses, he is hurled into an abyss, together with the chorus, the daughters of the Ocean.

Some fragments survive from the third play, *Prometheus Unbound*. Prometheus has resurfaced after thousands of years of burial, and is now suffering the additional punishment that an eagle comes daily to devour his liver. The hero Herakles arrives, learns from Prometheus where he must journey on his future wanderings—just like Io in *Prometheus Bound*—shoots the eagle, and (probably) then frees Prometheus. Prometheus reaches an accommodation with Zeus—presumably gaining the right to liberty in return for divulging his secret.

*Prometheus Bound* is a spectacular drama. There is little dramatic development, but the play is rich both in impassioned rhetoric and in scenic and theatrical effects: the daughters of Ocean, Okeanos himself, and Hermes all enter airborne, while Io rushes on in frenzy, maddened by a gadfly, and half transformed into the shape of a cow. These techniques, and the theme of the play, appealed powerfully to the Romantic imagination; and in the mid-nineteenth century it was accepted without question that the play, which appears in the manuscripts together with six undeniably genuine surviving plays by Aeschylus, was by his hand.

This ascription dates back to later classical times. In the Hellenistic and Roman periods, scholars familiar with the extravagant spectacle of contemporary productions accepted without question that Aeschylus, of the three great Athenian playwrights, was the most given to lavish and spectacular effects; and *Prometheus Bound* certainly demands the scenic resources which are popularly thought of as Wagnerian. However, doubts about its place in the Aeschylean canon have been raised on linguistic and stylistic grounds by several influential scholars in the twentieth century. Furthermore, Oliver Taplin has demonstrated convincingly that, with the exception of *Prometheus Bound*, the surviving plays ascribed to Aeschylus are far more economical in stage effects than those of Euripides, and arguably even of Sophocles (pp. 39ff.). It is also most unlikely that the *mēchanē* (the mechanical hoist employed in and after the late fifth century for airborne entrances by gods) was introduced into the Athenian theatre during Aeschylus' lifetime. *Prometheus Bound* uses it at least twice, possibly three times.

In the six plays which are undeniably authentic, Aeschylus uses no prop or stage effect which is not directly and richly related to the theme of the dramas. Aeschylus' is a theatre of severe economy, where the few props used are all of great significance, and physical action is restricted to a small number of paradigmatic actions and gestures which are set in deliberate opposition to the wealth of the playwright's verbal resources. The whole manner of *Prometheus Bound* lies in direct contrast to Aeschylus' normal practice.

The issue has now been resolved beyond reasonable doubt by the analyses undertaken by Mark Griffith. His book examines the play from a number of different perspectives, though the principal and most penetrating arguments revolve around questions of language and style. The conclusions seem irrefutable: *Prometheus Bound* could not have been written by Aeschylus, and is most unlikely to have been written by anyone within thirty years of his death in 458. The play is far more likely to be a product of the late fifth century, the age of Euripides and of the sophists—the period when spectacle for its own sake began to develop on the Athenian stage.

This certainly clears the way for a more profound analysis of Aeschylus' own dramatic style but it does not dismiss Wagner's claim to a genuine affinity with Aeschylus. It has never been clear to me why Wagner's admirers have sought to detect similarities between the *Ring* and *Prometheus Bound*. The rhetorical reference in the exordium to *Art and Revolution* is the only place in his extensive prose writings where Wagner mentions the play. And the resemblances which have been alleged do not rise above a trivial level.

The least fanciful of these comparisons are between Prometheus and Loge, Prometheus and Brünnhilde. Jacob Grimm was the first to draw the parallel between Prometheus and the Loki of Teutonic mythology; and Wagner's Loge has been said to share with Prometheus the characteristic that each fire-god is a free son of nature, the helper and friend of a god who initially established his rule through treaties; they are later tamed by the god. The parallels between Brünnhilde and Prometheus are even more numerous: they are both children of the Earth-goddess, and are punished for their love of mortal men by being bound on a rock by the fire-god. Both Prometheus and Brünnhilde prophesy to women (Io and Sieglinde) the heroic deeds of their descendants, and both are freed by heroes (Herakles and Siegfried); finally, both are visited during their captivity by a chorus of semi-divine, sympathizing kinswomen (in *Siegfried's Death* all eight Valkyries visited Brünnhilde on her rock in Act 1 scene iii).

None of these parallels is as close or as convincing as they appear at first sight: some of the elements in Wagner's story which have been ascribed to the influence of the Prometheus plays are in fact to be found in his Norse and German sources; and the alleged resemblances are all confined to superficial features of the plot. There is no affinity whatever between the subject-matter and the structure of the *Ring* and what we can guess to have been those of the Prometheus trilogy. In fact, only one Promethean echo can be certainly detected in the *Ring*; it comes not from the surviving drama but from Droysen's introduction. He conjectured that the Prometheus trilogy began in the dark beginnings of time, the *'dunkle Urzeit'* in which the 'dawn of existence' (*die Dämmerung des Werdens*) lay over land and sea. Wagner once wrote of the *Ring* (with pardonable exaggeration) as though it contained 'the very essence and meaning of the world in all its possible phases' (R 23/8/56). It seems probable that, as Schadewaldt claimed (pp. 361–2), this phrase of Droysen's stayed in Wagner's mind to inspire the music of the prelude to *Das Rheingold*, the prophecy of Erda, in which 'ein düstrer Tag/dämmert den Göttern', and the title finally given to the last drama in the *Ring* cycle.

These would be trivial questions, if it were not for the persistence of the view that Wagner's own stagecraft is Romantic to excess, extravagant in the employment of spectacle for its own sake—more akin to the theatre of Meyerbeer (and by implication to *Prometheus Bound*) than to the classical economy which we find in Aeschylus and Sophocles. There is, undeniably, far more spectacle in the *Ring* than in the *Oresteia*; Wagner was not the man to deny himself the resources of the modern stage (and indeed for its effective realization the *Ring* demands some facilities which were not yet available in 1876—in particular the full use of electric lighting). But the visual resources of the *Ring*—the scenery, the lighting and the stage effects—are harnessed, in close conjunction with the music, to precise expressive ends. Wagner's theatre is economical in its own way: just like Aeschylus, he employs direct but very powerful stage images in relationship to which the drama, which is carried primarily through the words and the music, gains its meaning.

# Select Bibliography

I have listed here all the books and articles of which I have made more than passing use while developing the argument of this book. This is not, of course, intended to be a complete record of everything that I have read—let alone of everything that has been written—about Aeschylus, Wagner, and related subjects.

### 1. AESCHYLUS; BACKGROUND MATERIAL

Adkins, A. W. H. *Merit and Responsibility: A Study in Greek Values.* Oxford, 1960.

Baldry, H. C. *The Greek Tragic Theatre.* London, 1971.

Dodds, E. R. *The Greeks and the Irrational* (Chapters 1–2). Berkeley, 1951.

Dodds, E. R. 'Morals and Politics in the *Oresteia*' in *The Ancient Concept of Progress and Other Essays.* Oxford, 1973.

Finley, M. I. *The World of Odysseus*, 2nd edn. Harmondsworth, 1979.

Lloyd-Jones, H. *The Justice of Zeus.* Berkeley, 1971.

Pickard-Cambridge, Sir A. W. *The Dramatic Festivals of Athens*, 2nd edn. Oxford, 1968.

Snell, Bruno. *The Discovery of the Mind* (trans. T. G. Rosenmeyer). Oxford, 1953.

### 2. AESCHYLUS; COMMENTARIES ON THE *ORESTEIA*

Betensky, A. 'Aeschylus' *Oresteia*: The Power of Clytemnestra' in *Ramus*, 1978.

Conington, John. *Aeschylus, 'Choephoroi'* (ed. and comm.). London, 1857.

Denniston, J. D. and Page, D. L. *Aeschylus, 'Agamemnon'* (ed. and comm.). Oxford, 1957.

Easterling, P. 'Presentation of Character in Aeschylus' in *Greece and Rome*, 1973.

Ewans, M. 'Agamemnon at Aulis; a Study in the *Oresteia'* in *Ramus*, 1975.

Fraenkel, E. *Aeschylus, 'Agamemnon'* (ed. and comm.) (3 vols.). Oxford, 1950.

Gagarin, M. *Aeschylean Drama*. Berkeley, 1976.

Jones, J. *On Aristotle and Greek Tragedy*. London, 1962.

Reinhardt, K. *Aischylos als Regisseur und Theologe*. Bern, 1949.

Snell, Bruno. *Aischylos und das Handeln in Drama*. (Philologus Suppl. 20.1.) Leipzig, 1928.

Taplin, Oliver. *The Stagecraft of Aeschylus*. Oxford, 1977.

Vickers, Brian. *Towards Greek Tragedy*. London, 1973.

### 3. AESCHYLUS; SPECIALIST WORKS ON IMAGERY AND LEITMOTIF TECHNIQUE

Goheen, R. F. 'Aspects of Dramatic Symbolism; Three Studies in the *Oresteia'* in *American Journal of Philology*, 1955.

Hiltbrunner, O. *Wiederholungs- und Motivtechnik bei Aischylos*. Bern, 1950.

Lebeck, Ann. *The 'Oresteia': A Study in Language and Structure*. Washington D.C., 1971.

Peradotto, John H. 'Some Patterns of Nature Imagery in the *Oresteia'* in *American Journal of Philology*, 1964.

### 4. WAGNER'S RELATIONSHIP WITH AESCHYLUS

Drews, A. *Der Ideengehalt von Richard Wagners dramatischen Dichtungen im Zusammenhang mit seinem Leben und seiner Weltanschauung*. Leipzig, 1931. (See also the review by Paul Maas in *Gnomon*, 1932.)

Droysen, J. G. *Des Aischylos Werke*. Berlin, 1832.

Droysen, J. G. *Aischylos; die Tragödien und Fragmente* (rev. with intro. by W. Nestle), 5th edn. Stuttgart, 1977.

Lloyd-Jones, H. 'Wagner and the Greeks' in *Times Literary Supplement*, 9 Jan. 1976 (reprinted in *Blood for the Ghosts—Classical Influences in the Nineteenth and Twentieth Centuries*. London, 1982).

Petsch, R. 'Der *Ring des Nibelungen* in seinen Beziehungen zur grieschieschen Tragödie und zur zeitgenössischen Philosophie' in *Richard-Wagner Jahrbuch*, vol. 2, 1907.

Schadewaldt, W. 'Richard Wagner und die Griechen' in *Hellas und Hesperien*, 2nd edn. Zurich, 1970.

Schaefer, Theodor. 'Aischylos' Prometheus und Wagners Loge' in *Festschrift 45er Versammlung deutsche Philologen und Schulmänner*. Bremen, 1899.

Westernhagen, Curt von. *Richard Wagner; Sein Werk, sein Wesen, seine Welt* (Chapter 6). Zurich, 1956.

Westernhagen, Curt von. *Wagner: a Biography* (trans. M. Whittall) (2 vols.) (Chapter 11). Cambridge, 1978.

Wilson, Pearl C. *Wagner's Dramas and Greek Tragedy*. New York, 1919.

Wrassianopolos-Braschowanoff, G. *Wagner und die Antike*. Leipzig, 1910.

## 5. WAGNER'S PROSE WRITINGS

Wagner, Richard. *Gesammelte Schriften* (14 vols.). Leipzig, 1914.

Wagner, Richard. *Richard Wagner's Prose Works* (trans. W. Ashton Ellis) (8 vols.). London, 1892–9.

Wagner, Richard. *Richard Wagner's Letters to his Dresden friends, Theodor Uhlig, Wilhelm Fischer, and Ferdinand Heine* (trans. J. S. Shedlock). New York, 1890.

Wagner, Richard. *Correspondence of Wagner and Liszt* (trans. F. Hueffer). London, 1888.

Wagner, Richard. *Richard Wagner's Letters to August Roeckel* (trans. Eleanor C. Sellar). Bristol, 1897.

Wagner, Richard. *My Life* (authorized English translation). London, 1911.

Wagner, Richard. *Skizzen und Entwürfe zur 'Ring'-Dichtung, mit der Dichtung 'Der Junge Siegfried'* (ed. O. Ströbel). Munich, 1930.


### 6. SOURCES FOR NORSE AND GERMAN MYTHOLOGY

Blackwell, J. A. (trans.) *The Prose Edda*. London, 1878.
Grimm, J. *Teutonic Mythology* (trans. J. S. Stallybrass) (4 vols.). London, 1883–8 and 1900.
Hollander, L. M. (trans.) *The Poetic Edda*. University of Texas, 1928.
Schlauch, M. (trans.) *The Saga of the Volsungs*. New York, 1930.
Taylor, P. B. and Auden, W. H. *The Elder Edda; a Selection*. London, 1969.


### 7. WAGNER; COMMENTARIES ON *THE RING*

Brink, Louise. *Women characters in Richard Wagner*. New York, 1924.
Buesst, Aylmer. *The Nibelung's Ring*. London, 1932.
Cooke, Deryck. *I Saw the World End*. London, 1979.
Dahlhaus, Carl. *Richard Wagner's Music Dramas* (trans. M. Whittall). Cambridge, 1979.
Donington, Robert. *Wagner's 'Ring' and its Symbols*, 3rd edn. London, 1974.
Gal, Hans. *Richard Wagner* (trans. H.-H. Schönzeler). New York, 1976.
Garten, H. F. *Wagner the Dramatist*. London, 1977.
Lorenz, A. *Der Ring des Nibelungen (Das Geheimnis der Form bei Richard Wagner, Band 1)*. Tutzing, 1966.
Newman, Ernest. *The Life of Richard Wagner* (4 vols.). New York, 1937–46.
Newman, Ernest. *Wagner as Man and Artist*. London, 1914.
Newman, Ernest. *Wagner Nights*. London, 1949.
Overhoff, K. *Wagners Nibelungen-Tetralogie*, 2nd edn. Salzburg and Munich, 1976.
Shaw, G. B. *The Perfect Wagnerite*, 4th edn. London, 1923.

Stein, Jack M. *Richard Wagner and the Synthesis of the Arts.* Detroit, 1960.

Tanner, Michael. 'The Total Work of Art' in *The Wagner Companion*, ed. P. Burbidge and R. Sutton. London, 1979.

Westernhagen, Curt von. *The Forging of the 'Ring'* (trans. A. & M. Whittall). Cambridge, 1976.

## 8. MISCELLANEOUS

Butler, E. M. *The Tyranny of Greece over Germany.* Cambridge, 1935.

Flint, W. *The Use of Myths to Create Suspense in Extant Greek Tragedy.* Princeton, 1922.

Griffith, M. *The Authenticity of 'Prometheus Bound'.* Cambridge, 1977.

Gründer, K. (ed.) *Der Streit über Nietzsches 'Geburt der Tragödie'.* Hildesheim, 1969.

Hegel, G. W. F. *Aesthetics* (trans. T. M. Knox). Oxford, 1975.

Jenkyns, R. *The Victorians and Ancient Greece.* Oxford, 1980.

Kamenka, E. *The Philosophy of Ludwig Feuerbach.* London, 1970.

Magee, Bryan. *Aspects of Wagner* (Chapter 1). New York, 1969.

Nietzsche, Friedrich. *The Birth of Tragedy and The Genealogy of Morals* (trans. F. Golffing). New York, 1956.

Rabkin, Eric. *Narrative Suspense.* Ann Arbor, 1973.

Rohde, Erwin. *Psyche* (trans. W. B. Hillis). London, 1950.

Schopenhauer, Arthur. *The World as Will and Representation* (trans. E. F. J. Payne) (2 vols.). New York, 1966 and 1969.

Silk, Michael and Stern, J. P. *Nietzsche on Tragedy.* Cambridge, 1981.

Skelton, G. *Wagner at Bayreuth*, revised edn. London, 1976.

Steiner, George. *The Death of Tragedy.* London, 1961.

Wagner, C. *Cosima Wagner's Diaries* (trans. G. Skelton) (2 vols.). London, 1978 and 1980.

Westernhagen, Curt von. *Wagners Dresdener Bibliothek.* Wiesbaden, 1966.

# Index